GEORGE GERSHWIN

His Life & Music

Design: David Houghton
Printed by: Staples Printers, Rochester

Published by: Sanctuary Publishing Limited, The Colonnades, 82
Bishops Bridge Road,London W2 6BB

Photographs used by kind permission of Culver Pictures Inc
Cover photographs: Redferns

ISBN: 1-86074-174-6

GEORGE GERSHWIN

His Life & Music

Ean Wood

CONTENTS

CHAPTER ONE

The Family

George Gershwin was born with two supreme gifts – the ability to write memorable tunes and an instinct for setting them with rich and unexpected harmonies. These are so closely interwoven with the melody that with him, more than any other composer of popular songs, the harmonies are part of the composition.

It is because of these harmonies that improvising jazz musicians value his work so highly. Without being over-complicated, they provide a constantly shifting pattern of chords to work with. From the twenties to today, numbers like 'Oh, Lady Be Good', 'I Got Rhythm' and 'Nice Work If You Can Get It' have been performed live and recorded over and over again.

His music, and the pleasure it gives to millions of people, have far outlasted his short life. He died in 1937, aged only thirty-eight, but in those thirty-eight years he poured out a torrent of songs such as 'Summertime', 'S'Wonderful', 'Embraceable You', 'They Can't Take That Away From Me', 'How Long Has This been Going On', 'The Man I Love' and hundreds of others. As well as these, there were his extended compositions like 'Rhapsody In Blue', 'An American In Paris' and 'Concerto In F', and his opera *Porgy And Bess*.

As well as the gifts he was born with, George was also fortunate in being born when he was – at a time when popular song in America was enjoying its first and greatest boom, and when the American theatre was poised to create the modern musical. It was in Broadway musicals that George would spend most of his energetic working life.

Both his parents were Jews from St Petersburg, the most Westernised of all Russian cities. His father, Morris Gershovitz, born in 1871, was the grandson of a rabbi and the son of an artillery mechanic. It may not have been George's grandfather's intention in life to become an artillery mechanic, but in Czarist Russia life for Jews was hard and circumscribed. After Catherine the Great had enthusiastically extended the Russian empire by annexing various neighbouring territories, especially a great chunk of Poland in 1795, Russia discovered it now had the largest Jewish population in the world. The Czars that followed Catherine were not too happy about this, and Jews were put under severe restraints. They had to live in prescribed areas, from which they were forbidden to move, and the men were liable to be conscripted for military service. This could be for as long as thirty years and during their time in the army great pressure was put on them to convert to Christianity.

George's grandfather, Yakov Gershovitz, was conscripted into the army of Czar Nicholas II at the age of ten, and served twenty-five years. Once a Jew had done such service, he and his family were rewarded with the freedom to live and travel anywhere. In addition, Yakov had designed an artillery piece that had won the approval of the Czar, and so had earned a fair amount of public esteem. He and his family moved to live near St Petersburg and he settled into a relaxed and fairly prosperous life as an inventor.

There was one privilege that Yakov's military service did not earn him, however. His son, Morris, would still be liable for such service himself.

By the end of the 1880s Morris was in his late teens, an amiable and easy-going young man who had already established himself with some success in the rather specialised trade of manufacturing fancy leather uppers for women's shoes. He also had a well-known fondness for card-games and billiards and attractive young women.

It was at around this time that he met Rosa Bruskin, then in her early teens. Rosa's father was a prosperous St Petersburg furrier. She was strikingly beautiful, and the impressionable Morris, himself around eighteen, fell in love with her. But within a couple of years, in 1891, she and her family emigrated to New York.

The notion of doing the same began to revolve in Morris's mind. After all, his mother's brother, whose name was Greenstein, was already settled in New York as a tailor.

Morris's decision to emigrate probably had several causes. The threat of national service might have been one of them. So might the view of

America as the land of opportunity, although Morris was never particularly ambitious. But what he was was romantic, and almost certainly the main reason for his eventual emigration was Rosa.

He set off optimistically by ship with the name and address of his main contact in America, his uncle Greenstein, tucked firmly inside the sweatband of his hat. It was sheer ill-fortune that as the ship approached New York, and he rushed to the rail to see the Statue of Liberty, the wind lifted the hat off his head and overboard, and the address with it.

With characteristic lightness of heart, he shrugged off this small setback. Disembarking, he rented a room in the Bowery, got himself into a pool game, and won thirty cents. This in spite of knowing not a word of English.

New York by this time, the early 1890s, already had a thriving population of Jewish immigrants. They were mostly poor, and there was a great sense of community among them. They formed themselves into committees to help each other, and there was a strong feeling of optimism about the opportunities available in this land of freedom.

So many actually did become successful that when later waves of Jewish immigrants arrived in the 1920s and 1930s, fleeing from the Communist order in Russia and from the Nazis, they expected to become rich in America. Many were disillusioned and embittered when this did not happen.

Probably the biggest Jewish community in New York when Morris arrived was on the East Side, and on his first morning in America he set off there to hunt for 'Greenstein the tailor', managing to get along by speaking Yiddish and Russian. It was suggested to him that he try Brownsville, in Brooklyn, where there was another thriving population of Jewish immigrants. He took a steam-train, crossing the ten-year-old Brooklyn Bridge, and three hours of hunting and questioning in Brownsville found him his uncle.

His life in the New World had begun, and one thing that marked this event was the changing of his surname to Gershvin. This may not have been Morris's own idea. Impatient immigration officials frequently gave immigrants with difficult foreign names some name that was close enough. This, for instance, was how Samuel Goldwyn (as he later became), entering America from Poland as Schmuel Gelbfisz, was registered in immigration as Samuel Goldfish.

Having the specialised skill he did, Morris soon found a job with a firm manufacturing women's shoes, and within a few years had risen to be foreman. He had also found his Rosa, and on 21 July 1895, they were married in a ratskeller on Houston Street on New York's East Side. He was twenty-four and she was nineteen. She was also pregnant.

Their first child, a son, was born on or around 6 December 1896. With a casualness about names that seemed habitual in the new family, Morris and Rosa (who had changed her own first name to Rose) always called him Izzy, which he believed was short for Isadore. It wasn't until he was applying for a passport in 1928, and needed a copy of his birth certificate, that the son discovered that technically his name was Israel. None of which mattered much by then, because in 1924 he had decided to call himself Ira.

Two years later, on 26 September 1898, a second son was born. His birth certificate read 'Jacob Gershwine'. 'Gershwine' seems to have been a simple clerical error, and the 'Jacob' was never used. From infancy everyone called the second son George. An American name in a family that were proud to have become Americans.

Later there would be two more children – a son, Arthur, on 14 March 1900 and a sister, Frances, on 6 December 1906. This was probably the same birthday as Ira, although nobody was ever quite sure when Ira's birthday was – the family never bothered to celebrate birthdays.

Nor did they bother much with the orthodoxies of the Jewish religion. Of the three sons, only Izzy, the eldest, had a bar mitzvah, and at home the family spoke only English, not Russian or Yiddish. So all the children spoke English as a first language.

Morris's casual attitude to life set the pattern for his family. Soon abandoning the shoe factory, he spent the rest of his life moving from business to business. He ran restaurants, Russian baths, Turkish baths, bakeries, a hotel, and a combination cigar store and pool parlour. For three exciting weeks he was a bookmaker at the Brighton Beach Race Track, but too many favourites won and the enterprise was a financial disaster.

As Ira said later in life, "My father loved to start businesses, but then he lost interest. He'd go and play pinochle and wouldn't supervise the latest venture." Fortunately Morris was often partnered in these ventures by one of his Greenstein cousins, and between them they somehow got along.

The family moved house (or more usually, apartment) even more often than Morris changed his business. By 1916, when Ira was twenty (and still known as 'Iz'), he calculated they had lived at twenty-eight different addresses, twenty-five in New York and three in Brooklyn.

Their family life, as well as being nomadic, was considerably sociable. Friends and relations came and stayed and went, and several nights a week Rose and Morris played cards with neighbours who ranged from local merchants to actors from the Yiddish theatre. All this gave their home life a slightly unsettled air. To add to this, it was less of a family unit than a collection of individuals, all slightly dissociated from each other. Frances, in later life, recalled that she almost had to raise herself.

Although the Gershvins lived perpetually on the edge of financial disaster, somehow they managed to live with a fair amount of style. As Rose once said, complaining about the way the biographical film *Rhapsody In Blue* had depicted George's early life as one of grinding poverty, "We were never without a maid." Well, hardly ever.

Not trusting banks (like many European immigrants), when the family did have money Rose invested it in jewellery, principally in a diamond ring. In his childhood, it was Ira's duty to pawn this when times were hard, and redeem it when things got better. By the time he was in his early teens he had completed this cycle half a dozen times, each time raising about four hundred dollars.

From time to time their restless life caused friction between Morris and Rose. Temperamentally they were very different. Morris was gentle, mild and humorous, taking life as it came. Rose was highly strung and purposeful. As George himself later wrote, "She was never the doting type. Although very loving, she never watched every move we made. She was set on having us completely educated, her idea being that if everything else failed we could always become schoolteachers."

In their different ways, however, Morris and Rose did have one trait in common, and that was emotional detachment, at least outwardly. Morris was amused and uninvolved, Rose was remote and undemonstrative. This, together with their somewhat unsettled family life, bred in both George and Ira a remoteness in personal relationships that stayed with them in different ways all their lives.

In their boyhood they were even remote from each other. Their temperaments too differed considerably. Gentle and withdrawn like his father, Ira's favourite occupation was reading. He began by renting nickel paperbacks of derring-do at two cents apiece from a library run from the back of a local laundry. He read these by the dozen. Then, in 1906, when he was ten, he happened on the first Sherlock Holmes novel *A Study In Scarlet*. This opened his mind to the rewards of good writing, and he went on over the next few years from Conan Doyle to Oscar Wilde and that most influential magazine of the decadent 1890s, *The Yellow Book*, preaching "art for art's sake" and the virtue in writing of always hunting for the most precise and expressive word, the *mot juste*.

From the age of about eleven he began to compile a scrapbook of articles and pictures clipped from newspapers, almanacs and catalogues, having the vague idea that it would be a useful source of information for him in later years, a sort of encyclopaedia. It contained a wide variety of material, from biographical articles (including one on Shakespeare) to "Help In Case Of Accidents" and "How Phrases Originate".

Later he would begin a second scrapbook, which would prove more significant to his future. In the 1900s there were scores of magazines and periodicals on the American market. New York alone had more than twenty daily newspapers, and there were scores of weekly and monthly magazines, American and British, pouring out a flood of short stories, jokes, essays, anecdotes and light verse. Ira's second scrapbook was of light verse that had caught his fancy.

He began to embellish his scrapbooks with small line-drawings, modelled on those he saw in popular magazines, and he became an enthusiastic sketcher, toying for a while with the idea of becoming an illustrator. He also became an enthusiastic theatre-goer, patronising the local vaudeville and silent movie houses, and the Grand Street Theatre which specialised in lurid melodramas. All his impulses were towards the arts.

George at about the age of eleven was a street kid. Restless and aggressive, his pleasures were physical and competitive. He played street hockey and punch-ball, and was regarded by his companions as the roller-skating champion of Forsyth Street. His nickname on the street, gained from the fact that his father was at that time running a bakery, was 'Cheesecake'. Tall for his age and muscular, he was well able to take care of himself in a brawl. Often he got into fights and came home with bruises or a black eye.

He was also frequently in trouble at school, usually for failing to do his homework or for being disruptive in class. Both he and Ira attended Public School 20, on Rivington and Forsyth Streets, and several times the respectable Ira had to intercede for him with the authorities. He did a little better when he moved on to PS25, on First Avenue and Second Street, but schoolwork continued to bore him and his marks were only passable.

His real education, however, had begun on the streets. New York in the 1900s was a lot safer city than today, although it could get rough if you got off your own turf. Indoors belonged to adults, but the streets belonged to the kids, and gangs of Irish, Italian and Jewish teenagers guarded their street territory and constantly battled with each other.

The prudent Ira picked up a few phrases of Italian so that if he was picked on by Italians he could pretend to be one of them, which sometimes saved him a sock on the jaw. Once, when there was a feud going on between the Irish and the Jews, George got caught on his own by some Irish. He had his roller-skates on, and trying to escape up the stairs of an apartment house he somehow managed to fall down an elevator shaft, landing on his head and sustaining concussion.

But as long as you avoided the rival gangs, in those days a kid could explore the whole city. As both George and Ira grew through their teens, they would wander the length and breadth of Manhattan by bus and subway, staying out until early morning and often venturing farther afield into Greenwich Village, Harlem and the East Side.

The sights and sounds and smells of New York in those days made a deep impression on both brothers, staying with them all their lives. Notes of his memories that Ira wrote out later included: "The horsedrawn streetcars on Delancey Street, their stoves hot in winter; the trips with other kids to Chinatown, to buy sugar cane at about a cent afoot; learning to swim in the mucky Harlem River; Hubert's Museum on Fourteenth Street (trained fleas, magic, card tricks for sale); the Eden Musée on Twenty-Third Street (horror and other waxworks); the Sheepshead Bay and Brighton Beach race tracks." An especially vivid memory was of the docks along the Hudson, where stevedores loaded and unloaded cargo, filling wagons with "large bunches of bananas and great piles of melons. Bananas would drop off the overloaded wagons; you picked them up ..."

And everywhere there was music – pianists in bars, hurdy-gurdys on the street, automatons in amusement arcades. America during the 1900s saw a huge flowering of popular music. Writing song lyrics became an obsession with Americans in all walks of life. Newspapers ran songwriting contests, and a vast sheet music industry sprang up.

As there was then no radio, the cinema was still silent, and the phonograph was still in its scratchy infancy, sheet music publishing was the heart of the popular song industry. This music would be bought by vaudeville and revue performers and producers for use in their shows, and hundreds of amateur singers and pianists would buy it for playing at home.

Most of the sheet music publishers were in New York. They would hire pianists to sit in their offices and play the new numbers to prospective customers, and soon there were so many of these pianists pounding away, especially in the brownstone houses on Twenty-Eighth Street, between Broadway and Sixth Avenue, that that area acquired the nickname 'Tin Pan Alley'.

The Gershvin family was not especially musical. Morris attended the opera from time to time, and possessed a fair singing voice and (according to George) "a musical whistle", but with none of them was music a passion. They were among the first in their circle to own a Victrola, but that was more a matter of social prestige than a thirst for melody and harmony. Nor did the young George seem to have such a thirst. To a street kid like himself and his companions, any boy taking music lessons would be marked down as a sissy. Nonetheless, music was already reaching out to him.

The first stirring he remembered was when he was six, and was standing on the pavement outside a penny arcade on Harlem's One-Hundred-And-Twenty-Fifth Street. Inside, an automatic piano was playing Rubinstein's *Melody In F*, and as George later said, "The peculiar jumps in the music held me rooted." For the rest of his life, he could never hear the piece without picturing himself in overalls and barefooted outside that arcade.

For some reason he did nothing about his newfound interest at the age of six, but when he was twelve he heard a fellow pupil called Maxie Rosenzweig play Dvorak's *Humoresque* at a school entertainment. George had not bothered to attend the entertainment, but he heard the sound of Maxie's violin floating out through the assembly-hall window. He was entranced and made up his mind at once to get to know whoever was playing. He waited outside for an hour-and-a-half, from three to four-thirty, in the hope of meeting the performer. It was pouring rain, and he got soaked to the skin, but no violinist emerged.

Going inside, he discovered the player's name and that he had already left by the teachers' entrance. He also found out where Maxie lived, about a hundred blocks from his own home and, still soaking, trekked there. Maxie had been home but gone out again. His parents, however, were so amused by this dripping enthusiast that they arranged for the two to meet.

George's musical instincts had been good. Maxie Rosenzweig, then aged eleven and a year younger than George, was a child prodigy who would go on in later years, his name shortened to Max Rosen, to be a successful violin virtuoso.

George and Maxie became close friends. They talked endlessly about music, and Max began George's musical education. He told him about the great composers and began to explain to him some of the rudiments of musical composition. George began to experiment on the pianos he found in the homes of Max and other friends, and he dreamed of one day becoming Max's accompanist, until one day Max told him to give up any ideas he might have of a musical career. "You haven't it in you, Georgie," he said. "Take my word for it. I can tell." As George himself said years later, "Max opened the world of music for me. And he came near to closing it too."

Fortunately, at around this time in 1910, George and Ira's mother Rose decided to buy a piano because her sister Kate had just bought one. She put down a first installment on a second-hand upright, and among much excitement from the watching neighbours it was hoisted in through the window of the Gershvins' apartment, above Saul Birn's phonograph shop on Second Avenue, where they were living at the time. Among the neighbours watching was a twelve-year-old school-friend of Ira's, Yip Harburg ('Yip' is a contraction of Yipsel, meaning squirrel).

Yip, like Ira, would go on to become a famous lyric-writer. Among the songs he wrote the words for are 'Brother, Can You Spare A Dime?', 'April In Paris' and 'It's Only A Paper Moon'.

Rose's idea when she bought the piano was that Ira, not George, should take piano lessons. After all, Ira was the quiet and studious son, not like George, who was showing all the signs of becoming a roughneck. In their oddly uncommunicative family, nobody had the slightest idea that George had been experimenting on his friends' pianos.

However, no sooner had the piano been installed in the apartment than George made a bee-line for it, twirled the piano stool down to size, lifted the keyboard cover and began confidently to play a popular tune of the day. The family were amazed, and Ira was especially struck by the harmonies produced by George's fluent left hand. Already he had something distinctive in the way he voiced a song.

Ira had already had a few piano lessons from his aunt Kate, but he was more interested in words than music, and was quite happy to be elbowed off the piano by his younger brother. The piano changed George's life. As he told an interviewer in 1924, "Studying the piano made a good boy out of a bad one. It took the piano to tone me down. It made me more serious. I was a changed person six months after I took it up."

The obsessive drive to create music that was to stay with him all his life had been generated. He began playing the piano constantly, and such was his singlemindedness that his parents at first were not sure what to make of this new behaviour. Morris, with his appreciation of opera and his easy-going approach to life, was encouraging. Rose, more practical, felt that perhaps it would be better if George thought less about the piano and more about his school-work.

Nonetheless, it was agreed that George should have piano lessons. First he went to a Miss Green, at fifty cents a lesson, then in succession to two other local lady teachers who charged the same. He quickly learned to read music, and soon was playing the piano for the morning assembly exercises at PS25. When he scraped through graduation there in 1912, at the age of fourteen, his mother, still doubtful about piano-playing as a livelihood, decided he had best become an accountant and sent him to the High School of Commerce, where he also played the piano for assembly.

While half-heartedly attending the High School, George continued obsessively listening to every piano player he could find, and to music of all sorts. Although his first interest in music had been fired by the light classics, he mixed the rhythms of ragtime and popular song into his playing. At no time did he make any distinction between different types of music. Classical music, ragtime, popular songs, all to him were simply music and all should merge into one another. Ragtime, both as popular song and as dance music, had become a national craze with the publication in 1911 of 'Alexander's Ragtime Band', written by a Jewish immigrant ten years older than George, and from the opposite end of Russia, from Siberia. His name had been Israel Baline, but when a printer's error on his first published song, 'Marie From Sunny Italy', had given his surname as 'Berlin', he adopted that to go with a new first name, Irving.

That was in 1907, and in those days Irving wrote only lyrics, but it wasn't long before he began writing music as well, and soon he was being billed as 'The King Of Ragtime', following his first hit with such numbers as 'That Mysterious Rag', 'Everybody's Doin' It' and 'Everybody Step'. In 1912, when his young bride died of typhoid contracted during their honeymoon in Cuba, he wrote the sad song, 'When I Lost You', which became the first of the Berlin ballads, selling more than a million copies and extending his range considerably.

From the 1890s until past the turn of the century the words of popular songs had been more important than the music. The melodies tended to be minor variations of familiar tunes that had been used before. It was Irving Berlin more than anyone who changed that. The stream of new and imaginative songs he produced made him for decades the king of popular composers.

In the year that 'Alexander's Ragtime Band' became a hit, George met a pianist called Goldfarb, who played classical pieces flamboyantly and with enormous gusto. This style of playing impressed the thirteen-year-old George, and he sought out Goldfarb's teacher, an impressively-moustached Hungarian conductor named Von Zerly, who mainly led theatre bands performing operettas.

Von Zerly took occasional pupils, and agreed to take George for the stiff fee of one-and-a-half dollars an hour. His methods were all his own. Instead of making his pupils practise scales, the basic equipment of any competent pianist, he hurled them straight into learning excerpts from grand opera and such pieces as the 'William Tell Overture', all simplified for piano by Von Zerly himself.

Probably more helpful to George's musical development were the concerts he began to attend. In 1912 and 1913 he heard recitals by virtuosos like Leo Ornstein, Efrem Zimbalist and Josef Lhévine. By early 1913 he was playing the piano in an amateur musical group organised by PS63 and calling itself the Beethoven Society Orchestra. It performed such popular pieces as Schubert's 'Unfinished Symphony' and the piece that had made such an impression on him three years earlier, Dvorak's 'Humoresque'.

In spite of his immersion in the classics, his interest in popular song remained as great. In his 1913 summer vacation from the High School of Commerce he got his first paid job as a pianist, getting five dollars a week for playing at a summer resort in the Catskill Mountains in New York State. The Catskill resorts were the refuge during the hot summer months for a million perspiring New Yorkers, mostly Jewish.

For this reason these resorts were nicknamed the Borscht Circuit and many performers struggling their way into show business, such as Phil Silvers, Eddie Cantor, Sid Caesar and Danny Kaye, made their ill-paid beginning entertaining in the hotels there.

George had by this time firmly decided that his mission in life was to be a composer of popular songs. With the example of Irving Berlin before him, he was convinced that popular song was not only an important music, it was also distinctively American, and as an American it was only right that he should use its rhythms and voicings.

His first song, never published, was written in 1913 and called 'Since I Found You' (a title possibly in imitation of Berlin's 'When I Lost You'). Its lyric was written by a Lower East Side friend of George's, Leonard Praskin. His second, also in 1913 and also with a lyric by his friend Praskin, was written in open admiration of Berlin, and was called 'Raggin' The Traumerei' (Berlin had done the same thing to Mendelssohn's 'Spring Song').

This second song was never published either, but in 1914 one of his songs did at least get a public performance. The Finley Club, a literary society that Ira belonged to, was putting on its annual concert. Ira, being on the arrangement committee, naturally arranged for his brother to appear. George, as well as accompanying a singer called Charles Rose, played a composition of his own as a piano solo. Its title is lost to history (although George would happily play it on request for the rest of his life). All we know is that it had a tango-like rhythm and that, according to Ira, its opening sounded like a later Gershwin song, 'Stiff Upper Lip'.

Another young pianist who played with the Beethoven Society Orchestra was Jack Miller. Impressed by George's enthusiasm, he suggested one day in 1914 that George should meet his tutor, Charles Hambitzer. He arranged the meeting, and Jack and George went to Hambitzer's studio. George played the 'William Tell Overture' as Von Zerly had taught him, with a great deal of showy style, exaggerated dynamics and uneven tempos. "Listen," said Hambitzer. "Let's hunt out the guy who taught you to play this way and shoot him. And not with an apple on his head either."

Charles Hambitzer was thirty-two. He had been born in Milwaukee, where his father owned a music store, and had turned out to be one of those natural musicians who absorbed musical knowledge without effort. He could play any instrument, almost on sight. As a child he could play piano, violin and cello, although none of his family was quite sure how or where he learnt. In adulthood he could play almost every instrument in the orchestra, at least competently.

He received his main musical training from Julius Albert Jahn, one of the finest piano teachers in the midwest, and became a piano virtuoso. As a young man he taught music at the Wisconsin Conservatory and later directed the Arthur Friend Stock Company Orchestra at the Pabst Theatre. He received further tuition from Hugo Kaun, a musician visiting from Germany, who taught him harmony, counterpoint and orchestration, and in 1908, when he was twenty-seven, convinced him he should move from Milwaukee to New York. There he opened a piano studio in the Morningside Park district, his teaching becoming so popular that soon he had seventy pupils.

He also became a member of a thirty-two piece orchestra, led by an ex-assistant of Toscanini's, Joseph Knecht, which gave serious concerts lasting from two to four hours, seven days a week, at the Waldorf-Astoria Hotel. A keen student of the newest developments in music, Hambitzer was among the first in America to play Arnold Schoenberg's atonal work *Six Short Piano Pieces* in public performance.

He also composed. He wrote suites and tone poems, and in the year George met him had just completed the score for an operetta, *The Love Wager*, which toured the country successfully for a year. This had been a commission. Most of his works were not, and he made little effort to get them published or performed, suffering from a mixture of impracticality, lack of ambition and a crippling sense of inadequacy.

His private life had been unfortunate. After a brief and unhappy first marriage and divorce, he had remarried in 1905. He and his second wife were devoted to each other, and they had a daughter, Mitzi, but after they came to New York his wife developed tuberculosis and became a hopeless invalid.

Passionate about music, he responded to George's serious enthusiasm and took him on as a pupil. It was the best thing that could have happened, giving George his first proper grounding in music. Hambitzer put him through a rigorous regime of exercises and scales. He introduced him to the great piano pieces by such as Bach, Beethoven, Chopin and Liszt, and even to composers then new on the scene, like Debussy and Ravel.

Although his main concern was to teach George to play, he also worked to make him conscious of harmony, theory and instrumentation. The two young men's enthusiasms fed each other. George would play Hambitzer current songs like 'Alexander's Ragtime Band' and point out their virtues, explaining that as far as he was concerned Berlin was America's Franz Schubert.

Soon after they had met, Hambitzer wrote to his sister:

> I have a new pupil who will make his mark in music if anybody will. The boy is a genius without a doubt; he's crazy about music and can't wait until it's time to take his lessons.No watching the clock for this boy! He wants to go in for this modern stuff, jazz and what not. But I'm not going to let him for a while. I'll see that he gets a firm foundation in modern music first.

It says a lot for Hambitzer's own awareness of all forms of music that he used the word 'jazz' as early as 1914. After all, jazz itself would only reach New York and become a craze at the beginning of 1917. The word itself first appeared in print only in 1913, and the most likely explanation of its origins is that it was an expression used in the dives of San Francisco meaning musical 'pep' or 'verve', and that it was first used of 'jazz bands' in Chicago. New Orleans, where the music was born, only began using the word later.

George revered and adored Hambitzer. As a pupil, he exerted himself to find him other pupils, eventually managing to dig up ten;

and in the years of his success he frequently acknowledged his indebtedness. Hambitzer, he said, made him "harmony conscious". They went to concerts together, and George acquired what he called "my habit of intensive listening. I... listened not only with my ears, but with my nerves, my mind, my heart... I became saturated with the music... Then I went home and listened in memory. I sat at the piano and repeated the motifs."

It was while studying with Hambitzer that George emulated his brother Ira and began to keep a scrapbook. In it he pasted pictures and biographies of great composers and performers, mainly clipped from a musical magazine, *The Etude*. He also inserted programmes of the concerts he more and more frequently attended – concerts by orchestras like the New York Philharmonic, the New York Symphony Society and the Russian Symphony, and by virtuosos like Leopold Godowsky and (naturally) Maxie Rosenzweig.

He also kept hearing exciting new compositions in the world of popular song. In 1914 his aunt Kate married. The wedding was held at the Grand Central Hotel, and the band there played a tune whose melody and harmonies so excited George that he raced to the bandstand to ask what it was. It was called 'You're Here And I'm Here', and it was from a 1914 show called *The Laughing Husband*, and it was by a composer called Jerome Kern, born and raised in New York and New Jersey, and then aged twenty-nine.

The band played another number by Kern, 'They Didn't Believe Me' (from an earlier show *The Girl from Utah*), and George knew he had found a model for the songs he wanted to write. In fact, as he himself said later, "I paid him the tribute of frank imitation, and many things I wrote at this period sounded as though Kern had written them himself."

What was it that was so new about these songs? They were not far different in structure from the standard songs of the day, having a sixteen-bar verse and a thirty-two-bar chorus (popular songs had settled into a more or less fixed form mostly so as to allow vaudeville and revue performers, with their established dance routines, to easily exchange an old song for a new one without having to rework their choreography).

But Kern used many devices that placed him far ahead of all other songwriters. In 'They Didn't Believe Me', for instance, he underlines a climax by using an unexpected change of key. When the chorus is repeated, a new four-bar phrase is suddenly interpolated. The rhythm unexpectedly changes from consecutive quarter and half notes to triplets. Countless fresh ideas like these, plus the essential gift of writing a charming melody, made Kern the man to emulate.

It was now becoming clear to George's family (it had been clear to George for some time) that his life was to be in music. The High School of Commerce had become an irritating irrelevance. George was anxious to leave it and when, in March 1914, he was told by a friend called Ben Bloom that there was a vacancy for a demonstration pianist at the music publishing firm of Jerome H Remick & Co, he applied for the job.

He was auditioned by the manager, Mose Gumble, who offered him the job at a salary of fifteen dollars a week.His piano-playing must have been impressive, because not only was George the first inexperienced employee that Remick's ever hired, he would also be, at fifteen, the youngest piano-pounder on Tin Pan Alley.

Fifteen dollars a week was good money for a poorly-qualified teenager, but when he announced his intention of quitting the High School and taking the job, his mother was unsympathetic. The suspicion had already grown in her mind that George would never make an accountant, but instead she had conceived the vague idea of getting him into the fur business. Anything rather than the uncertainties of the world of music.

Words were briefly exchanged between George and his mother, but his will was even more powerful than hers, and somewhat reluctantly she gave in. George quit school and went to work at Remick's. Morris's reaction was simply to shrug his shoulders.

CHAPTER TWO

Remick's

O nce employed at Remick's, George's life became even more hectic and exciting. There he met customers and music journalists and songwriters (some successful and some hoping to be successful), and began building up a useful range of contacts in the business. As he was an outgoing and sociable young man, many of these became close friends.

The firm of Jerome H Remick & Co had started off in Detroit, where it became successful by publishing hit songs such as 'Creole Belles' and 'Hiawatha'. In 1902, building on its success, the firm moved to Twenty-Eighth Street in New York City, to Tin Pan Alley. By 1914, when it employed George as a pianist, it had become one of the most powerful music publishers in America. Among the many songs that had made it so were 'Chinatown, My Chinatown', 'Put On Your Old Grey Bonnet', and 'By The Light Of The Silvery Moon'.

Songwriters would come to music publishers with songs they hoped to get published, and performers and producers would come looking for new songs to use in their shows. It was George's job to sit in one of a row of cubicles for eight to ten hours a day and demonstrate the latest numbers by pounding them out on a piano.

George, of course, did anything but pound. By now his personal style of playing was fairly well formed. His fingering was fast and clean, and as he played a tune he would embroider variations on it. In fact this became the way he would compose for the rest of his life, improvising at the piano.

Unlike most other Tin Pan Alley pianists, he had a thorough grounding in the harmonic theory of classical music, with its rich repertoire of resolutions, modulations and chord inversions. He used this knowledge in his improvisations, and also began to use in them the rhythms and intonations of American popular music, which at the time he joined Remick's, in May 1914, meant ragtime.

The original ragtime was a piano music that had grown up in the Southern and midwestern states during the 1890s. Originally the expression had been 'ragged time', 'ragging' being a slang word for syncopation, emphasising those beats in the bar that are usually weak in order to produce a stronger and more lively rhythm.

This syncopation would pass on into jazz, but ragtime, unlike jazz, was composed and written down. A typical ragtime piece was quite a formal composition. It would have three or four distinct sixteen-bar strains, which would be interwoven with considerable subtlety, both melodic and rhythmic, by such composers as Scott Joplin, who wrote his famous 'Maple Leaf Rag' in 1899, and Eubie Blake, who wrote his first rag, 'Sounds Of Africa' in the same year, when he was fifteen (he lived to be a hundred, dying in 1983).

Ragtime, in its classic form, became widely popular. Dances, based on the informal negro dances of the southern states and using ragtime rhythms, began to appear in the society dance-halls of New York, many of them with animal names reflecting their country origins – the turkey trot, the grizzly bear, the bunny hug.

The word 'ragtime' began to be used for any cheerful syncopated piano music, and in the 1900s 'novelty' pieces that were not true rags at all began to appear – 'Black And White Rag', 'Temptation Rag', 'Dill Pickles Rag' and hundreds of others. And when Irving Berlin wrote his song 'Alexander's Ragtime Band' in 1911, the craze swept the nation.

The pianists in a firm like Remick's worked closely with the song-pluggers. These were the firm's salesmen, and their energetic hustling was a great factor in making a song a hit. Using all the charm and contacts at their command they would plug the firm's songs to performers in vaudeville, revue, burlesque and musical comedy, to dance-band leaders, to singing waiters, and to the proprietors of stores selling sheet music, getting a song all the exposure they could.

Mose Gumble, who had hired George as one of his string of pianists, was himself one of the most successful song-pluggers of all time. Among the songs he energetically promoted into hits were 'Oh,

You Beautiful Doll' and 'In The Shade Of The Old Apple Tree'.

From time to time George would get a break from his piano cubicle and be sent out by Mose Gumble to play Remick songs in restaurants or music stores, sometimes as a soloist, sometimes to accompany a singer. On one such mission he was sent to the resort of Atlantic City, in New Jersey, to play in the sheet music department of a local five-and-ten-cent store during the day, and in the evening, after the store closed, to go out plugging songs himself in amusement arcades, saloons and the smaller cafés (the larger cafés would be the territory of experienced first-string pluggers).

When work was over, long past midnight, the song-pluggers of the various publishers would gather in Child's Restaurant on the boardwalk and talk shop. It was there that George first met another young pianist and song-plugger called Harry Rubinstein, who would become one of his lifelong friends.

Harry too would become a songwriter, changing his name to Harry Ruby. The writing partner he teamed up with was an ex-vaudeville dancer, Bert Kalmar, and together they wrote a fair number of mindless chirpy twenties numbers, such as 'I Wanna Be Loved By You' (boop-boopa-doo). One day, just to amuse themselves, they turned out a deliberately over-sentimental ballad which they had no intention of ever releasing. Somebody did release it, however, and 'Who's Sorry Now?' became their greatest hit.

Apparently realising that there was little difference between tongue-in-cheek nonsense and popular romance, from then on they divided their time between writing sentimental hits and some of the best and strangest numbers ever sung by Groucho Marx, such as 'Show Me A Rose' (and 'I'll Show You A Girl Named Sam') and the immortal 'Hooray For Captain Spaulding'. (As well as writing the songs for *Animal Crackers*, they worked on the screenplays of *Horse Feathers* and *Duck Soup*.)

Years later, remembering meeting George in Atlantic City, Harry wrote, "I still recall George's eagerness, his intense enthusiasm for his work, his passionate interest in every phase of the popular music business. Sometimes when he spoke of the artistic mission of popular music, we thought he was going highfalutin'. The height of artistic achievement to us was a 'pop' song that sold lots of copies, and we just didn't understand what he was talking about." And like almost everyone else, he was deeply impressed by George's playing.

George's love of piano playing stayed with him all his life. From time to time while he was employed at Remick's he would get evening jobs playing in cafés or night-clubs, sometimes as a soloist, sometimes in a small band. This was partly from love of playing, and partly to learn as much as he could about all aspects of the world of music.

He also began making occasional trips to East Orange, New Jersey, where he would make piano rolls, earning twenty-five dollars for six. In those days, when the phonograph was still a scratchy novelty, piano rolls provided the best-quality sound you could get in the home. The quality of the phonograph gradually improved, taking a great leap forward with the introduction of electrical recording in 1925. Shortly after that, the player-piano vanished from the scene, but George enjoyed recording piano rolls, and even after he had become famous, he still continued making them well into the twenties. He even cut a piano version of his 1924 masterpiece, 'Rhapsody In Blue'.

All this extra activity brought him in extra cash. He began to save money, and when his mother learned he had saved two-hundred dollars, she insisted he follow her example and buy a diamond ring for security.

On free evenings, he went as often as possible to classical concerts (a habit that many of his fellow song-pluggers found hard to understand – what did the concert-hall have to do with writing a big hit?). He also continued his studies with Charles Hambitzer. Only a few months after George had joined Remick's, Charles's invalid wife died of her tuberculosis. Charles was heartbroken, and to cope with his grief threw himself with even greater energy into his work – playing, composing and encouraging his pupils, especially George. Early the next year, feeling that he had now given George a good start in making him "harmony-conscious", he arranged for him to have additional lessons in theory from a colleague, Edward Kilyeni, a well-known teacher of composition. He told Kilyeni, "The boy is not only talented, but is uncommonly serious in his search for knowledge of music."

In his search for knowledge of music George combed New York, listening avidly to music of every sort. At around this time his family spent two periods living in the resort of Coney Island, which is not an island at all but the coast at the southern end of Brooklyn, where the Hudson River flows out into the Atlantic. The first of these periods was in the summer of 1914 and the second was in 1915, after one of Morris's business ventures, a small chain of restaurants, had collapsed and he was temporarily bankrupt. While in Coney Island George heard a ragtime pianist called Les Copeland, and was impressed. Possibly this was the first time he heard true ragtime, and not simply the popular music based on it.

But by the time George heard Les Copeland, popular music was already moving on from ragtime. By 1915 the first stirrings of jazz were beginning to be heard in New York, and the musicians leading the way were the black stride pianists – men like Willie 'The Lion' Smith, Luckey Roberts and James P Johnson, who would in time write the number that more than any other captured the carefree mood of the twenties – the Charleston.

These too, George soon made it his business to hear, dropping in at the bars and dance halls where they played, and even the rent-parties, where the tenant of an apartment, needing to raise the rent, would hire a pianist and charge his friends and neighbours a small fee to attend. Usually other pianists would drop in as well, and they would take turns trying to outshine each other at the keyboard. These 'cutting-contests' did a lot to raise the standard of their playing.

Stride piano was rhythmically freer than ragtime and brought the beginnings of jazz improvisation into popular music. Jazz itself would not become the popular craze in New York (and then the world) until a group of young white musicians from New Orleans, calling themselves The Original Dixieland Jass Band, arrived from Chicago to open at the fashionable Reisenweber's Restaurant in January 1917.

But the band that converted George for life to an enthusiasm for black music was working around New York earlier than that. In 1915 an entrepreneur called Barron Wilkins opened one of the first big night-clubs in Harlem, calling it Barron's Club, and in 1915 or 1916 George went there and heard the band of James Reese Europe.

The businesslike and gentlemanly Jim Europe was at that time the most fashionable band leader in New York. He had been born in 1881 in Alabama, and moved with his family to Washington when he was ten. There he completed his education and musical training, and in 1904 came to New York hoping to find a job as musical director and pianist in one of the black touring shows of the day. Ever since the end of the American Civil War in 1865, blacks had provided a large proportion of America's musicians – at first often in minstrel shows, later in black revues and musicals.

It took him till 1906 to get a job in one of these, when he went on the road with a revue called *Shoo Fly Regiment*. Returning to New York in 1909, he scraped a living by accompanying singers, playing in small dance orchestras, and giving lessons.

Many black musicians of his generation in New York tended to look down on the syncopated music that was being developed in the southern states, and especially in New Orleans. They regarded blues (if they ever heard any) as a low down primitive music, and even regarded ragtime as associated with the racially stereotyped minstrel shows of an earlier era.

But Jim Europe, who had decided that his future lay in popular music, realised the power of syncopation, even in the primitive form of those days, and decided to make use of it. In around 1910 he formed an orchestra and gave a concert at the Manhattan Casino.

They played light classics, some popular songs of the day, and a few ragtime pieces, and the show was completed by a variety programme and dancing. It was a great success, and was followed by other concerts, each more spectacular than the last.

By 1913 one of these concerts attracted an audience of four thousand, and in 1914 he even gave a concert at Carnegie Hall, ten years before Paul Whiteman's band played there, let alone Benny Goodman's famous appearance in 1938. His orchestra for that occasion had an extraordinary line-up including forty-seven mandolins, twenty-seven harp-guitars, eleven banjos, thirteen cellos, eight violins, eight trombones, seven cornets and ten pianos, plus two choirs.

This vast aggregation was probably assembled in an attempt to generate excitement. Another way he tried to do this was by playing at enormous speed. Two records he made in 1913, 'Down Home Rag' and 'Too Much Mustard' are played terrifyingly fast, at around two-hundred-and-eighty beats to the minute, with two notes to each beat.

He was by now becoming nationally famous, but his fame grew even greater after 1914, when one of his bands (a much smaller one) was heard playing at a private party by the husband-and-wife team of Vernon and Irene Castle, who were astounded by its rhythms and instrumental colour.

Following the popular-song boom of the first years of the century, there had grown up an equally enormous dance boom, spurred on by the popularity of ragtime. It was now that modern ballroom dancing began. The Castles were America's king and queen of the ballroom, and the rage of high society, devising new dances, giving demonstrations, and arranging tuition.

But they had trouble finding musicians who could play for the syncopated dances they wanted to create, and when they heard Jim Europe they knew that he was the answer. He became their musical director, and the most famous band leader in America. In an odd parallel to the life of Glenn Miller, at the height of his success he enlisted to fight in World War One. Given the job of assembling an army band, he succeeded so triumphantly that on its return from France the band (with Bill 'Bojangles' Robinson as its drum-major) was given a ticker-tape parade through the streets of New York. Quite an honour for a black band in 1919. He would undoubtedly have gone on to lasting fame if he hadn't been fatally stabbed, later the same year, by a drummer he had reprimanded.

By the time George heard The Jim Europe Band, in 1915 at Barron's Club, its tempos had become less frantic than they were, and its brass instruments in particular were beginning to use the voice-like intonations and the occasionally flattened notes characteristic of jazz. George was bowled over by its power and vitality, and it encouraged him to develop his interest in black music.

Among the tunes that Jim Europe frequently played were several by the pioneer blues composer, WC Handy, including 'Hesitating Blues', 'Memphis Blues' and Handy's most famous tune, which had been a big hit in 1914, 'St Louis Blues'.

Handy, who was from Alabama, led a sort of Sousa/ragtime brass dance-band around the southern states before coming to New York in 1917, and he did more than anyone to write down (and copyright) songs being sung by black blues singers in the South. George was so impressed by these songs that after his 'Rhapsody In Blue' had become the success it did, he autographed a copy of the score "For WC Handy, whose early blue songs are the forefathers of this work".

Meanwhile, at Remick's, George's own reputation was growing – at least as a pianist. One regular visitor to his cubicle was Max Abramson, a journalist working for the theatrical paper, *The Clipper*. Abramson was so impressed by George's playing that he started doing everything in his power to further George's career, referring to him, only half jokingly, as 'the genius'.

Another regular visitor to Remick's was a young would-be lyricist called Irving Caesar, later to write distinguished lyrics for (among many other things) the show *No, No, Nanette* (with composer Vincent Youmans, who also started out as a pianist as Remick's) and a less distinguished lyric for Shirley Temple, 'Animal Crackers' (with Ray Henderson, previously of DeSylva, Brown and Henderson).

But life at Remick's wasn't always fun. "Some of the customers treated me like dirt," George later wrote. Gospel singers would get him "to play them 'God Send You Back to Me' in seven keys". Chorus ladies would breathe down his back (although why he complained about this is unclear). "Others," he wrote, "were charming." Among the most charming were a young brother-and-sister dance team, Fred and Adele Astaire. They were still only teenagers. Fred had been born in 1899, and so was a year younger than George. Adele was a couple of years older.

They had started in vaudeville as children in 1905, at first being barred from the New York stage for being under-age, and so mainly performing on the West Coast. When George first met them at Remick's they were still trouping their act around the USA, building up their reputation and hoping to break onto Broadway.

Adele was bubbly and vivacious. Old-timers who saw her say she was the most talented partner Fred ever had. Certainly she was the partner he had longest, from 1905 until 1932, the year she retired from the theatre to marry Lord Charles Cavendish, the Duke of Devonshire's second son, and disappeared to live with him in Lismore Castle in Ireland.

"Wouldn't it be wonderful," the young George once said to Fred, "if some day I could write a show and you and Adele would star in it." Remembering the conversation years later, he said, "We just laughed then – but it came true."

George's worst aggravation from working at Remick's was that the firm resolutely refused to publish his songs. Among songs that he wrote there were 'Drifting Along With The Tide', 'Some Rain Must Fall' and 'Dancing Shoes'. Mose Gumble's reaction to these was, "You're paid to play the piano, not to write songs. We've plenty of songwriters under contract."

Trying to place his songs elsewhere, George took them to his first idol, Irving Berlin, who was by 1915 also in music publishing, a partner in the firm Waterson, Berlin and Snyder. Berlin praised the songs but made no offer to publish them. George put them away in a file for possible future use, a habit he continued all his life – no song or snatch of music that he thought had some value ever got thrown away, and many of his songs, initially rejected, found their way into later shows.

In 1916, George finally got his first song published. The lyric was written with a young colleague on Tin Pan Alley, Murray Roth (who went on to become a motion-picture executive) and its title was 'When You Want 'Em, You Can't Get 'Em, When You've Got 'Em, You Don't Want 'Em'.

The singer Sophie Tucker heard the song and liked both its well-constructed melody and its humorous colloquial lyric. She recommended it to publisher Harry Von Tilzer, and on 15 May 1916 it was copyrighted. The name of the composer was given as 'George Gershwin'. George had experimented with such alternative surnames as 'Gersh' and 'Wynne', but finally decided on 'Gershwin', and Gershwin he would remain. And in due course the rest of his family would follow suit.

Von Tilzer offered the young composer and lyricist a choice between a fee of fifteen dollars outright, or a percentage of the royalties with a five dollar advance against them. Roth took the fifteen dollars. George gambled on the royalties and the five dollar advance was all he ever got.

Unfortunately for the future of the newly-successful young team, shortly afterwards it broke up in rather an odd way. Whatever hidden tensions there were between them, George and Murray one day began to wrestle in a light-hearted way (after all, they were both still in their teens), and somehow the wrestling ceased to be quite so light-hearted. "Both were so shaken up," said Ira later, "that they never wrote another song together."

George's songwriting ambitions at this time were undergoing a subtle change. At first he had simply aimed at getting his songs published. A published song could be performed in vaudeville, or revue, or by dance bands, and through a combination of these become a hit. But there was another outlet for the sort of songs he wanted to write, and that was musical comedy. After all, Jerome Kern wrote only for musical comedy, and Irving Berlin a couple of years before, in 1914, had written his first complete score for the Broadway stage, a musical called *Watch Your Step* (starring Vernon and Irene Castle).

George's admiration for the work of Jerome Kern had made him realise that the songs in musical comedy were usually better-conceived than the songs of Tin Pan Alley. Not that a song from a musical comedy couldn't also become a hit – if the show was a success, songs from it would be published as sheet music and marketed in the usual way.

As far back as 1910, Ira and his friend Yip Harburg had listened for hours to the comic operas of Gilbert and Sullivan, played on the family Victrola. They were entranced by the combination of brilliant light verse and clever, tuneful music, and by the tightness of their overall construction. There was nothing like them at that time being produced in America.

Ira, in his own quiet way, had ambitions too. They were nothing like as intense as his younger brother's drive to create a truly American music, in fact they had more the feel of youthful enthusiasm than a holy crusade, but they were real. He had decided he wanted to become a writer, mainly in the field of light humour.

In spite of being a well-behaved schoolboy, Ira had not been an outstanding student. All the same, he did well enough at PS20 to be accepted at the age of fourteen for a three-year course at the academically demanding Townsend Harris School, his mother having the idea that he too might become a teacher. While there he wrote, illustrated and edited a one-page newspaper he called *The Leaf*, producing one issue a week for twenty-six weeks, and issuing it to its single subscriber, an older second cousin.

After *The Leaf* ceased publication he did illustrations for the school magazine, and also had to stay on an extra term at the end of his three years to retake two subjects which were necessary for his admission to the College of the City of New York.

He finally went there in February 1914, but never completed the course. Mathematics in particular floored him, and after two years he left, explaining, "The only possible way, seemingly, of getting a diploma, was to remain in college long enough to earn one by squatter's rights." While there, however, he did co-write a regular column for one college magazine with his friend Yip Harburg, and wrote solo sketches and verses for another.

In 1916 he transferred to a rather less demanding night college, but he had by now decided that he was no teacher. He had for a while the rather wild and impractical notion of studying medicine, and enrolled for an extension course at Columbia University. After one term he failed chemistry, and decided that maybe the sensible thing would be to give up all thoughts of further education and try to become a writer.

Uncertain as to exactly what form his writing should take, or whether he could make a living at it, he began a succession of routine jobs. The first, from 1916, was as desk clerk in a Turkish bath, or rather, two Turkish baths in succession. Both were ill-starred ventures of his father's – first the St Nicholas Baths on One-Hundred-And-Eleventh Street, and when that failed, the Lafayette Baths downtown.

He and George, who had not been especially close in their early teens, began to grow closer once George's discovery of the piano had opened in him a general awareness of the arts. (When Ira was publishing *The Leaf*, George even imitated him by producing a similar periodical of his own, which he called *The Merry Musician*, but his interest only sustained it for one issue.)

In around 1915, as well as going to concerts and shows and films with such Tin Pan Alley friends as Irving Caesar and Harry Ruby, George began going to them with Ira. And at the end of 1916 they were joined by a cousin, Harry Botkin, whose family lived in Boston, but who had come to New York to live. Harry was an artist who would eventually become a respected painter and art-connoisseur (as well as a lifelong friend of both George and Ira). The three of them often went together to shows and parties, and it was Harry who encouraged both his cousins to draw and paint.

For George, the painting came later. In 1916 his attention was firmly focused on learning to write for musical comedies. These, then and later, were usually written by a three-man team – a composer and a lyricist to do the songs, and a writer to provide the linking dialogue and plot (known in the business as 'the book'), although at times one person might perform two of these roles. The king of American musical comedy in the early years of the century, the energetic George M Cohan, habitually performed all three.

Most of Cohan's plots were mawkish and super-patriotic (he was even more proud than the Gershwins were of being American) and they have not worn well, but he did compose a few cheerful songs that have lasted, such as 'Yankee Doodle Dandy' and 'Give My Regards To Broadway'.

Cohan apart, the American musical of the first dozen years of the century was a mixture of romantic Viennese operetta and American revue. Those that tended towards the Viennese would have huge casts, over-lavish productions and fantastic plot-lines. Those looking towards revue, while equally lavish, would be haphazard collections of songs and vaudeville sketches, their music using syncopated ragtime rhythms instead of the flowing light-classical rhythms of operetta.

Kern, more than any other composer, changed all that. He felt that the songs and the plot should be tightly integrated. As he wrote in 1917: "The musical numbers should carry on the action of the play and should be representative of the personalities of the characters who sing them. Songs must be suited to the action and the mood of the play."

Why this approach makes for better musicals is not immediately obvious. Audiences tend to be excited by the music or the dancing or the singing or the comedy. People rarely come out of musicals saying, "My word, wasn't the way the songs were integrated into the plot magnificent?"

All the same, making the songs fit the characters and using them to advance the action of the plot allows the show to carry on telling a story without interruption. This keeps the audience involved in the plot and allows the show to build to a proper dramatic climax, in addition to whatever pleasure the songs would provide alone.

Kern got his chance to put his principles into practice at a New York theatre called the Princess. This tiny theatre, seating only two-hundred-and-ninety-nine, was on Thirty-Ninth Street. It was run by a manager called Ray Comstock and a theatrical agent called Bessie Marbury and, in 1910 they had been having a thin time of it. They were finding it hard to find the right sort of show for a house of that size.

Then Bessie had a brilliant inspiration. Why not try scaled-down musical comedy? The small theatre could not afford any of the big-name composers – they would have to get an ambitious youngster, and the obvious choice was Jerome Kern, who had already been making a name for himself. The additional numbers he had been hired to write into heavy imported Viennese operettas were usually the best things in the shows.

Kern suggested Guy Bolton to write both book and lyrics, and together they produced the first of what were to become famous as 'the Princess shows'. It was called *Nobody Home*, and was enough of a success for Ray Comstock and Bessie Marbury to commission them to write another. This was called *Very Good Eddie* (a catchphrase then made popular by ventriloquist Fred Stone), and by chance a young English writer, PG Wodehouse, who had moved to America the year before, was sent to review it for the magazine *The Smart Set*.

Kern had worked in London on a show called *The Beauty Of Bath*, and Wodehouse had collaborated with him there, writing excellent lyrics. Bolton was happier writing book than lyrics, and after Kern had introduced them, Bolton and Wodehouse decided to become a writing team.

The first show they collaborated on was not at the Princess. Bolton landed them the job of fitting a new book and lyrics to the existing score of a Viennese operetta, to be produced by the redoubtable Abe Erlanger, czar of Broadway, at his vast New Amsterdam Theatre. Guy Bolton's original name for the rewritten show was 'Little Miss Springtime', but Erlanger objected ("We don't have nothing little at the New Amsterdam"). It opened as simply *Miss Springtime* and was a considerable success.

Musicals were so popular by 1916 that there was an incessant demand for new material and, in that year, George learned that

Sigmund Romberg was composing a revue for the Shubert Brothers against a tight deadline, and was using additional contributions by other songwriters.

The Shubert Brothers were immensely successful theatre owners and impresarios, and Romberg, a Hungarian immigrant whose music was in the Viennese tradition, was their staff composer. Starting in 1912, when he was in his early twenties, he would compose no fewer than forty productions for the Shuberts, including *The Student Prince* and *The Desert Song*.

George brought Romberg five different choruses he had written. One was accepted. Romberg added his name to it as collaborator, lyricist Harold Atteridge was given the job of adding words, and on 27 June 1916 the song 'Making Of A Girl' was copyrighted (according to Atteridge, what makes a girl is her clothes). This was George's second published song, and it was his first to be premiered as part of a show (the revue was called *The Passing Show Of 1916*). Six months later he picked up his royalty cheque – a little over seven dollars.

Meanwhile, the trio of Bolton, Wodehouse and Kern had started work on a musical called *Have A Heart*, designed to follow *Very Good Eddie* into the Princess. As things turned out, *Very Good Eddie* carried on running and *Have A Heart* was produced instead by manager Colonel Henry W Savage at the Liberty Theatre on Forty-Second Street. It starred a singer called Louise Dresser, and George, who within a year would be touring in vaudeville as her accompanist, was at the New York opening night, on 11 January 1917.

Four days later, with Ira, he was at another opening, this time at the Shubert Theatre, of another Kern musical, *Love O' Mike*. It was the first time Ira had ever attended a premiere, and there, also for the first time, he met two of George's closest friends, Lou and Herman Paley.

Herman Paley, who was a cousin of the journalist Max Abramson, was a staff composer at Remick's some ten years older than George. A fellow-pianist, he was one of the few musicians around Tin Pan Alley who had as rich a musical background as George. After graduating from college he had studied composition under Edward MacDowell, and had gone on to study (like George) with both Hambitzer and Kilyeni. With this background he had written two songs that had modest success 'Billy' and 'I Can Hear The Ukeleles Calling Me'.

He and George hit it off as soon as they met and, in 1915, Herman had begun inviting George to the Paley family home, which was at that time on Seventh Avenue, near One-Hundred-And-Twelfth Street. There George met Herman's brother Lou. Lou, a schoolteacher (and lyricist), was widely read, and George both admired and enjoyed his literary knowledge and all-round culture. He also admired Lou's fiancée, the charming and sensitive Emily Strunsky, then studying German literature at Hunter College. There was also a young cousin of Herman and Lou, Mabel Pleshette, who was lively and effervescent and a pianist. George added her to the list of pupils he sent to Hambitzer.

The Paleys' apartment was always full of life and enthusiasm (at one time no fewer than ten assorted Paleys and Pleshettes were living there) and for George it became a home from home. For the first time he was part of a group of eager young people immersed in music and literature. They went out to shows and films and concerts, and at the apartment they played and ate and listened and argued. Its warmth was a considerable contrast to his own home (or succession of homes), where both his parents in their different ways were emotionally withdrawn.

This cultured circle in return were enchanted by George's joyous enthusiasm. He was still in some ways a half-educated street kid, but the Paleys recognised his talent, and all his life would remain his staunchest defenders. In later life Mabel Pleshette remembered his piano playing, saying, "George made the piano do things for him... he not only played what was written – he was improvising all the time. George could make the piano laugh, he could make it sad, he could make it do anything. And when he made it laugh, he chuckled, and you would chuckle with him. You just had to laugh... He seemed to love the keys and he made them do things for him. He loved to experiment. He was original."

When classically-trained friends of the Paleys were critical of his playing (as they frequently were, complaining that he "only played ragtime"), discussions at the apartment could become acrimonious, with Herman and Lou hotly defending him, and the sensitive Emily weeping.

George, a true son of his father, always appeared unmoved by both his attackers and his defenders. Nonetheless, the warmth of the Paleys' appreciation increased his growing dissatisfaction with working at Remick's. They were convinced he had talent as a composer as well as a pianist, and he wanted to immerse himself in the sort of music Jerome Kern was writing. He needed more time to write, and he needed a job that would bring him closer to the theatre. So on Saturday 17 March 1917, he quit.

CHAPTER THREE

Show Business

After leaving Remick's, George began to spend as much time as possible working on songs. At this stage in his life he was still developing his own voice, spending much time listening to and analysing songs by other composers that had become popular, then trying to write songs of his own in imitation.

His intention at this time was to break into the musical theatre, but oddly enough, the first member of the Gershwin family to become actively involved in a show was not George; nor was it Ira. It was the youngest member of the family, the ten-year-old Frances, or Frankie, as she was known.

On 6 May 1917, Ira, George and cousin Harry Botkin went to the Terrace Gardens on Fifty-Eighth Street to see Frankie perform in a school recital. She did a Russian dance which Ira noted in his diary "was a riot", followed by her singing 'M-I-S-S-I-S-S-I-P-P-I' as a solo, then duetted with another little girl in a song called 'So Long, Letty', which was "very charming indeed".

The next day mother Rose set off with singer and dancer Frankie for a week's booking she had got on a bill in Philadelphia. And by the end of the month Frankie had been hired to tour in a show called *Daintyland*, at a salary of forty dollars a week – more than either George or Ira would earn for some time.

This foray into show business seems to indicate some change in heart in Rose since the days when she urged her two eldest sons in turn towards schoolteaching. But after all, she was ambitious for her children, wanting to encourage any talent they might have, and in the past few years son George had at least made a living in the entertainment world, so it would have become less alien to her than before.

To some of the tunes George wrote, his friend Lou Paley contributed lyrics. The song they wrote together that became best known was 'Something About Love', although this wouldn't appear in performance until 1919. In the meantime, George played his songs at parties. And sang them. "My voice," he once said, "is what is known as small but disagreeable."

Already by this time George was beginning to show a zest for parties and night life. He had begun to dress well, and generally to present the outward appearance of a debonair man-about-town, courtly and well mannered. He was also something of a ladies' man, with a fondness for beautiful women. But all these diversions in his life fell a long way short of his passion for music, and in particular for the music of George Gershwin. Once at a party he was seated with a beautiful girl on his lap when someone asked him to play the piano. He immediately forgot the girl existed and stood up so fast that she fell to the floor.

On 6 April America had entered World War One and one of the songs George and Lou Paley wrote was a tongue-in-cheek patriotic sextet, 'We're Six Little Nieces Of Our Uncle Sam'. George managed to work into the music allusions to 'The Marseillaise' and to George M Cohan's current hit, 'Over There'.

With the war in France in mind, Lou Paley also wrote for George a lyric in praise of ragtime, supposed to be sung by a French mademoiselle, complete with 'Oo-la-las'.

The war otherwise had little effect on the lives of the Gershwins. George, wondering if he might get drafted, took the practical step of buying a saxophone and spent enough spare hours practising on it in a closet at home to become reasonably proficient. If he was going to get called up, at least he was going to have some hand in providing the music.

Meanwhile, he continued to play the piano professionally. The first job he got after leaving Remick's was found for him by one of the many contacts he had already made in the music business, the black band leader and arranger, Will Vodery, who for years was the musical director of the *Ziegfeld Follies*.

Florenz Ziegfeld, during the first quarter of the twentieth century was the undisputed king of revue. He had based his *Follies*, which ran from 1907 to 1929, on the Folies Bergère of Paris, although he removed almost all the French show's eroticism so as not to offend American respectability. Instead of being sexy, his shows were glamorous. The scenery and costumes were glittering and spectacular. His showgirls, in dignified parade, were statelier (and more nearly naked) than anyone else's, and his comedians were funnier, although Ziggy didn't really appreciate comedy, regarding even such performers as WC Fields and Will Rogers as something to fill the stage while his girls got ready for the next number.

Soon after George left Remick's, Will Vodery found him a job as pianist in a vaudeville house called Fox's City Theatre, on Fourteenth Street. George was to replace Chico Marx, who had been working there while the Marx Brothers' stage act *Home Again* was between bookings. George's salary was to be twenty-five dollars a week.

Most of the time the acts on stage were accompanied by an orchestra, but the theatre presented continuous performances and the orchestra members had to eat, so George's job was to fill in for them while they went for their evening meal.

On his first evening, he started out well. The practice he had got of playing sheet music all day at Remick's (and transposing it at sight into any key required) had made his ability to sight-read almost flawless. But unfortunately he got mixed up in his cues, and at one point found himself playing one tune while the dancers on stage were performing to another. Obviously Chico hadn't had this problem, in spite of the fact that by George's standards he was barely a pianist at all. But then, Chico was thirty, had been in vaudeville for half his life, and had all the chutzpah in the world, whereas this was George's first real experience of being part of a show.

The comedian in the show began capitalising on George's mistake, cracking jokes about the difficulty of finding decent piano players. The audience and the performers began laughing, and George felt so humiliated that he suddenly jumped up from the piano, red-faced, and fled, telling the cashier on his way out that he was quitting. He didn't even ask to collect his day's pay, and later said, "The whole experience left a scar on my memory."

Nonetheless, he quite soon found another job. Ziegfeld, together with fellow-impresario Charles B Dillingham, had mounted a mammoth revue the year before at the Century Theatre, a massive and opulent showplace at the bottom of Central Park West.

The revue, called *The Century Show*, had been a great success, and now Ziegfeld and Dillingham had decided to mount a sequel, with the working title *The Second Century Show* and with music by Jerome Kern and Victor Herbert. In July 1917 George got himself engaged as rehearsal pianist at thirty-five dollars a week. For the first time he would be part of a musical in the making. Also he would meet Jerome Kern.

Bolton and Wodehouse, who by now were the hottest writing team in musical comedy, had been employed to provide the book and lyrics. They already had four shows running on Broadway – *Oh, Boy!* at the Princess (with music by Jerome Kern), *Leave It To Jane*, *The Rose Of China* and *The Riviera Girl* (with music by the Hungarian composer Kálmán, and additional numbers by Kern).

Guy Bolton had a comedy running as well – *Polly With A Past*, which he had co-written, and after all this work both he and Wodehouse could have done with a break. But as they explained in their book *Bring On the Girls*, "Writing musical comedies is like eating salted almonds – you can always manage one more."

The thing that induced them to take on *The Second Century Show* was that Wodehouse had worked on a revue in London a few years earlier and had found it restful. In a London revue the acts employed generally provided their own material, and "all the author of a revue had to do was put his name to the thing".

They got a rude awakening. Writers of New York revues were expected to provide every word of the book and lyrics themselves. Rallying from the shock, and rising to the occasion, they decided to import Jerome Kern's principles into the show. This was going to be no mere succession of vaudeville acts, like that thing last year. They were going to give it a coherent plot, in which the songs would be an integral part.

Unfortunately, they soon discovered that the show had already been largely cast – those given contracts (according to Bolton and Wodehouse) included "three classical dancers, three acrobatic dancers, a Spanish dancer, forty-eight buck-and-wing dancers, two trained cows, and Harry Kelly and his dog Lizzie... (Harry would say 'Roll over' and

Lizzie would take not the slightest notice, and Harry would say 'Good dog' and the act would proceed.)"

Also in the cast were such famous names as Irene Castle, Marion Davies, comedian Lew Fields of the famous team of Weber and Fields, and the petite and lively dancer Ann Pennington, who some years later would make the Black Bottom famous by dancing it in *George White's Scandals Of 1926*. George White by then was Ziegfeld's closest competitor, but in 1917 he was simply a dancer – and also in *The Second Century Show*.

As the days went by, more and more acts were added – a juggler or a trapeze artist or a couple of cross-talk comedians, and a performing seal called Bertie. Bolton and Wodehouse did their best, but Bolton's attempt to create a plot that could accommodate all the members of this ill-assorted cast was doomed to failure. The show, which opened on 5 November, and which by then was called *Miss 1917*, was a flop. It ran for a mere thirty days.

George, however, was a considerable success in his modest role. Jerome Kern himself was impressed by his playing, and when he learned that George had ambitions to write musical comedy, advised him to get as much experience as possible of working in the theatre first.

Accompanying a wide variety of singers at Remick's had taught George a lot about how songs should be sung, and which songs suited which voices. So he was well able to accomplish that part of his job which involved coaching the chorus. And having to play the same pieces month after month for the dancers to rehearse gave him a chance to use his powers of improvisation. To keep from being bored, he would constantly make slight variations in what he played. This kept the dancers alert and on their toes, and so went down well with the management. So much so that once the show opened they gave him another job.

During the short run of *Miss 1917*, it was arranged that members of the cast (plus celebrity guests) would give Sunday evening concerts at the Century Theatre, and George was hired to accompany the singers, still at thirty-five dollars a week.

The first concert, on 11 November, was a star-studded affair, including Eddie Cantor, George White, Ann Pennington, Fanny Brice and the outstanding black comic, Bert Williams.

Lou Paley was not the only one writing lyrics for George's songs. His old friend from the Lower East Side, Leonard Praskin, with whom he had written his first two songs back in 1913, still occasionally collaborated with him. So did his Tin Pan Alley friend, Irving Caesar. George and Irving had written several songs, and at the third Sunday concert, on 25 November, George prevailed on singer Vivienne Segal to perform two of them – 'There's More To The Kiss Than The X-X-X' (the 'X-X-X' representing kissing noises) and 'You-oo Just You'.

A representative from Remick's was at the concert and at last they accepted one of George's songs for publication. 'You-oo Just You' appeared as sheet music early in 1918, with Vivienne Segal's picture on the cover. (This was the first published Gershwin-Caesar collaboration, and later that year it would become part of a revue called *Hitchy-Koo Of 1918*, sung by Adele Rowland.)

These songs gave George his first really big break. Harry Askins, the company manager of the short-lived *Miss 1917*, who had already been impressed by George's piano-playing, was impressed by the two songs Miss Segal had sung. He recommended George as a promising new songwriter to Max Dreyfus.

Max Dreyfus was the head of TB Harms Music, the most powerful and influential publishers in the world of musical comedy. Every producer of shows knew that the place to go to find the best talent was Harms Music. Among the composers they published were Victor Herbert, Sigmund Romberg, Rudolf Friml and Jerome Kern. Max Dreyfus, whose ear for music was exceptional, would in time sign up two other promising newcomers, Cole Porter and Richard Rodgers.

To get a Harms contract was every songwriter's dream. If you were with Harms, you were automatically established. Dreyfus was so impressed by what he heard of George's songs that he not only gave him a contract, he gave him one that was almost uniquely favourable. For thirty-five dollars a week, George would become a Harms staff composer, with no responsibilities but to write songs. No regular hours, no piano-pounding or song-plugging to show off the firm's wares. It was, as Ira noted, "Some snap". Furthermore, it did not restrict George to working exclusively for Harms music, except so far as songwriting was concerned.

As George became more involved in musical comedy, Ira began to be drawn towards it as well. While trying to find direction as a humorous writer, he was still earning a living (of sorts) outside the arts. His job at the Lafayette Baths (New York's oldest turkish baths) had evaporated in the middle of 1917 when his father succeeded in bringing them to bankruptcy.

Ira, looking for a little more stability, decided to get work with a firm not run by his father, and applied for a job at the advertising department of Gimbel's. Failing to get that, he applied to another store, Altman's, and got a job in their receiving department at fifteen dollars a week.

He started there in late September 1917 and only a few weeks later was delighted when he sold his first piece of writing, to the magazine *The Smart Set*. The piece was a very short – less than a hundred words – sort of poetic anecdote called 'The Shrine'. It was signed "Bruskin Gershwin", Bruskin being of course his mother's maiden name, and *The Smart Set* paid him one dollar.

Other small literary successes followed, but lyric-writing began to appeal to him more and more as a calling. After all, light verse had always been one of his main interests, and he had long admired the lyrics of WS Gilbert. During the last days of 1917 he tried his hand at writing a chorus to one of George's tunes, calling it 'You Are Not The Girl'. On the whole he was pleased with it as a first attempt.

As a result of George's work during rehearsals and at the Century Sunday concerts, he had acquired a reputation as a more-than-capable accompanist, and just before signing the Harms contract he had agreed to go on a vaudeville tour (on the prestigious BF Keith circuit) as accompanist to Louise Dresser, the actress he had seen a year before starring in *Have A Heart*.

Miss Dresser's act was made up of recitations and songs and Ira noted in his diary that among the songs were 'Down By The Erie' (from *Cohan's Revue Of 1916*), the Kern/Wodehouse song 'It's A Sure Sign' (from *Have A Heart*), 'Cheer Up, Father, Cheer Up, Mother' (written by George's friend Herman Paley) and her signature song 'My Gal Sal'. This had specially been written for her by a composer called Paul Dresser.

Paul Dresser, who had died in 1911, was no relation. His original surname was Dreiser and he was the brother of the well-known author

Theodore Dreiser, who was said to have collaborated with him on his best-known number, 'On The Banks Of The Wabash'.

George detested 'My Gal Sal', then and for ever, but his reaction to having to play it was completely in character. Every night he did everything he could to try and modify it into a more interesting piece. As Louise said, years later, "I knew [he disliked it], but oh! how he played it. There were times when I almost forgot the lyrics listening to Georgie trying to make that trite melody sound like a beautiful piece of music. It wouldn't have surprised me one bit had he banged the piano one day and walked off the stage. I wouldn't have blamed him too much – but that lovable, shy lad wouldn't have done such a thing."

To see George as a lovable, shy lad may seem odd after his early youth as a rough street kid, and given his steely confidence in his own musical ability. But after all, street-wise as he was, this tour was his first experience of life outside New York City. The tour went from Boston to Baltimore to Washington, DC, where one performance was attended by President Woodrow Wilson – it's hardly surprising that George, in spite of his growing persona as a man-about-town, was a little reserved.

As for being lovable, he undoubtedly had become so. Friend after friend commented on it. As he grew up, an endearing naivety emerged in his character. This was another manifestation of the Gershwin family detachment. George saw himself, quite objectively and openly, as a musical genius, being neither boastful nor modest about it.

In a famous story from later in his life, he once had Harry Ruby staying with him in a country house he and Ira had rented. It was a fine summer day and they began tossing a baseball back and forth. In the excitement of the game, they began throwing harder and harder, until suddenly George called a halt. "It's too risky," he said. "I must be careful of my hands. With you it doesn't matter."

"Why not?" asked Ruby. "I'm a pianist too." George shrugged. "It's not the same thing," he said.

Ruby, offended, said nothing, but after leaving the cottage at the end of his stay made no effort to keep in touch with George. Some while later they ran into each other by chance. George greeted Harry warmly and asked him why he hadn't kept in touch (it was natural in George to assume that keeping in touch was Harry's job). Then a thought struck him. Had he perhaps offended Harry in some way?

Harry decided to tell the truth. Yes, he said, he had been offended. He reminded George of the ball incident, and how George had said "It's not the same thing".

George, who didn't remember the incident, thought for a moment. "Well," he said. "It's not."

It should be mentioned here that Harry's reaction was unusual among George's friends, most of whom accepted George's disarming assessment of himself as a genius with amusement. They would even make jokes about his attitude and George would laugh at the jokes as freely and easily as anyone else.

Returning from his tour with Louise Dresser, he continued to compose songs and add them to his file of so-far-unpublished songs at Harms Music. He took another job as a rehearsal pianist, this time for a Kern musical called *Rock-A-Bye Baby*, which opened in New York in May 1918. During the out-of-town tryout for this show, he and Kern became quite friendly and Kern generously offered to give George any help he could when he felt he was ready to do his first show.

Back in New York, still incessantly writing, he engaged in his first full-blown collaboration with Ira. The date was 3 June 1918 and the song was in fact Ira's idea. (By this time Ira had had enough of working for Altman's and returned to his last baths but one, the St Nicholas Baths. Working on the admissions desk there he at least had time to jot down ideas for lyrics.)

The idea that came to him was to express in song George's feeling (and his own) that ragtime was the true music of America. He settled down to write a lyric and after toiling through about twenty different drafts, each an improvement on the last, he came up with a revue-type number whose first line was, "The Great American folk song is a rag".

He showed it to George, who liked it, and together they sat down at the family piano and began to develop the idea. George went through a similar process of trial-and-error and eventually came up with a raggy tune they both liked. Unfortunately, the line lengths of the tune were not the same as the line lengths of the song, so Ira had to go away and rewrite his lyric so that it fitted (which took him quite a few more drafts).

They called it 'The Real American Folk Song' and it turned out to be a fine effort for their first full collaboration. Words and music match well; George's music has a lively rhythm, with shifts in syncopation and unexpected harmonic changes and Ira's words catch the mood of the time, even though, years later, he was to comment that it was "too much like an essay".

A week later, on 12 June, Ira registered for the state census, and this made him eligible for the draft, which was a worry. But as things turned out he wasn't called up. Or rather he was, in October 1918, but then his enlistment was postponed. He was told to report again a month later, which he did – on 11 November, the day of the Armistice. After some delay and confusion, they told him he wouldn't be needed. They had beaten the Germans without him.

George's next job was as rehearsal pianist for the *Ziegfeld Follies Of 1918*. Around the same time he suffered a great personal loss when his mentor, Charles Hambitzer, died of the same TB that had killed his wife. That was the end of George's piano lessons for life – he never went to another tutor.

He did, however, continue his studies with Edward Kilyeni for another couple of years, learning about harmony, counterpoint and musical form by studying classical masterpieces. Kilyeni, who recognised George's natural talent, was always careful to keep him aware that the thousand-and-one devices and styles developed in music over the years were not 'rules'. He never stopped encouraging George to follow his own road and, although George at this time was devoting most of his considerable energy to trying to break into musical comedy, his overall view of himself was as a composer, pure and simple.

He wasn't only writing songs. From time to time, arising out of his studies with Kilyeni, he was also trying his hand at pieces more in the classical vein. Always delighted to play his music to anyone who would listen, one day in 1918 he contrived to get Sigmund Spaeth, the music editor of the New York *Evening Mail* to sit down and listen to some.

Among his 'serious' pieces were some novelettes and a toccata. When Spaeth heard them he felt they were merely weak distillations of Schumann and Liszt. He was not impressed. Then George played some of his songs. Spaeth sat up and paid attention. This was more like it. When George finished, he advised him to stick to popular music for a while and save the serious work till later.

That September, Harms at last published its first Gershwin song. It was called 'Some Wonderful Sort Of Someone', and it had a lyric by a Harms staff lyricist, Schuyler Greene.

The song was heard by the singer and comedienne Nora Bayes, who was about to star in a revue called *Look Who's Here*. Born in 1880, in Milwaukee (probably), Nora Bayes was one of the all-time top-liners in vaudeville. Off stage she could be warm and generous, but more usually was high-handed, stormy and temperamental. On stage she was poised and effortless and could dramatise a song like nobody else, wrapping the audience round her little finger.

The score for *Look Who's Here* was by a composer called A Baldwin Sloane, but between the two acts of the show there was to be what was known as a 'concert', in which the plot stopped dead while Nora was given the stage and a spotlight all to herself to perform what was essentially her vaudeville act. For this 'concert' she was going to choose additional numbers, among them 'Some Wonderful Sort Of Someone'. She also chose George to be her on stage accompanist.

The show (now called *Ladies First*) went for a week's tryout at the Trent Theatre in Trenton, New Jersey, and George went with it. As well as 'Some Wonderful Sort Of Someone', he had shown Nora Bayes 'The Real American Folk Song', and she agreed to include that in her act as well.

Ira, excited at the idea of having his first collaboration performed (and by such a star), took an afternoon off from the St Nicholas Baths and a train to Trenton, to hear the first performance. He was aesthetically dressed in a self-assembled outfit of purple shirt, dark blue knitted tie, and a mottled-green tweed suit, but unfortunately in his excitement he got off at Princeton Junction by mistake, some twelve miles short of his destination.

Too shy to ask anybody for directions, he made his way on foot through Princeton and eventually found a trolley-car that wound through the wilds of New Jersey and eventually got him to the theatre. Perhaps it was as well he made the journey, because soon after *Ladies First* opened in New York, 'The Real American Folk Song' was dropped – dropped almost from sight in fact, because it hadn't then been published, and it remained unpublished for around forty years.

George remained Miss Bayes' accompanist in New York and went with the show after its short New York run for a six-week tour. He was much impressed with her delivery of his song. While on tour he wrote from Cleveland to his music journalist friend Max Abramson, "Oh, Momma, what *she* does to it."

In Pittsburgh the show was conducted by Oscar Radin, a Russian Jew who had arrived in America in his early teens in 1890 and, by his late teens, was playing second violin in the theatre orchestra of the Pittsburgh Stock Company. He had gone on to become a musical director and conductor for the Shubert Organisation on Broadway and now had returned for a visit to his adopted home town to conduct the orchestra for *Ladies First.*

Because it was his home town, he invited his family to the show, and among them, seeing his first live show, was his eleven-year-old nephew, who was already regarded as something of a prodigy on the piano. This was Oscar Levant, later to become famous as a film actor and wit as well as a pianist. In the twenties he would become a prominent member of George's circle of friends and both then and later would be an outstanding performer of the major Gershwin works.

Young Oscar, already with several years of classical piano training behind him, later recorded his impressions of Nora and George, saying, "After one chorus of the first song, my attention left Bayes and remained fixed on the playing of the pianist. I had never heard such fresh, brisk, unstudied, completely free and inventive playing – all within a consistent frame that set off her singing perfectly."

It would be six years before George and Oscar would meet, but from that day Oscar's approach to the piano was modified by what he had heard. He was bowled over (and pale green with envy).

Nora Bayes, on the other hand, wasn't so happy with her accompanist. She did not like his impromptu additions of new phrases or bits of counterpoint and their rows reached a climax when she suggested he alter the ending of 'Some Wonderful Sort Of Someone' for her – adding that even Irving Berlin and Jerome Kern altered their songs when she asked them. George refused. "I like the song the way it is," he said.

That was the end of their association. George returned to New York without finishing the tour and somewhat agitated. Partly this was because of the row he had had, but it was also because during the tour he had learned what composer A Baldwin Sloane was hauling in in the way of royalties from the show.

This discovery fixed even more firmly in his mind that what he wanted to do was to write a whole show himself, not just contribute additional numbers to be slotted into other people's scores.

Fortunately, at the Harms office, Max Dreyfus had good news. There was a show for George to write. Not all the music, it was true, but five numbers, rather than just a couple.

What had happened was that a young producer called Edward B Perkins had come to Max with an idea for a revue. Perkins was a friend of comedian Joe Cook, another of the all-time great stars of vaudeville. He was so popular, in fact, that he was one of the few vaudeville stars who never went to Hollywood. The one film he did make, *Rain Or Shine*, was simply an adaptation of his stage show of the same name.

Cook was what was known in the business as a 'nut comic'. One of his most famous routines was a nonsensical monologue about why he would not imitate four Hawaiians. He also gave 'lectures', delivered in fast and dream-like double-talk and involving strange and elaborate props – life-size papier-maché gymnasts, mechanical contraptions with gears and levers and bells and mallets, doll's houses, banana stalks, mandolins, megaphones and so on. There seemed to be no end to his inventiveness, especially as he was also a juggler, wirewalker, sharpshooter, musician, magician, cartoonist, acrobat and dancer.

The revue, entitled *Half Past Eight*, as well as starring Joe Cook and his regular supporting troupe, was to feature the twenty-five-piece Jim Europe band, then just returned from the war in France. Perkins had come to Max Dreyfus looking for help in setting up the production, and Dreyfus, always helpful to promising youngsters, gave him a fifteen-hundred-dollar advance, offered to pay for the orchestrations, and offered the services of this promising young composer, recently signed to Harms Music, George Gershwin.

For the show, George eventually provided seven songs – 'There's Magic In The Air', with lyrics by Ira; three songs for which Perkins wrote the words; two songs with words by Irving Caesar; and the song 'Beautiful Bird', which he had written early in 1918, with lyrics by Herman and Lou Paley, and which was their attempt to write a song similar in feeling to the current hit, 'Poor Butterfly'.

Half Past Eight was a disaster, largely because it was underfunded. It opened for its out-of-town tryout in Syracuse, New Jersey, on Monday, 9 December 1918, and ran from quarter to nine to quarter to eleven, with a half-hour intermission. Not a generous playing time.

Furthermore, the show had mistakenly been advertised as having a Broadway chorus, but there was no chorus. George helpfully suggested that for the finale of the show all the members of Joe Cook's troupe should appear on stage in Chinese pyjamas and holding paper parasols so as to hide their faces. His idea was that this might at least keep the audience in their seats until the finale was over.

This might have worked (just possibly), if Perkins hadn't gone out and bought the cheapest umbrellas he could find, with the result that three of the 'chorus' couldn't get theirs to open and their unglamorous male faces were plain for all to see.

The consensus of critical opinion was well summed-up by *Variety* in its headline "Two-Dollar Show Not Worth War Tax". The article under the headline did however point out that the female star, Sybil Vane, "who sings four delightful songs... is not to blame for the poor entertainment".

Houses were poor and by the Wednesday matinee some of the cast were beginning to talk about not going on unless they were paid in advance. One of the acts did refuse to go on and Perkins, distraught, rushed up to George and asked him to go on in its place and play some of his hits while the next scene was set.

George, unshaven (he had the sort of blue chin that was liable to look a bit unshaven at the best of times) and in an unsmart blue suit, obliged as best he could. He didn't have a hit to his name at that time, but he improvised a medley of some of his unpublished tunes to a puzzled audience that was so bemused it didn't even give him a hand when he finished.

The show folded on the Friday night and George managed to at least liberate enough cash from the debacle to purchase a rail ticket back to New York. Philosophically, he consoled himself with the reflection that it had been good experience and at least he had had the thrill of seeing on the billboards for the first time, "Music by George Gershwin".

CHAPTER FOUR

The Hit And The 'Scandals'

Whatever discouragement George may have felt from the failure of *Half Past Eight* was soon dispelled. He continued turning out songs for his file at Harms Music and two he had written were chosen for inclusion in a Broadway show. It was called *Good Morning, Judge* and it opened on 6 February1919. One of the songs was 'There's More To The Kiss Than The X-X-X', and the other (in which Irving Caesar also had a hand in the lyric) was 'I Was So Young, You Were So Beautiful'. In the show it was sung by a brother-and-sister team, Charles and Millie King and, helped by their performance, it was the first of George's songs to become something of a popular success.

Another show, *The Lady In Red*, opened on 12 May and used two more songs. A revised version of 'Some Wonderful Sort Of Someone', the song Nora Bayes had asked him to change, and 'Something About Love', which he had written in 1918 with Lou Paley.

George's song output had now become prodigious and it would remain so all his life. André Kostelanetz, the conductor, once asked him how many tunes he wrote in a day and George guessed about fifteen. "That's the way I get the bad ones out of my system," he said. Most went straight into the waste basket, but maybe two or three would have something in them good enough to file for future use.

In the spring of 1919 he entered a competition sponsored by the New York *American* to write a national anthem. The anthem he wrote, 'O Land Of Mine' had words by Michael E Rourke (who wrote lyrics for Jerome Kern under the name 'Herbert Reynolds'). Among the judges for the competition were John Philip Sousa, John McCormack and Irving Berlin, and the first prize was to be five-thousand dollars.

George's anthem, entered anonymously, won the lowest prize – fifty dollars.

Occasionally he collaborated with Ira, as much for their own enjoyment as anything else. Ira had by now committed himself to becoming a lyricist and had left the St Nicholas Baths for a series of jobs closer to show business. At various times he worked as a photographer's dark-room assistant, as a vaudeville reviewer for the showbiz paper Max Abramson worked for, *The Clipper* (although this lasted for only three reviews and he got paid for none of them), and as the cashier for a circus, the Colonel Lagg Empire Show.

In 1919 he was amused by the names of four Russian-Jewish violinists then prominent in New York – Mischa Elman, Jascha Heifetz, Toscha Seidel and Sascha Jacobson. Together he and George wrote a song called 'Mischa, Jascha, Toscha, Sascha'. The song tells how, although all four have come to America and become successful playing the classics, they also "like to shake a leg to jazz". George's melody begins by having Russian overtones, but modulates into cheerful American vernacular. George and Ira, over the years, enjoyed performing it at parties.

Early in 1919 George also experimented further with the classics himself by writing a string quartet. He called it 'Lullaby'. It was never published or performed in his lifetime (except in private), but its main theme has a rather bluesy feel and George, never one to waste material, used the same theme again three years later for a song called, 'Has One Of You Seen Joe?'.

At around this time a young would-be producer named Alex A Aarons entered his life. His father, Alfred E Aarons, was a successful composer who had become general manager for the famous team of impresarios, Marc Klaw and Abe Erlanger, but Alex himself had gone into the garment industry. Early in 1919, however, when he was twenty-nine, he decided that he would rather be in show business. He would produce a musical comedy.

Raised with music around him, he had a well-trained ear and was looking for music that was new and original. He had liked the shifting harmonies of 'Some Wonderful Sort Of Someone', the unexpected chromatic shifts in 'There's More To The Kiss Than The X-X-X' and the extended melodic line of 'I Was So Young, You Were So Beautiful', in which George had stretched the length of the chorus to twenty-four bars instead of the conventional sixteen. This may seem like a very simple change, but no one in Tin Pan Alley in those days would have done such an unorthodox thing and it perfectly fitted the mood of the song.

Alex decided he wanted George to write the music for his show, which was to be called *La-La-Lucille!*. His father, Alfred, felt that hiring the established Victor Herbert would be a safer bet, but Alex doggedly insisted on George.

The author of *La-La-Lucille!* was Fred Jackson and essentially it was a farce. In it, John Smith, a young dentist, is left two-million dollars by a rich aunt on condition he divorces his wife Lucille, a former chorus girl. His lawyer suggests he divorce her, collect the money, and then remarry her. John agrees but, for his wife to divorce him, he has to be found in a compromising situation with another woman. He goes to a hotel where Lucille has selected the hotel scrubwoman as a harmless co-respondent.

The hotel is where most of the comedy takes place. For a start it turns out to have no fewer than thirty-eight John Smiths registered there, one of whom is with his bride in the adjoining bridal suite. Many embarrassing misunderstandings ensue, with hilarious results, but all turns out happily in the end.

This time George provided all the music, with lyrics by Arthur J Jackson and BG DeSylva. Buddy DeSylva would go on to become one third of the famous songwriting team of DeSylva, Brown and Henderson (and later to become head of production at Paramount Pictures), but in 1919 he was twenty-four and had only just decided to try and make a living in popular music. He had been employed as a lyricist by Remick's and one of his first commissions was *La-La-Lucille!*.

Between them, Gershwin, Jackson and DeSylva created thirteen songs. Nine of these ended up in the show, plus the Gershwin/Caesar number 'There's More To The Kiss Than The X-X-X'. George, with his usual economy, had also salvaged two tunes from *Half Past Eight* – 'From Now On' and 'The Ten Commandments Of Love'. But the most endurable song in the show turned out to be the rather Kern-ish 'Nobody But You', which George had composed during his days at Remick's and for which Buddy DeSylva provided lyrics.

During the preparation of *La-La-Lucille!*, George was at Harms Music one day and was called into Max Dreyfus's office. There he found Irving Berlin. Berlin, being an ex-Russian, had naturally been much affected by the Russian Revolution of 1917. He had responded by writing a number called 'The Revolutionary Rag'. For some reason he thought that Harms Music would be able to handle this better than his own firm of Waterson, Berlin and Snyder, and had come in to show it to Max.

Max asked George if he would take down the tune from Irving's dictation, which George did with impressive efficiency. Then Max asked him if he would play it. (Berlin was a notoriously poor pianist all his life – he could play only in the basic key of C, and eventually acquired a unique transposing piano that somebody had invented – by twisting a wheel on one end the whole keyboard could be shifted along relative to the strings, so that you could finger in C and any key you chose would sound.)

George played 'The Revolutionary Rag'. Wishing to impress his idol, he pulled out all the stops by improvising for it a rich and imaginative harmonic background. As Berlin later remembered, "I couldn't hear my own tune – but it was brilliant. It sounded like a different song."

Then George asked if he could play Berlin a couple of his own songs. One of them was a cheerfully rhythmic number written for *La-La-Lucille!* called 'Tee-Oodle-Um-Bum-Bo' and, whatever the other one was, Irving Berlin was sufficiently impressed by George and his songs to send for him shortly afterwards and offer him a job as his arranger and musical secretary. He said, "The job is yours if you want it. But I hope you don't take it. You are too talented to be an arranger and secretary. If you worked for me you might start writing the way I do, and your own style might become cramped. You are meant for big things."

George politely turned down the job (he didn't need telling he was meant for big things), but from these meetings a warm and lasting mutual respect arose between himself and Berlin.

It was also during the preparation of *La-La-Lucille!* that George suggested to Ira (who had just finished his stint as cashier with the circus) that he try writing songs with a young composer he had worked with at Remick's, Vincent Youmans. Youmans, born in New York, was the same age as George and would go on to write such hit musicals as *No, No, Nanette, Hit The Deck* and the first Astaire/Rogers musical *Flying Down To Rio*, before falling ill with the TB that finally killed him in 1946. Ira thought George's suggestion a good one and he and Vincent Youmans settled down to collaborate.

La-La-Lucille!, starring John E Hazard as John Smith and Janet Velie as Lucille, had one-week tryouts in Atlantic City and Boston. While they were in Atlantic City the conductor of the orchestra, Charles Previn, received a visit from one of the biggest stars of all time, Al Jolson.

Jolson, whose real name was Asa Joelson, was born in Lithuania in 1886. His family came to America when he was a child and at the age of thirteen, in New York, he made his first stage appearance, as part of a 'mob' chorus in a show called *The Children Of The Ghetto*.

He grew to have a fine rich voice, with a lot of rhythmic drive, but always regarded himself as a comedian as much as a singer. He worked in vaudeville and circuses and minstrel shows and it was as a member of Lew Dockstader's Minstrels in 1909 that he shot to fame. His on stage energy and magnetism were so great that his performances received rapturous ovations. So great did these become that the veteran Dockstader had to relinquish to him the traditional top spot on the bill, next to closing. No other act (except the finale) could follow Jolson.

In 1912, after starring in several hit musicals, he was signed by the Shuberts and, among other things, began giving Sunday evening performances at New York's Winter Garden. These became legendary, with Al holding the audience rapt for a full hour with an exhilarating torrent of songs and patter. Part of his act was to jump down off the stage into the aisles of the theatre and sing directly to the audience. He wasn't the originator of this trick, but it caused a sensation. His salary when he started with the Shuberts in 1912 was two-hundred-and-fifty dollars a week, but by 1919 it had risen eight-fold.

Jolson had such a burning need for audience approval, allied to a cast-iron confidence in his own performing ability, that he became notorious in show business as an incorrigible scene stealer. His wife, Ruby Keeler, once even referred to him bitterly as "the ego that walks like a man". But performing apart, he was amiable enough. He liked the songs in *La-La-Lucille!* and was delighted when Charles Previn introduced him to George.

On 26 May 1919 *La-La-Lucille!* had its New York debut, as the first production in the newly-opened Henry Miller Theatre. Billed as "The new up-to-the-minute musical comedy of class and distinction", what this meant in effect was that its dialogue was as saucy as a middlebrow audience could stand. Critic Percy Hammond, reviewing the Boston tryout, wrote: "For candour of speech it is rivalled only by the disease columns of the daily newspapers." (You'd think he was talking about the other Henry Miller!) He went on: "There was pretty music by someone named George Gershwin, and several pretty girls to dance to it."

On the whole the reviews were favourable and the show had what in those days was a respectable run of more than one hundred nights. This in spite of hot summer weather and a strike at one point by the actors' union, Equity.

One unfortunate situation did arise out of *La-La-Lucille!*. When George was hired to provide the score he remembered Jerome Kern's generous offer of help with his first full-scale show and mentioned it to Alex Aarons. But Aarons had a grudge against Kern for something Kern had said or done that he interpreted as a snub. He dissuaded George from taking up Kern's offer, which Kern then took as a snub, remaining angry at George for quite some time. Pique was practically Kern's home address.

Al Jolson kept in touch with the young composer whose work had impressed him in Atlantic City, and there was an odd episode during the New York run of *La-La-Lucille!* when he and George and Buddy DeSylva decided to go and stay in a country hotel in the town of Dixville Lodge. This is in the far north of New Hampshire, up by the Canadian border, about a day-and-a-half's train journey from New York.

The hotel was owned by the father of a composer and conductor called Paul Lannin, and the idea the three of them had was to spend a few days there resting and working. But after only a day or so George had had enough. The woodland life was far too peaceful and quiet for a city boy.

At this point he heard that there was a regular mail-plane flight between Dixville Lodge and New York. He was mulling over the proposition that four hours on a plane sounded a lot better than a day-and-a-half on a train, when Jolson dared him to make the flight. That did it. George got himself fitted into the second cockpit of a plane alongside the mail and flew home. Unfortunately it was a cold spring day (and colder at altitude), both cockpits were open to the elements, and he had no warm flying clothes. It was not a comfortable four hours.

Although George's ambition was to compose whole shows, he continued to contribute songs to shows mostly written by other people. In mid 1919, for instance, he was approached by a young actor-turned-producer called Vinton Freedley. Freedley had a problem with a show he was producing called *Dere Mable*, based on a popular series of letters supposed to be from a soldier, Bill, to his girl, and written by humorist Ed Streeter.

The problem was that part of Bill's character was his fondness for his dog, which demanded he have a song to sing to it. The show's composer had failed to come up with anything suitable, so Freedley approached George. George got together with Irving Caesar, and they came up with a pleasantly sentimental number called 'We're Pals'. This solved the problem, but did not, unfortunately, save the show. *Dere Mable* failed to make it into New York from its out-of-town tryout.

Ironically, it was one of George's isolated songs, not one written as part of a whole score, that was to become the biggest popular hit of his whole career and by far his biggest seller.

He met Irving Caesar one day in the summer of 1919 to discuss new ideas for songs. A recent big hit had been the song 'Hindustan'. Following the enormous success of the musical *Chu Chin Chow*, which opened in 1916, there had come a flood of songs with what was intended for an eastern or near-eastern feeling – 'On The Streets Of Cairo', 'Down The Nile (To Old Cairo)', 'Song Of Omar', 'Turque', 'Salome', 'Sphinx', 'Soudan', 'Palesteena' and so on.

'Hindustan' had been written in the dance tempo of a one-step (this was a ballroom dance in two-four time, with travelling steps that were walks rather than glides – a slightly stilted forerunner of the foxtrot). The song was beginning to fade in popularity and Irving suggested to George that they might do well to write another one-step as a successor, but using an American place-name as a title. "Just like Stephen Foster did in 'Swanee River'," agreed George.

That evening, over dinner at Dinty Moore's, they discussed the song further and decided to go on after the meal to the Gershwin family home and write it at the piano.

At that time the Gershwins were living in the Washington Heights area of New York, at 520 West One-Hundred-And-Forty-Fourth Street. George and Irving rode there on the top of a bus, still working out the song and, by the time they arrived, had the basic idea mapped out.

The Gershwins' piano was in an alcove, separated from their dining room by a beaded curtain. A mixture of family and friends, including George's father, Morris, were deeply embroiled in a poker game in the dining room, but George and Irving paid little attention, making a bee-line for the alcove.

It took them about fifteen minutes at the piano to complete both verse and chorus of their song. Verse and chorus was all most popular songs consisted of, but both George and Irving felt that this song needed an extra section, to come after the chorus and before each new verse. They began working on what became the trio section of the song.

The poker players had mixed reactions to all this playing and singing. Those who were losing were inclined to want the boys to shut up and go away, shouting such requests through the beaded curtain as, "Finish it some other time", but the winners on the whole wanted them to carry on, so as not to disturb the luck.

George and Irving soon did finish their song. They ran through it a few times to make sure and, by now, all the card-players were interested. The game stopped so they could listen properly and Morris Gershwin went off and fetched a comb-and-paper so he could join in. George and Irving (with accompaniment by Morris) played and sang the song over and over. And that was the first performance of 'Swanee'.

George had written another song, 'Come To The Moon', with words by his friend Lou Paley, which he submitted with 'Swanee' to producer Ned Wayburn, who at that time was preparing a revue to celebrate the opening of a new cinema, the Capitol Theatre.

The Capitol was on Broadway and Fifty-First Street and the revue, *The Capitol Revue*, was to appear on stage there, just before the main feature, during the opening week.

Ned Wayburn liked 'Come To The Moon' enough to use it (with some alterations to the lyric by himself), but he was so impressed by 'Swanee' that he decided to build a huge production number round it.

It would be performed by the Capitol Theatre's band – the famous Arthur Pryor band – and after it had been played through, the stage would be darkened and sixty chorus girls, with electric lights glowing on their slippers, would dance to its rhythms in the dark.

The public were not impressed. When the show opened, on 24 October 1919, George and Irving hung around in the lobby, where the sheet music for the song was on sale, to see how many copies were sold. Not many were. Nor did sales in the shops turn out to be much better. Irving was so discouraged that he considered selling his rights in the song for two-hundred dollars.

Although George talked him out of this, he was somewhat discouraged himself. Max Dreyfus tried to reassure him that, even if the song was not a popular success, it was a good piece and a credit both to its writers and to Harms Music.

At this point Al Jolson invited George to an elaborate party he was giving. George went and, of course, needed little encouragement to play some of his songs there. One of those was 'Swanee' and, when Jolson heard it, he at once said he wanted to sing it at one of his Sunday night shows at the Winter Garden. He did and the reception it got made him decide to incorporate it in the revue he was appearing in (also at the Winter Garden) during the week.

The revue was called *Sinbad* and most of its score was by Sigmund Romberg. But 'Swanee' was duly incorporated into it, rising swiftly into a major hit. Jolson recorded it and the record sold millions. Sheet music sales soared (eventually rising to two-and-a-half-million copies), and by early 1920 George and Irving found themselves regarded on Tin Pan Alley as important composers.

Meanwhile, George and Buddy DeSylva had provided half a dozen songs, some new and some from George's file of back numbers, for a revue called *Morris Gest Midnight Whirl*, which opened in the last week of 1919.

By that time George White, after ten years as a featured dancer in revues and musical comedies (including *Miss 1917*), had given up dancing to try and compete with Ziegfeld as a producer of lavish revues. He had already mounted the first of his 'Scandals' and was in Detroit planning a second.

The first had not been an unqualified success. The book, lyrics and music had been poor and the main thing the show had to recommend it had been the dancing of Ann Pennington, billed as "the shimmie queen".

George went to Detroit early in 1920 to talk to George White about doing the music for the new show and, riding on the success of 'Swanee', had no trouble landing the job. Unlike Ziegfeld, who habitually hired the best established talents around, George White would hire and encourage promising newcomers. One advantage of hiring promising newcomers is that you don't have to pay them much. George got fifty dollars a week and accepted it gladly, realising that the *Scandals* might prove a highly visible showcase.

The *Scandals* was to prove the centre of George's working life for the next five years. He would compose all the music for every annual edition from 1920 to 1924, his weekly salary rising from fifty dollars to seventy-five to eventually one-hundred-and-twenty-five dollars.

After their slightly shaky start the *Scandals* did succeed in becoming a genuine competitor to Ziegfeld, with grand and sumptuous settings through which near-naked girls paraded down glittering staircases between brightly-coloured curtains. Even after the first edition Ziegfeld had been sufficiently concerned to make George White a genuine offer of three-thousand dollars a week for himself and Ann Pennington to appear in the *Follies*. George White responded with a counter-offer of seven-thousand dollars a week for Ziegfeld and his wife Billie Burke to appear in the *Scandals*.

Ironically, George's Tin Pan Alley success with 'Swanee' meant that he never again had to write a one-off popular song. From now on, he would concentrate on songs for shows and on longer pieces. Mainly at first this meant the *Scandals*, which were revues not musical comedies, but his work for them enhanced his reputation and brought him closer to where he wanted to be.

Much of what he wrote for the *Scandals* was undistinguished, at least by his own later standards. Partly this was because he was still learning his craft and, partly, it was because the sort of music the show demanded could not be too challenging or out-of-the-ordinary. Nonetheless, there were some fine moments.

For the *Scandals Of 1920*, with the show's lyricist Arthur Jackson, he wrote a pleasant tune called 'Idle Dreams', and made his first attempt at writing a near-blues, calling it 'On My Mind The Whole Night Long', which is remarkably close in form to a genuine twelve-bar blues, complete with pauses between phrases.

George was slightly ahead of his time in writing a blues. Although he had heard and been impressed by the blues of WC Handy as early as 1915, blues did not become a popular craze until two months after *Scandals Of 1920* opened, when Mamie Smith and her Jazz Hounds made their historic recording of 'Crazy Blues'.

This was no more a genuine blues than 'Alexander's Ragtime Band' was genuine ragtime, but within six months of its release it became a surprise million-seller. In fact it sold so well in Harlem that the record company (Okeh) sent agents there to check that somebody wasn't giving copies away. Blues became the new craze after jazz which, by 1921, had after all been around for four years.

Ira by now was devoting himself seriously to becoming an established lyricist. As George had suggested, he had written a number of songs with Vincent Youmans which George played for producer Alex Aarons. Aarons was impressed and, again taking a chance on two unknowns, hired Vincent and Ira to write his next show after *La-La-Lucille!*. It was called *Two Little Girls In Blue* and it opened in 1921.

Youmans had written a fine score and Ira's witty lyrics were singled out for praise by several critics. But he had felt uncomfortable about using his real name on them, in case people thought he was trading on his brother's growing fame. So he had concocted a pseudonym from the first names of his younger brother and sister and, for some time, would work under the name of Arthur Francis.

Later in 1921 Arthur Francis engaged for the first time in an extended collaboration with George Gershwin. Together they wrote all the songs for a "play with music" called *A Dangerous Maid*. A couple of these songs were based on tunes that George had failed to sell to Remick's when he was working there – 'Some Rain Must Fall' and 'Dancing Shoes'. But probably the best of them was one called 'Boy Wanted'.

This maiden venture was a failure. *A Dangerous Maid* played out of town tryouts in Atlantic City and Pittsburgh, but it never reached New York. An interesting detail about the production is that in the cast (as well as Vivienne Segal, who had sung George's two songs at the

Century Theatre) was Vinton Freedley, who had gone back to acting after the failure of his production *Dere Mable*. This was only temporary. Soon he would team up with Alex Aarons, whom he already knew, for a producing partnership which would produce a string of successes, many with Gershwin and Gershwin.

In the *Scandals Of 1921* George and lyricist Arthur Jackson again had a couple of goodish numbers, the sprightly 'She's Just A Baby' and a reworking of another number he had written back in his days at Remick's, with words by Lou Paley. Then it had been called 'You're The Witch Who Is Bewitching Me', but with Arthur Jackson's new lyric it became 'Drifting Along With The Tide'.

George was continuing to develop as a composer, spending hour after hour experimenting with harmonies and rhythms. In the summer of 1921, when he was writing for his second *Scandals*, he enrolled in a summer course at Columbia University, taking two courses, one on 'Nineteenth Century Romanticism in Music' and one, which began at the ungodly hour of eight-thirty am, on 'Elementary Orchestration'.

At this time George's life revolved around two households. There was the Gershwin home, which seems to have started staying in one place for at least a few years. The family had been in the house on One-Hundred-And-Tenth Street and Amsterdam Avenue where 'Swanee' was written since 1919.

Also there was the Paley household. In 1920 Lou Paley had married his fiancée, the delightful and sensitive Emily, and they had taken an apartment at 18 West Eighth Street. It was George's habit to go there on Saturday evenings, where there might be Ira, or friends like Irving Caesar and Vincent Youmans, or various members of the Paley clan, such as brother Herman, or cousins Max Abramson and Mabel Pleshette (the girl he had sent to study with Charles Hambitzer).

These were not lavish evenings. Lou and Emily had little money, and Emily's younger brother, English Strunsky, would remember later that "practically nothing but Fig Newtons and cheese was served at those Saturday nights". George tended to bring recently-acquired girlfriends to these evenings, to see how they reacted to the 'Bohemian' atmosphere. "If a girl didn't fit in," recalled Emily, "he didn't think much of her."

Between Emily and English Strunsky in age was a sister, Leonore, whom everybody called Lee. She looked very like her sister, was almost as charming, and was a bundle of energy. She and Ira fell in love, and in the mid-twenties would marry. As George rather plaintively said to her mother at that time, "You gave Emily to Lou, and Lee to Ira, but who do you have for me?"

Often at Lou and Emily's was another Paley cousin, George Pallay. Two years younger than George, he was Max Abramson's brother and a more-than-successful stockbroker. In 1918, at the age of eighteen, while working as a twenty-five-dollars-a-week clerk in an investment house, he had contrived to gather enough inside information to wind up owning several hundred thousand dollars of stock securities.

With all this wealth, he had become a sophisticated man-about-town and George, from the time they met, in around 1919, regarded the younger man with admiration and envy. It was his ambition to become equally suave and sophisticated himself.

As his own success grew, he began to buy well-tailored suits and generally to dress in style. He and George Pallay would make the rounds of the night spots together, spending lavishly and entertaining chorus girls. In time, as their friendship deepened, Pallay would become one of George's very closest friends, one with whom he could discuss his most private concerns.

With his growing sophistication and success, George began to find himself accepted in high society and found this world very much to his liking. His first taste of it came in 1921 when Dorothy Clark, the pianist at the Ziegfeld Roof, took him and Vincent Youmans to a party at the fashionable home of Jules Glaenzer, on Fifth Avenue.

Jules Glaenzer, then in his early thirties, was a man-of-the-world such as George could only dream of becoming. Courteous and charming, he was like something out of a more gracious era. His father had been New York's most fashionable interior decorator, and Jules was raised in a world of elegance and culture. He became a bon vivant, a raconteur and a gourmet. Also a capable tennis player, polo player, swimmer, yachtsman, pianist and ballroom dancer.

Since 1910 he had been first vice-president of the famous jewellery house of Cartier, where his salesmanship was legendary; but in 1922 he had recently embarked on his real passion in life, which was giving parties. Eventually he would give about two hundred a year – cocktail parties, dinner parties, brunches, supper parties and, the ones he loved most, first night parties. To all these he invited a carefully chosen mixture of guests from society (often including royalty) and from the worlds of the theatre, music, politics and big business. He liked to see people having a good time and he enjoyed bringing people together.

He liked the artists to entertain the rich and was pleased when the rich were entertained enough to invest in the artists. A few among his regular guests over the years were Maurice Chevalier, Mistinguette, Irving Berlin, Jerome Kern, Cole Porter, Richard Rodgers, Douglas Fairbanks, Mary Pickford, Charlie Chaplin, Gertrude Lawrence, Beatrice Lillie, Judy Garland, Edgar Bergen, Charlie McCarthy, Jascha Heifetz – the list is almost endless.

Entertainers and musicians enjoyed performing at his parties, because when this was happening he insisted on total silence, fiercely shushing anyone who dared to talk. Noel Coward once said, "Jules is the only host who knows how to keep people quiet when others are entertaining."

He found George, when they first met, to be almost completely lacking in social graces. "Why," said Glaenzer, "I even had to take him aside and tell him to get the cigar out of his mouth when I introduced him to a young lady. But George learned quickly. In a short time he was as well-poised and completely at ease on Park Avenue as he was on Broadway."

George and Jules became friends and, over the years, George would frequently attend Glaenzer parties and always play the piano. Once Jules ran into Hoagy Carmichael, who was having trouble finishing a song he was writing. Jules solved the problem by arranging a dinner party and inviting both Hoagy and George. He managed, without much difficulty, to get them both seated at the piano and quietly told the other guests to keep away.

The two played their songs for each other until, inevitably, Hoagy played the piece he had got stuck in, as far as it had got. George, now totally involved, offered a suggestion. He played an unusual harmonic progression, ending on a diminished seventh. "That's the chord I've been looking for all month," said Hoagy.

George's playing was a wonderful asset at parties. The writer SN Berhman, in his book, *People In A Diary*, wrote: "I felt on the instant, when he sat down at the piano, the newness, the humour, above all the rush of the great heady surf of vitality. The room became freshly oxygenated; everybody felt it, everybody breathed it." And another writer, Cecelia Ager, who was often at the Paleys', added: "You can't imagine what a party was like when he was expected and he did *not* appear."

By 1921 George was beginning to develop a musical voice of his own. Towards the end of the year he wrote a song he was particularly proud of, called 'Do It Again'. The words to it were written by Buddy DeSylva and it would remain one of George's favourites all his life, its harmonies changing from bar to bar in true Gershwin style.

Soon after writing the song he played it at a Glaenzer party and an actress there called Irene Bordoni asked him if she could introduce it in her new show. In fact what she said was, "I muss have dat dam song." The show was called *The French Doll* and, with 'Do It Again' duly interpolated, it opened on 20 February 1922.

Another show that opened on the same night was called *For Goodness Sake*, which marked the first coming together of an historic partnership. It was produced by Alex Aarons and, although most of the score was composed by Paul Lannin and Bill Daly, it had three of George's songs interpolated into it – 'All To Myself', 'Someone' and 'Tra-la-la' – all of them with lyrics by "Arthur Francis". But that wasn't all. It also had Fred and Adele Astaire, starring on Broadway for the first time.

Aarons and his friend and future colleague, Vinton Freedley, had admired the Astaires' dancing for some time and had talked about trying to co-produce a show starring them. Although *For Goodness Sake* was produced by Aarons alone, Freedley did have a small financial investment in it. The team was beginning to come together.

George, who had known the Astaires since his days at Remick's, played the piano for rehearsals and was impressed by how far their ideas in dancing mirrored his ideas in songwriting. Their dances tended to have a dramatic structure and the routines they invented used elements from all forms of dancing – from tap, from vaudeville, from ballet, from the ballroom. Just as George took ideas from all forms of music.

When *The Scandals Of 1922* came along, George White hired as his orchestra the Paul Whiteman Band, which had just become and would remain through the twenties, the most popular and successful band in America.

Paul Whiteman, whose name will for ever be closely linked with Gershwin's music, was a large, portly man, weighing around three-hundred pounds and somewhat resembling a taller Oliver Hardy. He had been born in 1890 in Denver, where his father, Wilberforce Whiteman, was conductor of the Denver Symphony Orchestra and head of musical education for the Denver schools.

As a boy he was trained to professional standard on both the violin and the viola. But he rebelled against the sort of musical career his fond parents had in mind for him and, by 1915, had made his way to San Francisco, where the Panama-Pacific Exposition was providing a lot of work for musicians.

Being an affable man who liked drinking and associating with women, he spent a good deal of time in the sleazy dance halls of the area of San Francisco known as the Barbary Coast. At that time jazz was beginning to spread out from Louisiana to the rest of America, and one of the first places that New Orleans musicians migrated to was San Francisco.

Like Gershwin, Paul Whiteman enjoyed this new music and in 1920, aware of the success that a band leader called Art Hickman was having in California, decided to form a band himself. Hickman, a year or so before, had been the first leader to introduce saxophones into his dance band, at that time he had working for him a young arranger called Ferde Grofé.

Grofé, who has a strong claim to being the first person to establish the principles of arranging for a big band, also had a strong family background in classical music. His maternal grandfather, Bernhardt Bierlich, had been solo cellist for the Metropolitan Opera in New York; an uncle, Julius Bierlich, was for a while concertmaster of the Los Angeles Symphony; and his mother played violin, viola and cello, sometimes professionally. His father was a comedian and baritone.

In his late teens Ferde himself was briefly in the Symphony, playing viola, but to make a living in music he also had to work in popular music and so he too became familiar with the new sounds. Although he never became a great jazz player, he was one of the very few musicians at that time thoroughly at home in both jazz and classical music.

In 1920, having left Art Hickman, he was asked by Paul Whiteman to be the pianist and arranger in the band he was about to form. Grofé accepted. Whiteman formed his band, talked the Alexandria Hotel in Los Angeles into hiring it and was on his way.

The Victor Phonograph Company hired the band to compete with Columbia, who were recording Art Hickman, and almost the first records Whiteman made were an enormous success. His coupling of 'Japanese Sandman' and 'Whispering', recorded in 1920, sold two-and-a-half-million copies, while his record of 'Three O'Clock In The Morning' sold a million more. One for every second phonograph in the country.

In the *Scandals Of 1922*, whose cast included the great WC Fields – hijacked from the Ziegfeld *Follies* – George made two major (and very different) contributions. His main lyric writer for this edition of the show was Buddy DeSylva and, towards the end of their writing it, Buddy remembered a number George had written with Ira a little while before. It was a cheerful love song referring to the continuous flood of new dances that kept appearing. The lyric began "I can dance the old gavotte, I can shimmy, I can trot" and ended "I'll build a staircase to Paradise, with a new step ev'ry day".

Buddy thought that, as George White liked staircases, the song might be a good one to base a *Scandals* production number on. He asked Ira if he and George had any plans for the song. Ira said no, and in fact he didn't think it was all that great a song anyway.

Buddy suggested his production number idea and Ira was delighted by the idea of having one of his songs featured in the *Scandals*. The next night he and George went round to have dinner at Buddy's apartment in Greenwich Village, and after dinner, at about nine pm, they all three began re-writing. By two in the morning they had the new version completed, verse and chorus. It had changed a lot. The word 'staircase' had even become 'stairway', and it was now titled 'I'll Build A Stairway To Paradise'.

George's music, as well as having a haunting melody, was more complicated than was usual. The verse had twenty-four bars instead of the usual sixteen and it had unusual jazz-like flattened thirds and sevenths, or 'blue notes'. The chorus, in addition, had unusual key changes. Ira himself had doubts about a song with such ambitious music ever being a hit and resigned himself to getting a nice credit in the programme and not much else.

When George White heard 'Stairway To Paradise' he was delighted. He had a lavish setting designed to feature the song, with two gleaming white spiral staircases rising up out of sight and dominating the stage. Fifty beautiful girls danced up and down them, costumed in shiny black patent leather that glinted in the spotlights.

The number was a smash. Bands and record companies seized on the song as the best thing in the show and played it incessantly. The sheet music was published and the song became a hit. Ira's first cheque for one-third of the royalties came to three-thousand-five-hundred dollars, enough to support him for a year.

George's other contribution to the show would turn out to be more significant. For some time he and Buddy DeSylva had been discussing the idea of writing a one-act opera, lasting maybe twenty minutes, and using blues inflections in the music.

They suggested such a piece to George White for the *Scandals*, but he rejected the idea on the grounds that the sets and costumes would be too expensive. Then, three weeks before the show was due to open, he changed his mind and said yes. If they wrote their opera he would include it in the show as the opener to the second act ('Stairway To Paradise' being spotted to close the first.)

George and Buddy got to work and in five days and nights wrote their opera. It was the tension and excitement of this concentrated burst of work that first brought on the minor ailment that would plague George all his life. He called it "composer's stomach", but in fact it was nervous constipation.

Will Vodery helped out by writing the arrangements for the opera, and it was entitled *Blue Monday*. Set in a basement saloon in Harlem, its plot concerns two lovers, Vi and Joe. Another character, Tom, is jealous of Joe and when Joe goes out of town to visit his mother, Tom tells Vi that he is seeing another woman. When Joe returns, she shoots him. He dies, but not before she learns the truth.

Although *Blue Monday* is technically a true opera, the dialogue being sung, not spoken, its overall effect is still that of a string of unrelated songs and the music is frankly not all that good. For a start, it isn't really very dramatic. The piece's main interest today is mostly to musical historians, showing, as it does, George taking his first tentative steps towards the extended works of his later years.

The best song in it is probably the opening number, 'Blue Monday Blues', which really does have something of the feel of the music in the Harlem night spots where George continued to go as often as possible. Also fairly good is 'Has One Of You Seen Joe?', the aria he based on the main theme of his string quartet, 'Lullaby'. But other pieces, such as the spiritual, 'I'm Gonna See My Mother', sung by the dying Joe, really does not come off at all.

Whatever led the usually-shrewd George White to change his mind and include the piece is hard to imagine. Even if it had been a masterpiece, a downbeat drama like *Blue Monday* was completely out of place in his otherwise-cheerful show. So conditioned were the audience to expecting entertainment in fact, that one critic castigated the opera as "The most dismal, stupid, and incredible blackface sketch that has ever been perpetrated. In it a dusky soprano finally killed her gambling man. She should have shot all her associates the moment they appeared and then turned the pistol on herself."

'Blackface', although then still common in vaudeville, was probably also a mistake. It is hard to take seriously white singers with their faces masked in black greasepaint, even singing 'Massa's In De Cold Cold Ground'.

The piece survived the out-of-town tryout, but after the opening night in New York George White dropped it from the programme.

All the same, even with its faults, quite a few people, both in the audience and in the show, had liked it. Prominent among these were Paul Whiteman and Ferde Grofé, who found it exciting and original. As the Whiteman Band grew in popularity, size and ambition, they would remember George.

CHAPTER FIVE

'Rhapsody In Blue'

Towards the end of 1922 George began for the first time to work closely with a man who would become a long-time musical colleague and friend: William Merigan Daly, known to everyone as Bill.

Bill Daly was shy and bespectacled, with habitually untidy hair. In contrast to George, with his immaculate dress sense, he dressed for comfort in old sweaters with the elbows out and scuffed old shoes. He was also an extremely talented musician – a pianist, a composer and a conductor.

Some ten years older than George, he had been a boy prodigy as a pianist, but in his teens gave up performing completely. He went to Harvard, graduating in 1908, and from there entered journalism, becoming the managing editor of *Everybody's Magazine* (where he helped to discover and encourage the writer Edna Ferber).

In 1914 he was asked to conduct a choral concert being given in honour of Paderewski. He did and his conducting made such an impression on the maestro that Paderewski not only urged him to return to music, but recommended him to the Chicago Opera.

They offered to hire him as a conductor and he accepted, but before he could take up the post, they temporarily ceased mounting productions. So Bill took a job conducting a Broadway musical called *Hands Up*. This was in 1915, the same year that George began work at Remick's and, in fact, they briefly met while George was there.

During the next few years, Bill continued to conduct musical comedies, with great success, and to do a certain amount of composing – he had been co-composer of the Astaires' first starring show, *For Goodness Sake*. George had met him then and on several other occasions, but late in 1922 they found themselves working closely together on a score for a rustic musical comedy called *Our Nell*. It was described as 'A Musical Mellowdrayma' and for a while it had been known as *Hayseed*.

The lyricist was the show's co-author, Brian Hooker, while George and Bill Daly divided the writing of the score between them. George's numbers included 'By And By', 'We Go To Church On Sunday' and 'Walking Home With Angeline'. This last number was a good one, musically witty and with a catchy rhythm, but the best number in the show was a delicate and graceful little song written by George and Bill (and Brian Hooker) in collaboration, called 'Innocent Ingenue Baby'.

Our Nell was a fair success, running until well into 1923. It was at around this time that Jerome Kern finally got over the feeling that he had been snubbed by George at the time of *La-La-Lucille!*. As George's reputation rose, Kern made his peace by announcing that he would soon retire and turn over to George all his unfulfilled show contracts. As things turned out, he did neither.

Early in 1923 George made his first trip abroad, to London. British dance bands looked to America for the best numbers, and the biggest and most lasting hit in Britain at the beginning of the twenties was 'Swanee'. There was also a considerable two-way traffic between the London musical theatre and Broadway – Kern, for instance, had worked in London, Wodehouse had moved to America and producers on either side of the Atlantic looked to the other side for shows and talents.

As a result of all this, Albert de Courville, the London producer who had brought the Original Dixieland Jass Band, and thus jazz, to London in 1919, hired George to come to London and write the music for a revue at the Empire Theatre in Leicester Square, offering him fifteen-hundred dollars and his return boat fare.

George had no real notion of the success his song had been in England and, when his boat docked at Southampton, he was taken aback and delighted when a customs official checking his passport said, "George Gershwin, writer of 'Swanee'?" The man went on to ask him what he was writing now and, as George wrote next day to Ira, "I couldn't ask for a more pleasant entrance into a country. When I reached shore a woman reporter came up to me and asked for a few words. I felt like I was Kern or somebody."

On his first night he was taken to a London revue starring comedian George Robey. He liked Robey, feeling he put over a lyric song as well as anybody he'd seen, but noted that, from what he'd seen and heard and been told, England was years behind America in the field of musical comedy. There were almost no ingenues or leading men who could perform the sort of songs he had been writing and most of the music he heard was from America.

Even the most popular thing in the revue, the Savoy Havana Band, was being led by an American, Bert Ralton. Ralton had been one of the original two saxophonists imported into his dance band by Art Hickman in 1918 and George had met him in America in 1922, when Ralton had been in a band recording a 'Mexican' number written by George and Buddy DeSylva. Never used in a show, it was called 'Tomale (I'm Hot For You)'.

Bert Ralton was not the only American colleague he met in London. Alex Aarons was also there. *For Goodness Sake*, the show he had produced with the Astaires', was transferring to London, where it would be retitled *Stop Flirting*, and Alex hired George to revise the score and contribute a few new numbers.

By now Aarons and Freedley had serious plans to co-produce shows and had put the Astaires under contract to appear in a new show in New York as soon as *Stop Flirting* closed. What they had in mind was to produce a new kind of musical. It was to have something of the same intimate feel as the Princess shows written by Bolton, Wodehouse and Kern and have the songs integrated into the action in the same way, but it would have more realistic and contemporary characters and use popular music in the more expressive way that George was working towards.

Alex insisted to Vinton Freedley that George must be the sole composer. He had to insist because Vinton had doubts. He thought George's music was too complex and subtle for successful musical comedy. In a way he can hardly be blamed. After all, he and George had been associated in two flops. There had been his production *Dere Mable* (even though George only contributed the song 'We're Pals' to it), and *A Dangerous Maid*, which he had performed in, and for which all the songs had for the first time been co-written by

George and 'Arthur Francis'.

Arthur Francis had also written the lyrics for the Aarons musical *Two Little Girls In Blue*, with music by Vincent Youmans, in 1921. Aarons had run out of money during the preparation of that and the production had been taken over by the domineering Abe Erlanger, who kept it running all summer at a loss so as to compete with Ziegfeld's *Follies* (Erlanger hated Ziegfeld for poaching his most beautiful girls). Although the show hadn't been a great success, its lyrics had won a lot of praise. Aarons wanted Arthur Francis to write the lyrics for the new show as well. Inexorably the two brothers were being drawn together into a songwriting team.

While in London, Alex Aarons had long discussions about the plot and settings for the proposed show with Fred Astaire. It was unusual for a star to be so closely involved in a show so early in its production, but Fred was an unusual star. As well as performing and choreographing, he could write tunes and was a useful pianist and drummer.

Fred and Alex decided that it made sense to cast the Astaires as brother and sister, rather than as the conventional romantic couple; in fact, to cast them as a brother-and-sister dance team and build the comedy on sibling rivalry rather than romantic misunderstandings. Guy Bolton and Fred Thompson were contracted to write the book around this idea.

While in London, George came up with a highly rhythmic fragment of melody, eight bars long. He was very proud of it. It sounded distinctively American and he was intrigued that he had hit on it in a foreign city. At one of his meetings with Alex Aarons, he played it and Alex asked him to keep it aside for use in the planned show. George agreed.

The revue that he was in London to write, initially called *Silver Lining*, but eventually called *The Rainbow*, turned out to be a disaster. The book, written by Edgar Wallace, Noel Scott and producer Albert de Courville, was weak. The lyrics were better. One thing George had noted England did have was half a dozen good lyric-writers, and fortunately he was to work with one of these, Clifford Grey.

Unfortunately their schedule was mercilessly tight and, perhaps for this reason, the songs George and Clifford Grey turned out were perfunctory and below George's usual standard. Later in life he admitted that this score was the weakest he ever wrote.

The songs included 'Sunday In London Town', 'Eastern Moon', and a lively enough number called 'Oh! Nina'. Also in the show was the song he had written with Bill Daly, 'Innocent Ingenue Baby', only with the lyric slightly altered by Clifford Grey for English ears and the title changed to 'Innocent Lonesome Blue Baby' (as George had noted, the musical comedy ingenue was almost unknown in England).

To make the show work as well as possible, Albert de Courville had hired a number of American and French performers for his cast. But in a way this made matters worse. The leading comic, who was English, had had difficulty learning his lines and his part had been considerably cut in rehearsal. On the opening night, 3 April 1923, he stepped forward during the show and began to harangue the audience about the iniquities of hiring foreigners to compose and perform in shows when English artists were clearly so much better. Eventually he had to be forcibly removed from the stage.

Before returning to New York, George took a plane to Paris to visit Jules Glaenzer, who had an apartment at 5 Rue Malakoff, near the Bois de Boulogne. Buddy DeSylva was also visiting Glaenzer and the three of them made the rounds of the city's most famous restaurants and night clubs.

George was bowled over by Paris. He fell in love with it at first sight. One day, while they were driving down the Champs Élysées in Glaenzer's car, he exclaimed with his characteristic combination of boyish enthusiasm and naivety, "Why, this is a city you can write about!" "Don't look now, George," said DeSylva, "but it's been done."

Back in New York, George and Buddy began collaborating on the 1923 edition of the *Scandals*, this time with two additional lyric writers, E Ray Goetz and Ballard MacDonald. The show, which opened on 18 June, contained a dozen or so songs, the best of which was 'Where Is She?', with its mingling of blues inflections and popular song in a way that George was now beginning to master.

Somewhere around this time he began to study with Rubin Goldmark, who also taught the American composer (and George's near-contemporary) Aaron Copland. George did not get on with Goldmark and one almost wonders why he went to him. Goldmark was a solid traditionalist who had no sympathy for George's new ideas. At his third lesson, George brought in a copy of his string quartet, 'Lullaby', written in 1919 when he was studying with Edward Kilyeni. Goldmark looked at it and said, "It's good. Yes, very good. It's plainly to be seen that you have already learned a great deal of harmony from me." Three lessons were all George took.

Not all lovers of classical music were as hidebound as Rubin Goldmark. Towards the end of 1922 signs had started appearing that George was attracting notice in the world of 'serious' music, as well as the world of popular music and Broadway shows. On 6 September that year there appeared a newspaper interview with a respected classical musician, Beryl Rubinstein. In his interview Rubinstein, who was a concert pianist and a member of the faculty of the Cleveland Institute of Music, referred to George as "a great composer", saying:

> This young fellow has the spark of musical genius which is definite in his serious moods... [he] has the fire of originality... With Gershwin's style and seriousness he is not definitely from the popular music school, but one of the really outstanding figures in the country's musical efforts... I really believe that America will at no distant date honour [him] for his talent ... and that when we speak of American composers George Gershwin's name will be prominent on our list.

Almost a year later, in August 1923, came an article by Gilbert Seldes, the critic who would become famous in 1924 for writing a book, *The Seven Lively Arts*, which championed such despised forms as vaudeville, the strip cartoon and the silent cinema. In the highbrow magazine *The Dial*, which he then edited, he wrote: "Delicacy, even dreaminess, is a quality [Gershwin] alone brings into jazz music. And his sense of variation in rhythm, of an oddly-placed accent, of emphasis and colour, is impeccable."

Another writer who was impressed by George's music was Carl

Van Vechten. He too was an encourager of the overlooked and undiscovered. During his long life he fought for recognition for composers like Schoenberg, Stravinsky and Satie, and for writers including Ouida and Ronald Firbank. He was also one of the main moving spirits behind the 'Harlem Renaissance' of the twenties, fighting for recognition for black poetry, painting, drama and music, and he and George had frequently visited Harlem's night spots together.

In the spring of 1923 Van Vechten was asked by the French concert singer Eva Gauthier to suggest ideas for a programme she was booked to give at New York's Aeolian Hall that autumn. He suggested some modern American songs. When she looked dubious, he added, "Jazz". At this she looked more interested, but nothing further happened until later in the year when she returned from a visit to Paris. There, she told Van Vechten, Maurice Ravel had suggested the same thing.

Impressed by this, she asked Van Vechten whom he could recommend as an accompanist (and as a guide in this unknown field) and immediately he suggested George, whom he had known since he heard him play 'Swanee' at a party in 1919, before it had been performed in public.

She sought out George and together they assembled a programme of seven American songs: 'Alexander's Ragtime Band' (Berlin), 'The Siren's Song' (Kern), 'Carolina In The Morning' (Walter Donaldson) and by George – 'I'll Build A Stairway To Paradise', 'Do It Again', 'Innocent Ingenue Baby' and 'Swanee'.

The *Recital Of Ancient And Modern Music For Voice* took place at the Aeolian Hall on 1 November 1923. For her performance, Mlle Gauthier, standing in front of a black backdrop, wore a long-sleeved black velvet dress and enormous diamond earrings. This produced a powerful effect, her face, hands and earrings standing out dramatically in the blackness.

The American section of her programme was the third of six, the other five being labelled 'Ancient', 'Modern Hungarian And German', 'Austrian', 'British' and 'French'. Among the composers represented were Purcell, Byrd, Bellini, Bartok, Hindemith, Schoenberg, Bliss and Milhaud.

For these other sections she used her regular accompanist, Max Jaffe. For the American section she used George. It was his first appearance on the concert platform and his bustling nervousness contrasted strongly with the sedate composure of Jaffe. The sheet music he carried as he dashed on from the wings, with its lurid Tin Pan Alley covers, brought titters from the sophisticated audience. But from the moment he launched into 'Alexander's Ragtime Band', the audience was his.

When he slyly slid a quotation from Rimsky-Korsakov's 'Scheherezade' into 'Stairway To Paradise', the audience purred with recognition. This tall, dark-haired young man knew about real music. It was all right to like him.

Music critic Deems Taylor, reviewing the recital in the New York *World* wrote: "[The songs] stood up amazingly well, not only as entertainment but as music... What they did possess was melodic interest and continuity, harmonic appropriateness, well-balanced almost classically severe form and subtle fascinating rhythms – in short the qualities that any sincere and interesting music possesses."

The American section of the programme was such a success that the audience demanded an encore, so Mlle Gauthier and George reprised 'Do It Again'. Twice. And they repeated the whole recital three months later, in Boston, at the end of January 1924. But by then George had made another, and more significant, appearance at the Aeolian Hall.

At the same time as the *Recital Of Ancient And Modern Music For Voice*, George had been collaborating with Buddy DeSylva on the songs for a musical called *Sweet Little Devil*. This was being promoted as the show which would bring its star, Constance Binney, back to Broadway from Hollywood. While working to complete the score for this, George was approached by Paul Whiteman with a proposition.

Since they had worked together on the *Scandals Of 1922*, the Whiteman Band had gone on from success to success. By 1924 it was getting seven-and-a-half-thousand dollars a week for appearances in vaudeville.

Both Whiteman and his arranger, Ferde Grofé, liked jazz. As well as being aware of its commercial popularity, they realised it was capable of being both exciting and emotionally expressive. But with their classical backgrounds they thought of it as a coarse rough music and believed that the best way of bringing out its virtues would be by using the techniques of nineteenth century classical music.

Whiteman decided to give a formal concert, performing the new music he was creating to an influential audience which might otherwise never hear the new music he was creating. It was his intention, he said, to "make a lady out of jazz". Remembering how impressed both he and Grofé had been by George's one-act opera, *Blue Monday*, he asked George if he would write an extended composition to be featured in the concert.

George wasn't too enthusiastic. *Sweet Little Devil* was due to open in New York on 21 January and before that there was to be a tryout in Boston, beginning on the 7th, which would undoubtedly call for revisions to the score. He didn't feel he would have time to write an extended piece. Besides, he felt he wasn't yet ready to write a major work for an orchestra. He told Whiteman he would think about the proposition, but was making no promises.

On the evening of 3 January, with their songs for the tryout mostly completed, George and Buddy went to relax at the Ambassador Billiard Parlour, on Broadway. This was a favourite hangout for songwriters, and Ira went with them.

At around eleven pm, while George and Buddy were playing billiards, Ira sat reading the next morning's edition of the New York *Tribune*. An item on the amusement page caught his eye. It announced a concert to be held on Tuesday, 12 February, at the Aeolian Hall by the Paul Whiteman Orchestra, on the theme of "What is American Music?", and it mentioned that pieces were being specially written for the occasion by Irving Berlin and Victor Herbert, and that George Gershwin was "at work on a jazz concerto".

This was news to Ira. When George and Buddy finished their game (George lost), Ira read them the item. George didn't seem surprised, or even disconcerted. "So he's really going through with it," he said. Calling Whiteman, he learned that the concert was going on earlier than planned because another band leader, Vincent Lopez, was also preparing a serious jazz concert, to feature a WC Handy composition called 'The Evolution Of The Blues'. Lopez had even announced its date.

Fortunately, it turned out that while George had intended to turn down Whiteman's offer, he had been unable to stop thinking about it, and ideas for an extended piece had started coming unbidden into his head. At a party, for instance, while improvising at the piano, a melody had occurred to him that might well (and did) become the basis for a slow movement.

Now that he seemed to be faced with actually having to write a piece, his mind began to work faster. En route to Boston for the tryout of *Sweet Little Devil*, the rhythms of the train began giving him further ideas.

His first plan, remembering *Blue Monday*, was to write a symphonic 'blues'. But then he thought that maybe that would be too restricting and he should look to jazz for inspiration. As he later put it, "There had been so much chatter about the limitations of jazz, not to speak of the manifest misunderstandings of its function. Jazz, they said, had to be in strict time. It had to cling to dance rhythms. I resolved, if possible, to kill that misconception with one sturdy blow."

Not wishing to tie himself down to any definite musical structure, such as a concerto, he elected to call his work a 'rhapsody' (defined in the Oxford English Dictionary as "an instrumental composition enthusiastic in character but of indefinite form"). At one point he thought of calling it 'Rhapsody For Jazz Band And Piano', but then, in keeping with his lifelong feeling that he was writing the music of his country, he thought a possible title for the work might be 'American Rhapsody'.

By the time he returned to New York after the Boston opening of *Sweet Little Devil* on 7 January, he had the framework of the piece fairly well worked out. In a back room at the Gershwin apartment on One-Hundred-And-Tenth Street, a second piano had been installed for himself and Ira to work at. George settled himself down there and got seriously to work, composing the piece as if it were for two pianos, but making occasional notes on the score as to which instruments should actually be used where.

Not only did he not yet consider himself competent to score for an orchestra, there was an added complication in scoring for the Whiteman Band. In the early days of big band music, the musicians in the bands were by no means as well-schooled as orchestral musicians, and it was necessary for an arranger to know the weaknesses of each player. Also the strengths, because some might have a personal intonation that no other musician could emulate. The only way to arrange the 'Rhapsody', especially in the short time available, was for Ferde Grofé to do it.

For the period of the composition Grofé almost moved into the Gershwin home. Mother Rose kept him and George copiously supplied with Russian tea and father Morris, listening amiably to George's progress with his composition, is said to have remarked, in the heavy Russian accent he never lost, "Make it good, George, it's liable to be important."

Ferde Grofé took George's completed pages of manuscript from him one by one as they were completed and got straight down to working on the arrangements. It is a good indication of the way the members of the Whiteman Band had individual strengths and weaknesses that he did not write on his scores the instruments to be played, but rather the names of the players.

One of the Whiteman musicians was clarinettist Ross Gorman and one of his strengths was his ability to play a long glissando on the clarinet, which being a keyed instrument was not designed to do any such thing. George, when Gorman played such a glissando during rehearsal as a joke, decided that it would make a perfect opening, establishing the mood of the piece at once. (When he explained the precise emotional effect he was after to Gorman, however, Gorman balked. He said that no clarinettist could produce the effect George wanted. George insisted and Gorman had no option but to go away and experiment with reeds of different stiffnesses until he could manage it. Which he did triumphantly.)

During this time of concentrated composition, George played some of what he had written, during a social evening at the Paleys'. Asked what he was going to call it, he told them he was thinking of 'American Rhapsody'. Ira, who that afternoon had been looking at

Whistler paintings with titles like 'Nocturne In Blue And Green' and 'Harmony In Grey And Green', suggested, "Why not call it 'Rhapsody in Blue'?"). George liked the idea, and 'Rhapsody In Blue' it became.

On 21 January, *Sweet Little Devil* opened at the Astor Theatre in New York. In spite of the winsome and likeable presence of Constance Binney as the leading lady, it didn't do well. Its plot, telling how the simple home-loving heroine competed against a glamorous Follies girl for the love of a South American engineer, was a bit thin even by the standards of 1924. It survived on Broadway for less than four months.

By 25 January, four days after *Sweet Little Devil* opened, George had more or less completed the 'Rhapsody'. By 4 February, Ferde Grofé had done the arrangements. At that time the Whiteman Band were appearing at the Palais Royal night club on Forty-Eighth Street, and for five days they rehearsed sections of the piece there after work, late into the night.

The first complete rehearsal also took place at the Palais Royal, but at the more convenient hour of noon. About thirty guests were invited, including Walter Damrosch, conductor for the New York Symphony Society, several serious music critics (some of whom had never heard of George Gershwin) and Victor Herbert.

Some were enthusiastic, some were less certain. Victor Herbert, who was impressed, suggested to George that he could make his middle melody more effective by preceding it with a rising passage ending in a held note. Which George did.

One thing George hadn't done was to put the last touches to his own piano part. He continued to tinker with the score, eventually completing it in a back room at the Aeolian Hall while the first part of the concert was in progress.

The concert attracted a huge audience, made up, in Paul Whiteman's words, of "Vaudevillians, concert managers come to have a look at the novelty, Tin Pan Alleyites, composers, symphony and opera stars, flappers, cake-eaters, all mixed up higgledy-piggledy". ('Flappers' and 'cake-eaters' were current slang terms for the fashionable young, female and male, 'cake-eaters' being young men who hung around female company at social occasions like tea-parties.)

Some of the audience were in evening dress, as for a classical concert. Some were simply in everyday suits. Famous names who were there (by invitation) from the world of music included Sergei Rachmaninov, Igor Stravinsky, Fritz Kreisler, Mischa Elman, Leopold Stokowski, John Philip Sousa and the Harlem stride pianist Willie 'The Lion' Smith. There were socialites like banker Otto Kahn, publisher Condé Nast and (of course) Jules Glaenzer and performers such as Gertrude Lawrence. The critics present included Carl Van Vechten, Gilbert Seldes, Heywood Broun and the one regarded as most influential of all, Deems Taylor.

Whiteman went on to report that: "Even though it was snowing, men and women were fighting to get into the door, pulling and mauling at each other as they sometimes do at a baseball game, or a prize fight, or in the subway." He became so nervous of what he had let himself in for and whether he really had anything to offer, that he "vowed I'd give five-thousand dollars if we could stop right then and there". But there was nothing for it. Soon the curtain went up and writer Hugh C Ernst, who had co-written the programme notes with Gilbert Seldes, was beginning the opening announcement: "The experiment is to be purely educational. Mr Whiteman intends to point out, with the assistance of his orchestra and associates, the tremendous strides which have been made in popular music from the day of discordant jazz, which sprang into existence about ten years ago from nowhere in particular, to the really melodious music of today..."

The concert opened with a dixieland-style rendition of the Original Dixieland Jass Band number 'Livery Stable Blues'. This was intended as an example of the raucous sort of music that 'symphonic jazz' was going to improve on. Unfortunately, many people afterwards agreed that this was the most exciting number of the evening. That is, until 'Rhapsody In Blue':

The full programme was this:

I. True Form Of Jazz
    (a) Ten years ago – 'Livery Stable Blues' . . . . Nick La Rocca
    (b) With modern embellishment –
'Mama Loves Papa' . . . . Abel Baer

II. Comedy Selections
   (a) Origin of 'Yes, We Have No Bananas'...... Frank Silver
   (b) Instrumental comedy –
   'So This Is Venice' .... Theodore Thomas
   (adapted from *The Carnival Of Venice*)
III. Contrast – Legitimate Scoring vs Jazzing
   (a) Selection in true form – 'Whispering' John Schoenberger
   (b) Same selection in Jazz Treatment
IV. Recent Compositions With Modern Score
   (a) 'Limehouse Blues' .... Philip Braham
   (b) 'Linger Awhile' .... Benson Rose
   (c) 'Raggedy Ann'..................... Jerome Kern
   V Zez Confrey (piano)
   (a) 'Kitten On The Keys' .... Zez Confrey
   (b) Three Little Oddities:-
      Romanza
      Impromptu
      Novelette..................... Zez Confrey
   (c) 'Nickel In The Slot'................. Zez Confrey
   (accompanied by the orchestra)

INTERMISSION

VI. Flavouring A Selection With Borrowed Themes
   'Russian Rose'............. Ferde Grofé/Peter DeRose
   (based on 'Volga Boat Song')
VII. Semi-Symphonic Arrangements Of Popular Melodies
   (a) 'Alexander's Ragtime Band' .... Irving Berlin
   (b) 'A Pretty Girl Is Like A Melody' .... Irving Berlin
   (c) 'Orange Blossoms In California' .... Irving Berlin
VIII. A Suite Of Serenades, By Victor Herbert
   (a) Spanish
   (b) Chinese
   (c) Cuban
   (d) Oriental
IX. Adaptation of Standard Selections To Dance Rhythm
   (a) 'Pale Moon'................ Frederick Knight Logan
   (b) 'To A Wild Rose'.............. Edward MacDowell

(c) 'Chansonette'. . . . . Rudolf Friml

X. Rhapsody In Blue, By George Gershwin
(George Gershwin at the piano, accompanied by
the orchestra)

XI. In The Field Of The Classics
'Pomp And Circumstance'. . . . . Sir Edward Elgar

After 'Livery Stable Blues', the rest of the programme raised little
enthusiasm, even among the many Whiteman fans (the flappers and
cake-eaters) who had managed to gain admission. Too many of the
pieces had the same orchestral colouring and by the time the
programme had wound its slow length along to George's piece,
boredom was setting in.

'Rhapsody In Blue' changed all that. Ross Gorman's upward wail
on the clarinet grabbed the audience by the ears at once and the
music held them spellbound right to the end. Whiteman was
overwhelmed with pleasure and relief. "Somewhere in the middle of
the score I began crying," he later admitted. "When I came to myself
I was eleven pages along, and until this day I cannot tell you how I
conducted that far."

The audience gave George and the orchestra an ovation that
went on for several minutes and George was called on to take
several bows. He had changed the concert from a well-meant but
slightly dull experiment into a major musical event.

After the Aeolian Hall concert it was obvious to everyone that the
dance band of the future would be playing some sort of arranged
jazz. Whiteman had succeeded in giving jazz a veneer of social
acceptability. The concert and others like it, coupled with his
publicity tag of being 'The King Of Jazz', allowed the more daring
among the respectable to listen to anything called 'jazz' without
feeling they had to apologise more than a bit and it did much to
allow a hearing for the real thing.

The success of the concert had been far greater than Whiteman
had even dared to hope for and it was all due to 'Rhapsody In Blue'.
Serious musicians and critics discussed it deeply and at length and
the whole concert was repeated at Aeolian Hall on 7 March and
again, this time at Carnegie Hall, on 21 April. The Whiteman Band

would perform the 'Rhapsody', both as part of the concert and otherwise, eighty-four times in 1924 alone, often with George at the piano.

In June, George and the band got together in the Victor studios and recorded an abridged version of the 'Rhapsody' on two sides of a twelve-inch seventy-eight. This record has the distinction of being the one that remained on sale the longest. It was never out of catalogue from the day it was issued until seventy-eights stopped being produced almost fifty years later.

George played a piano version of the 'Rhapsody' that same year at a Glaenzer party. Present was a young English actor and playwright, then relatively unknown – Noel Coward. Soon, when writing what was to be his first hit play, *The Vortex*, he came to a critical scene where the hero, Nicky Lancaster, has to play the piano. He remembered the 'Rhapsody', and got George's permission to use some of it. When the play opened in London (also in 1924), this was the first time anything of the piece had been heard in England. Demand for the recording soared.

And what has been the consensus of opinion about the 'Rhapsody'? Well, for a start, it isn't really jazz. George cannot be blamed for this, because although the word 'jazz' had indeed been around for nearly ten years by 1924, the term was popularly being used to describe any sort of hot dance music.

Real jazz, even in its earliest flowering, had hardly got going in 1924. The first of Louis Armstrong's historic Hot Five recordings was still a year in the future. What was there, then, for George to have heard? Among the trendsetters in music there had been the Original Dixieland Jass Band in 1917 and the freer and more inventive white group, the New Orleans Rhythm Kings, who were based in Chicago and started recording in 1922. Outstanding on the 1924 scene was the great band leader Joe 'King' Oliver, also working in Chicago. He started making records with his Creole Jazz Band in 1923, but there is no evidence, musical or anecdotal, that George ever heard him or them.

So the jazz available for him to try and base his music on was thin and inexpressive compared with what was soon to come along, good fun though much of it was.

He was not alone in this situation. Igor Stravinsky wrote his piece 'Ragtime' well before 'Rhapsody In Blue', and he remained so convinced that he now understood the rhythms of jazz that when he came to write 'Ebony Concerto' for the Woody Herman band in 1945, it was clear that the rhythms in the new piece were still closer to the ragtime of thirty years before than they were to the rhythms of the swing era.

From a classical music point of view the piece also has its faults. The harmonies in it, while adventurous by musical-comedy standards, were to symphony-goers nothing new. The overall structure is weak, the various themes and sections tend to follow one another in succession, without proper development or interplay. Furthermore, some of the sections seem to run out of ideas and drift off into meaningless repetition.

But what it does have is great rhythmic inventiveness (especially by the standards of its time), moments of great drama (beginning with the beginning) and possibly the thing that has contributed most over the years to its continued popularity, a succession of memorable and evocative melodies, each with such a personal quality that they could have been composed by nobody but Gershwin.

After the Aeolian Hall concert, there was naturally a party. George had gone out of his way to invite three of the Harlem pianists he frequently went to listen to – Willie 'The Lion' Smith, James P Johnson and James P Johnson's nineteen-year-old protege, Fats Waller.

At the party, George naturally made for the piano. As Willie 'The Lion' later wrote, "It looked as if he was going to stay seated at the piano all night himself and hog all the playing... I finally went over and said to Gershwin, 'Get up off that piano stool and let the real players take over, you tomato.' He was a good-natured fellow and from then on the three of us took over the entertainment."

George wouldn't have worried about being out-played at the party. From now on he would be regarded as a serious composer, in a country that generally believed all serious music came from Europe.

This acceptance was underlined the following June, when

conductor Walter Damrosch came to him with a proposition. He had talked the president of the New York Symphony Society into offering George a commission to write a piano concerto. George accepted the challenge and signed a contract that committed him to performing the concerto, when it was written, at seven performances – in New York, Washington, Philadelphia and Baltimore.

But performing was to be some way off. Having signed the contract, it took George almost a year to begin the actual writing. Life was to continue being as hectic as ever.

CHAPTER SIX

'Lady Be Good'

George's next assignment after the success of 'Rhapsody In Blue' was to compose the music for *George White's Scandals of 1924*. Again Buddy DeSylva provided the lyrics, this time on his own, except for one number on which he collaborated with Ballard MacDonald.

This turned out to be the best number in the show. It was 'Somebody Loves Me' and not only was it George's biggest hit since 'Swanee', it was really the first of his songs to have an unmistakably Gershwin sound. He had found the secret ingredient that would characterise all his best-loved songs – the ability to write a haunting melody.

The 1924 *Scandals* was the last edition that George composed for. To write the next year's show, he told George White, he would need a considerable increase in salary from the one-hundred-and-twenty-five dollars a week he was now getting. He was relieved and unsurprised when White refused. That was really what he wanted. After the success of 'Rhapsody In Blue', he was now more determined than ever to establish himself as a composer of musical comedies, and his work for the *Scandals* was eating up too much of his time.

The main project he had in the offing was the musical that Aarons and Freedley were planning for the Astaires. They didn't yet have all the backing they needed, but Guy Bolton and Fred Thompson had already written their first version of the book and it was obvious to everyone concerned that this production was to be something special. It was to be called *Lady Be Good* and by the spring of 1924 George and his brother were beginning to think about writing songs to fit the plot.

His brother had by now decided that he was well enough established as a lyricist to admit publicly that he and George were related. He was happy to use the last name 'Gershwin', but not so sure about a first name. He didn't want to use his real name (or what he then thought was his real name), Isadore, because he felt it was too common. At the same time he felt he would be more comfortable if he could keep the same initial. He considered calling himself 'Irving', but then decided there were too many Irvings around in the music business already.

Eventually, after a lot of consideration, he chose the name 'Ira', which he liked because it was unusual. Also because he thought it meant 'sweet' or 'gentle'. It was only when doing a crossword some years later that he discovered to his amazement that it is a synonym for 'watchful'. Or so he claimed. But according to the *Oxford Dictionary of Christian Names* it is Aramaic for "the stallion" and was the name of a priest of David. 'Watchful' is probably more appropriate, even though Ira was never entirely sure for the rest of his life that the name he had chosen was the right one. (He would use it for the first time on the lyrics he wrote for a musical called *Be Yourself*, which opened in the autumn of 1924. It was written by the famous team of George S Kaufman and Marc Connolly, with music by the less famous Lewis Gensler and Milton Schwartzwald.)

In the spring of 1924, Ira was working on the lyric to a chorus George had composed. He showed it to George, who liked it, and sat down with Ira to compose the introductory verse. The melody he came up with turned out to be not quite right. He had based it on a piano fragment from 'Rhapsody In Blue' and it came out far too strong and moody to match the chorus they had started with. It was so strong in fact that it seemed worth developing as a song on its own. On hearing it, Ira almost immediately came up with a line that fitted – "Some day he'll come along – the man I love".

These last four words at once became the title and, realising they were onto something good, the brothers settled down to develop the new song into one for Adele Astaire to sing in *Lady Be Good*.

It was with this song that George and Ira completely merged as a team. The stronger mingling of popular song and blues and classically-based harmonies that George had created for 'Rhapsody

In Blue' transferred itself into his songs and the rhythms and melody lines he created inspired Ira to write in a new style, employing the speech rhythms and vocabulary of the New York they had both grown up in. Their songs became urban and up-to-the-minute and, having the shared background of brothers, their talents matched perfectly.

From then on, George would write almost all his songs with Ira. Their partnership was well-balanced, each inspiring the other. George would always remain the by far more energetic of the two (Ira, as one of their friends once said, was a hard man to get out of an easy chair), but from the time he took up music he always had great admiration and respect for his elder brother.

Ira's artistic insight and influence helped to mould and direct George's talent, most obviously in the structure of the songs they wrote together, each one setting and developing a small dramatic situation. But there was more to George's admiration than that. As Ira once said, "George's drive had nothing to do with money or the lack of it. He never knew how much money he had in the bank. He was really doing what he did because he felt he had to do it... To me George was a little sad all the time because he had this compulsion to work. He never relaxed. He had to be doing something all the time... [I think] George admired me because I was relaxed..."

At around the time they wrote 'The Man I Love', George and Ira also developed a couple of other songs in preparation for *Lady Be Good*. One was written as a sort of tribute to a famous female impersonator of the time, Bert Savoy, who the year before, in the summer of 1923, had been struck by lightning and killed, with another actor, while watching a storm on the sands at Long Beach, about fifteen miles east of Coney Island.

Extremely popular both on stage and off, Bert Savoy had been the comedy half of an act called Savoy and Brennan. A large man, wearing drag and a striking red wig, he would reel drunkenly round the stage muttering things like, "You don't know the half of it, dearie!". George and Ira wrote a wry bittersweet comedy number for the show called 'The Half Of It, Dearie, Blues'. This would be Fred Astaire's first-ever solo number and the nearest that his diffident on stage character of the mid twenties could get to a declaration of love.

The other number they worked up was based on the rhythmic eight bars that George had played for Alex Aarons in London the year before, the tune that Alex had asked him to save for the Astaires. Using those eight bars as the basis for the chorus, George added a verse (again borrowing from 'Rhapsody In Blue'), and Ira wrote a lyric for the whole thing, basing much of it on a song he had written in 1923 with music by Bill Daly and Joe Meyer, but which was never used. That had been called 'Little Rhythm – Go 'Way''. The new number he called 'Fascinating Rhythm'.

But *Lady Be Good* was still a few months off. The Astaires were still in London, appearing in *Stop Flirting* (known previously in America as *For Goodness Sake*) and Aarons and Freedley were still trying to find the rest of the backing. In the meantime they hired George to write the score for a show that was to be put on in London at the Winter Garden Theatre. So before his last edition of the *Scandals* opened, which it did at the end of June, George again found himself on a boat crossing the Atlantic.

The London show, a revue called *Primrose,* was produced by Aarons and Freedley in collaboration with a pair of English producers, Grossmith and Laurillard – 'Grossmith' being George Grossmith, who had also collaborated with Guy Bolton on the book.

This George Grossmith – the third of that name, which can be confusing – was a comic actor, writer and impresario. His father, of the same name, was a famous performer in Gilbert and Sullivan and even more famous as the author of *The Diary Of A Nobody*. His father in turn, also George Grossmith, was famous for giving public readings and entertaining lectures and for dying of an apoplectic fit at the dinner table at the Savage Club, immediately after giving a comic recitation.

George (Gershwin) was the sole composer for *Primrose* and most of the lyrics for the show were by an English writer, Desmond Carter. George did, however, manage to slip in a few lyrics by Ira, including 'Boy Wanted', salvaged from their flop of three years before, *A Dangerous Maid*. Another was a quartet in four-part harmony (which was rare in a musical) called 'Four Little Sirens We' and it was a sort of tribute to Gilbert and Sullivan, being an echo of

'Three Little Maids from School'.

Primrose was George's most ambitious and varied score so far. As well as the quartet, it had ensemble numbers, duets, love songs and comedy songs. Not only that, George for the first time orchestrated several of the numbers himself (this was not usual practice for show composers, who rarely had either the skill or the time).

George, when he could spare time from his music, was highly susceptible to the charms of a pretty face and during his involvement in *Primrose* he also became involved with an attractive dancer in the chorus. Her name was Sylvia Hawkes and if their relationship didn't last, it was possibly because she was, in her own way, as ambitious as he was. She went on to marry Lord Ashley, heir to the Earl of Shaftesbury. And Douglas Fairbanks, Sr. And Lord Stanley of Alderley. And Clark Gable. As Guy Bolton put it, "Nobody ever cut a wider swathe than Sylvia Hawkes."

In London George also spent a fair amount of time socialising with the Astaires and discussing their forthcoming project. He played them 'The Half Of It, Dearie, Blues' and reported in a letter to Ira that they were crazy about it, going on to say, "I would if I were you, get several ideas for the show without writing any of them up yet. There is a lot of work to be done on this show."

Primrose, which opened on 11 September, was a fair success. It ran for two-hundred-and-fifty-five performances and made George as much of a favourite in London as he already was on Broadway, which encouraged the English music publishers, Chappell, to publish for the first time the complete score of a Gershwin show.

George had set off back to America two weeks before *Primrose* opened. On the boat he ran into the banker Otto Kahn, a frequent backer of shows. Alex Aarons had already approached him about putting money into *Lady Be Good*, but Kahn had turned him down with the wry excuse that he never backed sure hits. Now he asked George how the music for the show was coming along and George, needing little coaxing, found a piano and played him first 'Fascinating Rhythm', and then 'The Man I Love'.

Hearing 'The Man I Love' changed Otto Kahn's mind. He decided he would invest in the show after all, and put up ten thousand dollars.

Now all was set. The money was in place, the book was more or less completed and the Astaires had finished their London run. George and Ira got down to completing the songs. Wanting to get things right, they eventually wrote nineteen numbers, including 'So Am I', 'We're Here Because', 'The Man I Love', 'Fascinating Rhythm', 'The Half Of It, Dearie, Blues' and the title number 'Oh, Lady Be Good!'. Eleven of them ended up in the show.

Rehearsals began towards the end of September and the show was to start its tryout in Philadelphia on 17 November and open in New York, at the Liberty Theatre, on 1 December.

In the cast, as well as Fred and Adele, were comedian Walter Catlett and the singer Cliff Edwards, also known as 'Ukulele Ike'. The orchestra was conducted by Paul Lannin, whose father owned the hotel in Dixville Lodge where George had failed to stay for the whole weekend, and who had co-composed *For Goodness Sake* with Bill Daly.

George had been impressed by how well two pianos worked with the Paul Whiteman Band, so he made the innovation of augmenting the orchestra with the two-piano team of Phil Ohman and Victor Arden, whose playing he admired.

The plot of *Lady Be Good* concerned the brother/sister dance team of Dick and Susie Trevor, who are down on their luck. Each separately gets involved in a scheme to make money and each scheme causes trouble in their respective love lives. But as this was still a musical comedy, albeit rather more realistic than usual, all ends happily in the end, with both Dick and Susie rolling in love and money.

Aarons and Freedley had got together a perfect team. Everyone involved felt involved in the whole show and offered each other support and suggestions. For instance, during rehearsal the Astaires were having trouble with finding an exit step for their dance to 'Fascinating Rhythm'. Fred had been worrying about it for days and the tryout in Philadelphia was fast approaching.

Then one day George happened to be there. Fred asked him to look at the routine. George went to the piano and, as Fred later wrote:

We all went through the thing, reaching the last step, before the proposed exit and George said, 'Now travel, travel with that one.' I stopped to ask what he meant and he jumped up from the piano and demonstrated what he visualised. He wanted us to continue doing the last step, which started centre stage, and sustain it as we travelled to the side, continuing until we were out of sight off stage.The step was a complicated precision rhythm thing in which we kicked out simultaneously as we crossed back and forth in front of each other with arm pulls and heads back. There was a lot going on and, when George suggested travelling, we didn't think it was possible. It was the perfect answer to our problem, however, this suggestion by hoofer Gershwin and it turned out to be a knockout applause puller.

'Fascinating Rhythm' came in the middle of Act One (although it was reprised as the finale of both acts). For the beginning of Act One, Guy Bolton had come up with what he thought was a marvellous opening. The setting was the street outside Dick and Susie's lodgings. After an exhilarating chorus by way of overture, the first scene was of Dick and Susie being evicted, their few possessions being thrown out onto the sidewalk. In Guy Bolton's words:

> Adele, behaving as she would unquestionably have done in real life, arranged the furniture neatly about a lamp post, hung up a 'God Bless Our Home' motto and with the help of a passing workman – destined to become the hero – attached the percolator and fixed the hydrant so that water would be constantly available.
>
> After which, of course, it began to rain and she and Fred did a number called 'Hang On To Me', dancing together under a big umbrella.

Guy was proud of this idea. It was just the sort of charming little scene that had worked so well for him in the Princess shows. But

Alex Aarons didn't like it at all. Only Guy's protestations that it would have to be thrown out over his dead body kept it in the show during rehearsal.

"Alex remained sure it would be a flop. On the first night of the tryout in Philadelphia, Guy was backstage during the number and at the end of 'Hang On To Me' Alex dashed up to him. 'I told you!' he shouted. 'I told you how it would be if we kept that scene in. They're howling and booing.' 'Not so much howling and booing,' Guy explained, 'as cheering their heads off.'

Among the other outstanding numbers in the show was 'Oh, Lady Be Good!', which was sung to Susie (Adele) by Walter Catlett, playing her lawyer, J Watterson Watkins. He is trying to talk her into impersonating a Mexican heiress (which she is uneasy about, seeing she doesn't speak Spanish) and at the same time making a pass at her.

There were also two lyrical love songs, giving a change of pace from the Astaires' rhythmic excitement – 'So Am I' and 'We're Here Because' – and in Act Two, to complement 'Fascinating Rhythm' in Act One, the Astaires performed an eccentric 'nut dance' to the tune 'Swiss Miss'. It brought the house down.

During the Philadelphia tryout one change was made. 'The Man I Love', the song which had brought backing from Otto Kahn, was dropped from the show. This was partly because Vinton Freedley objected that it slowed things down, but also partly because such a moody song was not ideally suited to the singing of Adele Astaire, whose personality, both on stage and off, was bubbly and vivacious (it seems to have been partly as a defensive reaction to this that her brother, from boyhood, overlaid his natural uncertainty with an air of well-bred detachment).

In Philadelphia and then in New York, the show was a smash and a popular feature turned out to be George's innovation of having two pianos play against the orchestra. Ohman and Arden put his music across so successfully that Aarons soon asked them to play during intermission as well as during the performance, with the result that many of the audience stayed in their seats instead of going out for a drink or a cigarette. As George explained a couple of years later, "I think that one reason for the success of this novelty was that the piano is the most telling instrument for music like mine that requires the quickest accent which falls on the full chord."

They also took to playing on after the final curtain, taking it in turns for one to play straight while the other improvised – "For the fans who refused to go home," explained Fred Astaire in 1953. He felt that their playing was a large factor in the success of the show.

Naturally the Astaires got most of the critical attention at first, but quite soon the media began to pay attention to the Gershwins as well. The fact that this ground-breaking show was largely created by two pairs of siblings gave reporters something to write about and helped it to get press coverage far beyond anything expected.

A typical reaction came from a critic of the day called Alexander Woolcott, who wrote: "I do not know whether George Gershwin was born into this world to write rhythms for Fred Astaire's feet, or whether Fred Astaire was born into this world to show how the Gershwin music should really be danced, but surely they were written in the same key, those two."

Lady Be Good ran in New York for a year, then transferred to London. For the London production George contributed three new songs. Two had lyrics by his old collaborator Desmond Carter: 'Buy A Little Button From Us' and 'I'd Rather Charleston' (written to capitalise on the current dance craze). The third was actually one he had written with Lou Paley back in 1919 – 'Something About Love'.

After a two-week tryout in Liverpool, the show opened on 26 April 1926 at the same theatre where George's first London show *The Rainbow* had played – at the Empire in Leicester Square. It was as resounding a hit in London as it had been in America. During the week before it opened Fred and Adele went twice into the recording studios and recorded a total of four songs from the show, all accompanied by George at the piano – 'Hang On To Me', 'Fascinating Rhythm', 'I'd Rather Charleston' and Fred's solo 'The Half Of It, Dearie, Blues'. On this last he can be heard dancing and George's voice can briefly be heard encouraging him, exactly as they used to do in rehearsal.

The day after the show opened, Fred and Adele went back into the studios again and recorded 'Swiss Miss', this time accompanied by the Empire Theatre Orchestra, under its leader, Jacques Heuvel. At the same session the show's principal comedian, William Kent (who had taken over from Walter Catlett) recorded the title song, also with the Empire Theatre Orchestra.

Sadly, *Lady Be Good* was the last live show ever to appear at the famous Empire. In late Victorian and Edwardian times it had been a music hall whose promenade was famous to the ends of the actual Empire as a parade ground for frail beauties. In 1916 public opinion caused the owner, Sir Alfred Butt, to close the promenade. The theatre did less well after that and, with the rise of the cinema, it did even worse. It closed for conversion into a cinema itself on 22 January 1927 and *Lady Be Good*, which was still running, was forced to close with it.

CHAPTER SEVEN
Light-Hearted
And Serious

By the beginning of 1925, George Gershwin, now aged twenty-six, had established himself in the world of musical comedy as a leading composer and, to the concert-going public, as an enjoyable talent, worth listening to with respect.

By now it had become a popular pastime among his friends to advise him to opt for one thing or the other. Some advised him to concentrate on his songwriting talents. Others, impressed by the success of 'Rhapsody In Blue', urged him to get down to concentrated study so as to mature as a serious composer.

George listened and smiled and paid no attention to either side. As ever, he made no distinction between his various composing activities. He would work just as hard on a song as he would on his concert pieces, regarding each of his compositions as part of a whole. As far as he was concerned, it was all Gershwin music. And from a practical point of view, this attitude worked well. He enjoyed writing for musical comedy and that subsidised his more prestigious work.

As part of his 'serious' work, he had composed, more or less as an exercise, some short piano pieces. They were not much more than sketches for future use and he called them 'Novelettes'.

Towards the end of November 1924 he was visited at the Gershwin apartment on One-Hundred-And-Tenth Street by a violinist friend called Samuel Dushkin. Dushkin saw the 'Novelettes' and asked George if he would consider using the material in them to produce a piece for him to play.

George thought this sounded interesting, and together they chose two of the pieces – one slow, one faster and more rhythmic – and worked them into a piece for violin with piano accompaniment, calling it 'Short Story'.

Dushkin, with George's blessing, performed this in a recital at the University Club in New York City on 8 February 1925 and, whereas 'Short Story' has barely been heard of since, it did encourage George (some little while later) to turn various of the 'Novelettes' into a suite of preludes for the piano.

At the same time as this was happening, George and Ira and Buddy DeSylva were busy composing the songs for a new musical comedy for Alex Aarons. This was originally entitled *My Fair Lady* (it was the song with this title, which remained in the show, that gave Lerner and Loewe their title years later). Before it opened, however, the show had been renamed *Tell Me More*.

The show's plot was hardly inspired. It was the one about the rich heroine who meets the hero at a masked ball and pretends to be a poor shopgirl in order to test his affections. Whether it was the result of having to work with such hackneyed material, or whether George and Ira were suffering a reaction after the excitements of *Lady Be Good*, or whether they were simply working to too tight a deadline – for whatever reason, the songs were well below their usual standard and none is remembered today.

The show opened in New York on 13 April and survived for less than a month, by which time George was again in England, working on the London production of the same show.

The evening before he sailed, he met the woman who in many ways would become closer to him than any other. Her name was Kay Swift. She was at that time married to a banker (although the marriage didn't last) and George was brought to their house by a friend, Marie Rosanoff, who was the cellist of the Musical Art Quartet.

Kay was a musician and composer herself. She had a formidable background in classical music and would, within a few years, write the score for a musical, *Fine And Dandy*, and compose the hit song 'Can't We Be Friends?'. She had a fine intellect, a ready wit, culture, charm and social position and she worshipped George Gershwin, both the man and the musician.

For the rest of his life she would selflessly submerge her talent in his – taking down musical dictation, editing his manuscripts, playing the second piano in his two-piano versions of compositions and offering him valuable criticism. George was never proud about accepting criticism, he would happily discuss both his own and other people's music by the hour. Once Kay said to him that she thought his music had greater variety and interest than Irving Berlin's. Affronted at this disparagement of his first idol, George went to the piano and for over an hour played Berlin songs, demonstrating their subtleties. "He's a master," he kept saying. "Let's make no mistake about *that*."

Their friendship took a couple of years to develop, but eventually it became extremely deep. Kay continued his education in the art of gracious living, decorating his apartment with flowers, teaching him horseback riding (although she never managed to stop him miscalling it 'horse riding') and extending his appreciation of painting and sculpture.

Being tall, handsome, amusing, talented and moderately well-off, George by 1925 had become one of the most eligible bachelors in America. But in spite of the many beautiful women who pursued him – and as he became more and more famous there were very, very many – he always hung back from involvement.

In spite of the fact that he was too diffident to do the pursuing himself, he had many affairs with those who pursued him. He kept one little waltz tune he had written unpublished and, from time to time, would say to some young woman, "You're the kind of girl who makes me feel like composing a song," and lead her off to his suite. It got so his friends would tiptoe after to listen outside his door as he 'composed' the waltz, saying soulfully, "It will be dedicated to you."

But always he seemed to hang back emotionally. One girl who had fallen for him decided she had had enough when the most romantic thing he could find to say was that she was good for his 'composer's stomach'. Nor did he go in for giving lavish gifts – except to Kay. To her he gave two valuable paintings.

The real truth is that George's greatest passion in life, far outstripping all others, was his music. He was one of those fortunate people who have found something that gives them so much reward and pleasure that everything else becomes secondary. Kay Swift was the one woman with whom he could share this passion deeply and fully.

The London production of *Tell Me More* turned out to be considerably better than the New York one. George wrote a couple of new numbers for it, with lyrics (as usual in London) by Desmond Carter, but they were no more outstanding than the rest of his score. In the end, the main reason why the London show turned out better was that it had two outstanding light comedy actors in its leading roles – Leslie Henson and Heather Thatcher, both of them popular favourites. It opened on 26 May and had a long and successful run.

While George was in London, Eva Gauthier was also there, and he joined with her in recreating her 1923 concert, the *Recital Of Ancient And Modern Music For Voice*. After the concert a reception was given for Mlle Gauthier and himself by Lord and Lady Carisbrooke, who were cousins of the then king, George V. George (Gershwin) had by now become as much of a social lion in London as he was in New York.

It was also on this visit to London that he began planning the piano concerto he had been commissioned to write by the New York Symphony Society almost a year before. After he had received the commission, through the urging of Walter Damrosch, he had gone out and bought the scores of several well-known concertos, in order to study how major composers handled the form. It was not true, as one story had it, that he had to go out and buy a book so as to find out what the actual form of a concerto is. After all, he had attended dozens of concertos in performance and his musical memory was formidable. But it is still fair to say that his formal training was thinner than his studies with Charles Hambitzer and Edward Kilyeni might imply.

Such studying was mainly of piano technique and the theory of harmony, rather than a detailed grounding in the music of the past. An instance of the incompleteness of his knowledge came one day at Harms music, where another of his social circles used to meet at noon on most weekdays. Whenever George was in New York, he went there as often as he could manage, which was usually about three times a week.

Among the other regular attenders were Harry Ruby, Buddy DeSylva, Vincent Youmans, Harold Arlen, Bill Daly and Irving Caesar. One day, Bill and Irving were there first. While waiting for the others to arrive, Bill went to the piano and started playing the well-known aria 'Depuis Le Jour' from Gustave Charpentier's opera *Louise*. Irving, the group's comedian, hummed along. Then George came in with Vincent Youmans. "Why," he said to Bill, "it's wonderful, really wonderful. When did you write it?"

George was and, would always remain, much more an instinctive musician than a trained one. And to orchestrate a complete concerto, allotting the different notes of the score to different instruments or sections of a symphony orchestra, represented a considerable challenge. Ira always considered George's concerto to be the bravest thing he ever undertook.

At around the end of May, after the London opening of *Tell Me More*, he made a brief visit to Jules Glaenzer in Paris (the city that had so entranced him two years before). Glaenzer, always delighted to give parties and introduce celebrities to each other, made sure that George met several important French musicians, notably Francis Poulenc, a leading member of the group of experimental composers known as Les Six, who dominated French music between the wars.

In early June, George sailed home, and soon was hard at work on what he had decided to call his 'New York Concerto'. Late in July, Ira wrote to his and George's friend Max Abramson: "[George] is now working on his 'Concerto' at the rate of about a page a day. If he doesn't speed up, I'm sorry for the show we are supposed to start writing in a couple of weeks. So far, about fourteen pages, the concerto sounds marvellous. He's setting a standard for himself he may find difficult to keep up."

How George managed to get through the volume of work he did at this time is amazing, even for him. While wrestling with the piano concerto, which he had now decided to call by the more neutral title 'Concerto In F', he was also writing one complete musical and half of another.

The one he was writing the complete score for was the one mentioned by Ira. It was to be called *Tip-Toes* and it was being put together by Aarons and Freedley as a follow-up to *Lady Be Good*. The book was again by Guy Bolton and Fred Thompson and it was to open in December at the same theatre, the Liberty.

The show that George was writing half of was giving him a chance to try his hand at operetta. Called *Song Of The Flame*, it was described by its producers as a 'romantic opera' and its setting was the Russian

Revolution. George was sharing the writing of the score with Herbert Stothart and the lyric writers were Oscar Hammerstein II and Otto Harbach, who had already worked with Rudolf Friml and Jerome Kern, and would go on in 1926 to collaborate with Sigmund Romberg on *The Desert Song*.

To add to the pressures of George's life, in the summer of 1925 the Gershwin family moved from their apartment on One-Hundred-And-Tenth Street to a whole house on One-Hundred-And-Third Street, near Riverside Drive.

It was a five-storey house of white granite. On the ground floor was a billiard room where young people of the neighbourhood used to meet – some were friends of the two youngest Gershwins, Arthur and Francis, by then twenty-five and eighteen years old, some were neighbours, some were complete strangers. From that floor a service elevator led to the upper floors and father Morris was so entranced by this that for some time after they moved in he spent much of his time simply riding up and down in it.

On the first floor above ground were the living rooms and dining rooms, where the Gershwins would welcome their friends and relations, including all the Wolpins and Bruskins, to drink tea and play cards and generally socialise.

The next two floors were mostly bedrooms and the top floor was George's. He had comfortable chairs, a brick fireplace and a grand piano (as well as the two pianos downstairs that the family had brought with them). One room was his study, lined with books and music and with a cupboard built in to house his manuscripts. Through the study was his bedroom.

George by no means regarded his floor as a private sanctum. Everyone seemed welcome. Composers and musicians, from the famous to the most struggling beginner, from the concert hall or from Tin Pan Alley, called in to ask advice or make a pilgrimage. Journalists from high-powered newspapers and periodicals, or from school magazines, came seeking interviews. Even casual acquaintances were welcome to drop in on him at any time.

People have said that George was always able to work in a hubbub of noise and conversation, but that is not quite true. It would be more accurate to say that he was enormously sociable and could not bear to turn people away. And while he could work surprisingly well in crowded chaos, there were many times in his life when he took steps to find somewhere quieter to work, even if that went against his gregarious nature.

During his hectic late summer of 1925, he definitely began to feel the need for a bit more privacy. A friend of his, Ernest Hutcheson, who was giving piano master classes at the Institute of Musical Art (which later became the famous Juilliard School of Music), suggested he go there and work on the 'Concerto In F' in peace and quiet.

The Institute was at Chautauqua, in the extreme west of New York State, close to Lake Erie, and George did go there for a while, but peace and quiet was still hard to come by. Ernest's piano students were fascinated by both his reputation and his playing and would ask to come and listen. Ernest, after conferring with George, laid down the rule that under no circumstances was a single one of them to invade George's privacy before four pm. With the result that at four sharp every day a horde of students would burst in to hear him. And George, obligingly, would not only let them, but break off from working on the concerto to play and sing them his songs.

After he returned to New York, when he felt the need for a quiet retreat, George took to renting a couple of rooms at the nearby Whitehall Hotel, on One-Hundredth Street and Broadway. He continued to go there and work occasionally for several years.

Sometimes, when he was at work on the top floor, his proud father would sit on a chair in the hall outside his door, listening. As long as the piano kept playing, he would beam with pleasure. But if there came a long pause, or the playing was hesitant and repetitive, his face would grow grave and concerned, knowing that his son was wrestling with a problem.

On one of these occasions, when the pause grew so long it became unbearable, Morris at last quietly opened the door, put his head in and whistled a short phrase. "Does that help you, George?" he asked.

George's way of working was all his own. Composing by playing the piano, he seemed to pour out musical ideas in an endless flood. Even at parties, he didn't simply play things he had written, with variations. Whole new ideas would come to life as he played, many of them often reappearing later as part of completed songs or orchestral works.

Yip Harburg, who worked with many composers, once said: "[George's] method of composing was the nearest to playfulness that I've ever known. Most composers sit down at the piano and say a little prayer: Please God, let me have it. But George never did. George sat down at the piano as if he were going to have fun with it." In fact he usually had so much fun composing that frequently he would have to be reminded to stop and eat.

With women pursuing George the way they did, naturally there was a great deal of speculation among his friends as to which woman might land him. One of his most serious affairs was still in progress while he was at work on the 'Concerto In F'.

For many months he had been in a fairly steady relationship with a girl who taught physical culture in Chicago. Few of his friends had met her, so she was generally referred to among them as the 'Dream Girl', and it was generally agreed that she might be the one. Then Ira got news that she had got tired of waiting for George to come to the point and had married someone else.

Ira was distressed, knowing that George would be devastated. Ducking out of the unpleasant task of telling him, he instead begged a friend, the writer SN Behrman, to break the news. Sam Behrman went up to the top floor, where George was working. As he later told the story:

> [George] was working on the 'Concerto In F'. He played me a passage; he completed a variation on it.
>
> "George," I said, "I have bad news for you. Dream Girl is married."
>
> His brown eyes showed a flicker of pain. He kept looking at me. Finally, he spoke. "Do you know?" he said. "If I weren't so busy, I'd feel terrible."

At around this time, in August 1925, an article written by George appeared in *Theater Magazine*, expressing some of his thoughts about the America he was living in and whose spirit he was trying to capture in music. "Modern life," he wrote, "is, alas! not expressed by smooth phrases. We are living in an age of staccato, not legato. This we must accept. But this does not mean that out of this very staccato utterance something beautiful may not be evolved ..."

By late September, as well as working on the two musicals (and writing the odd article), George had finished the third and final movement of his concerto. But the whole thing was still only in two-piano form. Now it was time to begin the orchestration. During this process his friend Bill Daly helped him by playing the orchestral parts on one piano while George played the piano parts on another. He finished the whole job some six weeks later, triumphantly writing the date at the bottom of the last page of the manuscript – 10 November.

Soon after this momentous date he borrowed the Globe Theatre for an afternoon from producer Charles Dillingham. He hired sixty musicians and, with Bill Daly conducting, had a run-through of the whole concerto for Walter Damrosch (and a few friends). So happy was he with the way it sounded that after the run-through he made only six small revisions.

The concerto was clearly ready to be performed and, towards the end of November, formal rehearsals began at Carnegie Hall, with Damrosch conducting the New York Symphony Society Orchestra, and George featured on piano. He was feeling so cheerful about his concerto (and life in general) that at one rehearsal he showed up wearing an extremely tweedy suit and smoking an enormous briar pipe, which he carried on smoking even as he played. At least it was a change from his usual cigar.

The premiere was to be on the afternoon of Thursday, 3 December, with a second performance in the evening. On the Sunday before, in the New York *Tribune*, an article by George describing his concerto appeared. "The first movement," he wrote, "employs the Charleston rhythm. It is quick and pulsating, representing the young enthusiastic spirit of American life... The second movement has a poetic nocturnal atmosphere which has come to be referred to as the American blues, but in a purer form than that in which they are usually treated. The final movement reverts to the style of the first. It is an orgy of rhythms, starting violently and keeping up the same pace throughout."

At the performance, the concerto was part of a programme that included Glazunov's 'Fifth Symphony' and Rabaud's 'Suite Anglais'. They were played before the intermission and the 'Concerto In F' was in the second half.

George, who, almost up to the performance, had seemed so calm that he had to be hurried out of a leisurely bath at two o'clock, became more tense and agitated as the big moment approached. In the artist's room during the intermission he was pacing up and down, rubbing his fingers. He was anxious to show the concert-going public that the 'Rhapsody In Blue' hadn't been just a happy accident. He was going out there to let them know that (in his words) "there was plenty more where that had come from".

Walter Damrosch, sitting quietly as George paced, said, "Just play the concerto as well as it deserves, George, and you'll come off with flying colours."

The audience, similar to the one for the first performance of 'Rhapsody In Blue', was an eclectic mixture of socialites, song-pluggers, music lovers, musicians and fans of George's shows. The performance went well, although the 'Concerto In F' did not arouse the enthusiasm that 'Rhapsody In Blue' had. Again the critics were divided. Some hailed George as a genius who had a lot more to say musically than certain highly regarded 'modern' composers. Others found the concerto conventional, trite, fragmentary and uncertain in form. Discussion raged for weeks, with arguments to and fro about the relationship between popular and high culture and the whole nature of modern American music.

All in all, the 'Concerto In F' is a deeper, more mature piece than the 'Rhapsody'. It is fuller of musical ideas, its themes develop more naturally from one to another and it is richer in contrasting moods. Although it has not got the catchy dramatic quality that keeps the 'Rhapsody' so popular, it does have a number of theatrical moments, including the rhythmic figure on the kettledrum at the very beginning. Interestingly, George's additions to the conventional symphony orchestra were almost all in the percussion section – bass drum, snare drum, cymbals, 'Charleston stick', xylophone and bells.

Rather surprisingly, he used no saxophones in the 'Concerto' and hardly ever would in anything he wrote. This was less remarkable in 1925, when jazz musicians had not yet learned how the saxophone could be played to best effect. But by the end of the twenties it had come into its own as a powerfully expressive instrument and George's indifference to it does suggest that after about 1924 he stopped keeping abreast of new developments in jazz. In spite of his having begun his career in Tin Pan

Alley, in spite of his extended works, in spite of his sense of all Gershwin music being one, his creative centre in his adult life was always musical comedy. That was where he was really most at home.

Of all his extended works, he would always remain proudest of the 'Concerto In F'. In it he felt he had achieved what he set out to do, to write "a piece of absolute music".

Two parties were given to celebrate its premiere. One was given by Walter Damrosch and his wife at their home at 168 West Seventy-First Street. The house was packed with Gershwin friends and admirers and the whole atmosphere was of praise and celebration.

The other party was given by (naturally) Jules Glaenzer. There George was presented with that symbol of the twenties and thirties, a solid gold cigarette case. It was inscribed with the signatures of twenty-eight of his friends. At a dinner party soon afterwards, George produced the case and passed it round the table for admiration. It won the expected ooh and aahs, making the complete circuit back to him. As he was stowing it away again in his inside pocket, Ira produced a battered pack of Camels. "Anybody want a cigarette?" he asked.

At the end of the month, on 28 December, *Tip-Toes* opened at the Liberty Theatre. Somehow George, while writing the concerto, had managed to turn out a score that was a worthy successor to *Lady Be Good*. This in spite of a re-treaded plot line in which Tip-Toes, a lively and pretty dancer, is brought to Miami by her brothers to trap a millionaire into marriage. The millionaire, Steve the glue king, duly falls for her, but she also falls for him. This causes complications and they only manage to get united for the final curtain after she manages to convince him that it truly is him she loves and not his glue money.

Although the show didn't have the Astaires (who were about to set off for London with *Lady Be Good*) it did have the clever and lively Queenie Smith in the title role and George had written some spirited numbers, including 'That Certain Feeling' and 'Sweet And Low Down', as well as the touching and tender 'Looking For A Boy'. But the person whose talent shone brightest in the production was Ira.

He himself said in later life that it was in *Tip-Toes* that he first felt satisfied with his lyrics. Reflecting his brother's music, they had now become assured and flexible and witty. Unfortunately his wittiest number, 'The Harlem River Chantey' got dropped from the show, but his disappointment was more than made up for by a fan letter he received from the equally witty lyricist, Lorenz Hart, who only the previous May had had his first big hit with the immortal Rodgers-and-Hart song, 'Manhattan'. The letter read:

> Your lyrics... gave me as much pleasure as Mr George Gershwin's music and the utterly charming performance of Miss Queenie Smith... I have heard none so good this many a day... It is a great pleasure to live at a time when light amusement in this country is at last losing its brutally cretin aspect. Such delicacies as your jingles prove that songs can be both popular and intelligent. May I take the liberty of saying that your rhymes in *Tip-Toes* show a healthy improvement over those in *Lady Be Good*. You have helped a lot to make an evening delightful for me – and I am very grateful.

The day after *Tip-Toes* opened, on 29 December, George found himself back at Carnegie Hall. Not performing, but attending a concert by the Paul Whiteman Band, entitled *A Second Experiment In Modern Music*.

Whiteman had never forgotten George's one-act opera *Blue Monday*, which his band had provided the music for in the *Scandals Of 1922*. Needing something to follow on from the success of 'Rhapsody In Blue' and believing that *Blue Monday* deserved a second chance, he had decided to re-stage it as part of his concert.

This time it would be performed without scenery (or blackface), but simply with a few props – a bar, a table, some chairs – to suggest the night club setting. It was also re-titled *One-Hundred-And-Thirty-Fifth Street* (after one of the main thoroughfares of Harlem). In spite of fine performances from the original cast – Blossom Seeley, Jack McGowan, Charles Hart and Benny Fields – the show impressed the serious music critics no more than it had impressed the *Scandals* audience, although they did admit that it contained a couple of good melodies.

The reception it got probably wasn't helped by the fact that the opera was staged in front of the band, so the audience had the unsettling distraction of seeing through the action to Paul Whiteman waving his baton in front of two dozen musicians. Nonetheless, if the piece had been stronger it might have surmounted this. What was now obvious was that

George's music had come a long way since 1922.

The next day, making three Gershwin events in three nights and making the end of 1925 even more hectic than the rest of it, *Song Of The Flame* opened, at the Forty-Fourth Street Theatre on Broadway. Its Russian Revolution-inspired plot, an attempt to marry political awareness and fairy-tale romance, did not really succeed.

In it, the heroine, Aniuta, is a noble-born rebel who becomes the leader in a peasant uprising and acquires the soubriquet, 'The Flame'. Somewhere along the way she meets and falls in love with the reactionary Prince Volodyn. The main conflict is between their attraction for each other and their conflicting ideologies, but eventually each assimilates enough of the other's point of view for a rapprochement to be achieved and they end in both Paris and each other's arms.

The production was mounted in true operetta style, with vast and ornate sets, colourful costumes, a Russian-inspired *corps de ballet* and a huge orchestra. Although George had written only some of the songs (with Oscar Hammerstein II as his lyricist), his were no more distinctive than the rest of the score, which had throughout a sort of pseudo-Slavic flavour. It was not George's scene and he never messed with operetta again.

After his swift succession of triumph and failure at the end of 1925, George took a short rest, then sailed off back to England early in 1926 to supervise the London production of *Lady Be Good*. He rented an apartment in Pall Mall and began to enjoy the London social scene, often in the company of the Astaires.

One night at a party they met the Prince of Wales (later Edward VIII), who invited them to Buckingham Palace. George also became friendly with Lord and Lady Mountbatten and with another member of the Royal Family, Prince George (later the Duke of Kent), who became especially fond of him. He often invited George to parties he gave and even more often dropped in at the Pall Mall apartment. When George returned to New York, he proudly hung a photograph of the Prince in his top floor retreat. It was inscribed "From George to George".

Lady Be Good began its four-week tryout in Liverpool on 29 March. It wasn't due to open in London until four weeks later, so George took the opportunity of nipping over to Paris for a week. Mabel Pleshette, the Paleys' cousin who had studied with Hambitzer, had recently married. Her husband's name was Robert Schirmer and they were visiting Paris. George arranged to stay with them in their rented apartment.

While he was there, he hit on the idea of trying to capture in music the feel of this city he so enjoyed; to write a musical impression of Paris. He came up with a sort of walking theme to open the piece, then got stuck. As he said to Mabel, while working on it in the Schirmers' apartment, "This is so complete in itself, I don't know where to go next."

He and Mabel usually spent part of the day shopping and sightseeing and, a day or so later, he said to her that he wanted to go to the Avenue de la Grande Armée. This rather surprised her, as it was an inelegant street with not much in it but shops selling car spares.

It turned out that George wanted to shop for taxi horns. He bought several and the sound of them helped him past his creative block. Before setting off back to London on 11 April he presented the Schirmers with a signed photo of himself, inscribing on the back the opening bars of the new piece (marked "Very Parisienne") and the title 'An American In Paris'.

Also on hand to help with the London production of *Lady Be Good* was its co-author, Guy Bolton. His friend and partner, PG Wodehouse was in London as well and one night they went to the Vaudeville Theatre to see a revue called *Rats*. One of its stars was Gertrude Lawrence.

Wodehouse had seen her before – in revues that offered her less scope – but Bolton had never seen her. Both were bowled over by her performance, as they later wrote: "She had everything. She could play sophisticated comedy, low comedy, sing every possible type of song, and she looked enchanting."

Getting back to the Mayfair Hotel, where he was staying, Guy wrote her an enthusiastic note saying that "if she came to New York he would guarantee to star her in a revue, a musical comedy or a straight comedy, whichever she preferred". She replied with a six-page telegram that essentially said 'Okay'. She was going to New York anyway, being engaged to play there in the second Charlot revue (she had been in the first on Broadway in 1924), but after that, probably towards the end of the summer, she would be available.

Now that he had the prospect of writing a musical comedy for Gertrude Lawrence, Guy had to interest a producer. He hesitated between approaching Ziegfeld or Aarons and Freedley. It was the latter partnership's connection with George that finally decided him in their favour. He took his proposal to Alex Aarons, who accepted it instantly, agreeing that the book for the show should be written by the old firm of Bolton and Wodehouse.

After *Lady Be Good* opened at the Empire, George and Alex set sail back to New York, already laying plans for the new musical. Both of them had seen Gertrude Lawrence in the first Charlot revue, and both were enthusiastic about working with her.

George's first job on his return, however, was writing a one-off song with Ira for the 1926 edition of a revue called *Americana*. The result was a gentle witty song, 'That Lost Barber Shop Chord', one of George's best and most neglected numbers.

Bolton and Wodehouse, still in England, came up with a first draft of the book for the Gertrude Lawrence musical, giving it the title *Oh, Kay!*, while George and Ira began working on the songs.

During this same period George also began working on his 'Novelettes', developing them into piano Preludes. Ira, on 14 September, married Emily Strunsky's sister Lee. They moved into the Gershwin home on One-Hundred-And-Third Street, taking over the floor below George.

Also in September, George and Ira were approached by a producer called Edgar Selwyn, who had an interesting proposition. The top comedy writer in the American theatre, George S Kaufman, had written a play that Selwyn, with Kaufman's blessing, wanted to turn into a musical.

The craftsman-like Kaufman, whose plays were as ingeniously and carefully assembled as clockwork, had written this play alone, although usually he wrote with a collaborator. Partly he did this because comedy writing often comes better from two people throwing ideas back and forth, and partly because his dry and witty nature shied like a frightened horse from anything resembling emotion, so he needed somebody to handle the obligatory love scenes.

One of his collaborators was Morris Ryskind, who had been a friend of Ira's, then of George's, since well before 1920. He was a regular attender at the Paleys', and had even co-written the occasional lyric with Ira. His first break in show business had come when he wrote the lyric for a song for Nora Bayes – a mock-Chinese number called 'One Dumb Goy'. In 1925 he worked with Kaufman on the book for the Marx Brothers' Broadway musical *The Cocoanuts*.

Kaufman was a pacifist by nature, but not nearly so much so as

Ryskind, who used to preach endlessly about the futility and barbarity of war and everything connected with it. This constant preaching got Kaufman so worked up that one day he went away on his own and started writing a play attacking warmongers, war profiteers and the military-minded in general. The result was the play he had brought to Edgar Selwyn, called *Strike Up The Band*.

After writing it, Kaufman, having a good showman's instinct for what the public would stand, became uneasy that he had pitched things a little too strong. He decided that if it were transformed into a musical, that would sugar the pill and the obvious people to write the songs were the Gershwins. They were delighted to be asked and agreed to get to work on it as soon as possible.

Meanwhile, there was *Oh, Kay!* to be completed. Gertie Lawrence finished her stint in the second Charlot revue and returned to England, where she met Bolton and Wodehouse and discussed her role with them.

Soon all three returned to New York and rehearsals got under way. This was naturally a time of hard work and excitement and one night George, too stimulated to sleep, reached for a book on his bedside table. It didn't do much for his sleeping. He became so engrossed that he read the whole book, finishing it at four in the morning. At which point he leapt out of bed and wrote a letter to the author saying he would be interested in writing an opera based on the book. The author was called DuBose Heyward and the book was *Porgy*.

George's thoughts had been turning towards opera for over a year. In 1925 he had told a reporter, "I used to think – if I could write a popular song hit that my ambition would be realised. Then I wanted to write a successful musical show. Playing my own music in a concert at Carnegie Hall seemed a milestone – but my sights are still higher!... I hope someday to write an opera in the American idiom."

His idea then had been that possibly Carl Van Vechten would be the ideal librettist – a deeply cultured writer and critic who loved the popular culture of America and who was a moving force behind the Harlem Renaissance of the twenties, encouraging black writing, painting and music. George did speak to him about his idea and Van Vechten came up with a proposed plot for a black opera, involving a rather Svengali-like character. But its structure was too complex and over-sophisticated and

George turned it down.

Porgy was simpler and more direct in its emotions and, in it, DuBose Heyward kept the reader constantly aware of the music heard and played by his South Carolina characters.

Heyward, who himself lived in South Carolina, replied to George's letter, saying that he liked the idea of an opera and would be glad to discuss it next time he came north, which would be sometime within the next few months. George was happy to wait. He had quite enough on hand to keep him occupied.

On 18 October, *Oh, Kay!* began its tryout at the Shubert Theatre in Philadelphia. Its plot involved bootlegging. By 1926 Prohibition had been in force in America for six years, the Eighteenth Amendment to the US Constitution laying down the law that no person shall "manufacture, sell, barter, transport, import, export, deliver, furnish or possess any intoxicating liquor except as authorised in this act".

As a result, within six months of the law being passed, speakeasies had sprung up all over America. There were far more of them than there had ever been saloons. By the middle twenties there were estimated to be one-hundred-thousand in New York City alone. Women, to whom the saloon had been socially off-limits, flocked to them as often as men and they became the fashionable place to go.

So bootlegging was already a fashionable subject and Bolton and Wodehouse's decision to use it in their plot was not that original. The story, such as it was, concerned a hard-up English duke and his sister, Kay (played by Gertrude Lawrence).

Down on their luck since the Great War, they sail to America in their last remaining possession, a yacht, and set about using it for rum-running. Pursued by government prohibition agents, they seek refuge in the palatial home of one Jimmy Winter, whom Kay has previously saved from drowning. He falls in love with Kay and she and her brother arrange to hide their stock of liquor in his cellar. Unfortunately it turns out that another rum-runner, Shorty McGee, is also secretly storing his stock of contraband liquor there, meanwhile posing as Jimmy Winter's butler. After many confusions and misunderstandings, including the pursuit of Jimmy by various blondes, all ends happily and Kay and Jimmy are united.

In spite of what British critic James Agate described as "the cretinous imbroglio of this piece", George and Ira turned in a stunning score, their numbers including 'Clap Yo' Hands', 'Do, Do, Do', 'Maybe' and, probably best of all, 'Someone To Watch Over Me'. This was touchingly performed by Gertrude Lawrence, in spite of the fact that her weakest attribute (apart, possibly, from her dancing) was her singing voice, which tended to be inaccurate and inaudible (her friend Noel Coward once described it as "horrid"). But everything was made up for by her comic acting.

In the words of James Agate, reviewing the show when it came to London, she showed "astonishing command of character and power of mimicry. In quick succession, without any alteration of pose and by the mere expression of her face and inflection of her voice, she will present to you a scullery-maid, amorous or dejected, or a heroine from one of Mr Lonsdale's comedies, *insouciant*, challenging and deliciously over-mannered. Or she will take up a doll and by holding it to her breast and crooning to it, take you straight into the infantile heart of woman and, in the next moment, holding the wretched thing by the ankle, plunge you into a world of mockery from which sentiment and sentimentality have been banished."

The doll, as it happened, was an inspiration of George's. Later he told the story himself:

> In the second act of *Oh, Kay!* the glamorous Gertrude Lawrence had the stage to herself to sing 'Someone To Watch Over Me'... it was all very wistful and, on opening night, somewhat to the surprise of the management, Miss Lawrence sang the song to a doll. This doll was a strange looking object I found in a Philadelphia toy store and gave to Miss Lawrence with the suggestion that she use it in the number. That doll stayed in the show for the entire run.

The other acting triumph in the show was by Victor Moore, playing Shorty McGee. He was a sad faced, helpless looking little man who by 1926 had been appearing in American musicals for almost quarter of a century. During rehearsals, he had made so poor an impression that Vinton Freedley seriously considered buying out his contract and replacing him, but from the first night of the Philadelphia tryout he brought down the house, scoring the biggest personal triumph of his acting career so far.

The show opened in New York on 8 November and went on to have the longest run of any Gershwin musical to date. George's score had more musical unity than any he had written previously, finding endless variations on the same thematic material. As composer Phil Springer put it, "He would take a little motif and play with it to the point where he had extracted the most you could." James Agate, who loved music but didn't much like musicals, put it differently when reviewing the show – "As far as I can judge, Mr Gershwin's score was largely made up of two tunes, one of which was plugged at least fourteen times. Shade of Sullivan!"

With *Oh, Kay!* launched, George returned to the concert platform. On 4 December, at the Roosevelt Hotel, he took part in an attempt to repeat the success of Eva Gauthier's song recital of three years before.

The singer this time was the Peruvian Marguerite D'Alvarez, an operatic contralto. George had met her the previous January at a party given by Carl Van Vechten and it was Van Vechten who persuaded her, as he had Eva Gauthier, that she should incorporate 'jazz' songs into her repertoire.

At the performance, she sang Jerome Kern's 'Babes In The Wood' and three numbers by George – 'Nashville Nightingale' (which he had written with Irving Caesar in 1923), 'Clap Yo' Hands' (from *Oh, Kay!*) and, as an encore, 'Oh, Lady Be Good'.

As well as accompanying her for these songs, George played one of the pianos in a two-piano arrangement he had made of 'Rhapsody In Blue'. He also performed five of his new 'Preludes For Piano'. These turned out to be attractive miniatures, each consisting of three sections, with two rhythmic movements framing a haunting blues-tinged slow one. They are among the most sensitive compositions he ever created.

At around this time, DuBose Heyward made his promised trip north. He and his wife Dorothy took a short vacation in Atlantic City and George went there to meet them. Walking up and down on the boardwalk, he and DuBose discussed *Porgy*.

DuBose Heyward was then forty-one years old. A tall, rather frail man, gentlemanly and quiet spoken, he had been a partner in a small insurance company, but at heart was a poet. Eventually he had achieved enough success with his poetry to decide to try and make a living by writing. By selling his share in the insurance company, plus a small house he owned in Charleston, he and his wife Dorothy, who was herself a playwright, had just enough to live on and he set to work writing the novel that became *Porgy*.

Although DuBose had been delighted to receive George's letter, it caused something of a situation in the Heyward household. When the novel had come out, in September 1925, it had been highly praised by the critics as the first realistic depiction of black life in America and it sold well. As a result, several theatre companies had approached DuBose with the suggestion that it be turned into a play. He turned them down, feeling his book would not work on stage, and even discouraged his wife Dorothy from trying her hand at dramatising it.

Dorothy, convinced he was wrong and that the book's plot and characters would adapt naturally to the stage, had secretly set about turning it into a play, intending to surprise her husband with the finished result. She had been at work on this for seven months when George's letter arrived. Realising that a Gershwin opera based on the book might render her work useless, she was forced to admit what she had been doing.

Fortunately, when he read what she had written, DuBose was so impressed that he completely changed his mind about his book's dramatic possibilities. Not only that, when he met George he confessed that he did not want to disappoint his wife, and that her stage version (on which he had now started to collaborate) must have precedence.

George was completely amenable. He was quite happy for *Porgy* to be presented as a play, as he felt that would in no way compete with any operatic version. He also explained to Heyward that he had no immediate intention of writing such a version, partly because he had a lot of other commitments and partly because he felt he was not yet technically equipped for the job.

Porgy certainly appealed to him as a possible subject for turning into an opera, but not yet. All he could say at the moment was that he was interested. Both he and DuBose Heyward agreed to keep in touch.

CHAPTER EIGHT

An American
In Paris

During the twenties, theatre in New York was more popular than it had ever been, or ever would be again. It had the field of entertainment more or less to itself. Vaudeville was more an ally than a competitor and, among the media that would eventually challenge the stage, radio was still rising in popularity and the cinema did not begin to talk until near the end of the decade.

The first talkie, *The Jazz Singer*, starring Al Jolson, was made in 1927, which was the busiest year Broadway ever saw. More than two-hundred-and-sixty plays opened, among them more than fifty new musicals, the hit of the year being *Show Boat*, based on the book by Edna Ferber, with music by Jerome Kern and lyrics by Oscar Hammerstein II. (Hammerstein's wife Dorothy was always jealously protective of his reputation. If she heard anyone refer to Jerome Kern's 'Ol' Man River', she would say, "Excuse me, but Oscar Hammerstein wrote 'Ol' Man River'. Jerome Kern wrote 'Ta-ta dum dum, ta ta-ta dum dum'.")

Early in the year, George and Ira began work on George S Kaufman's anti-war musical, *Strike Up The Band*. The meticulous Kaufman was still revising the book, but it was already close enough to its final form for them to start writing songs.

Its plot was this: Horace J Fletcher, the rich owner of the American Cheese Company (of Hurray, Connecticut), has his market protected by a fifty per cent tariff on imported cheese. Switzerland protests at this financial handicap on Swiss cheese and Fletcher, to teach Switzerland a lesson, persuades the US Government to force them into a war, happily agreeing to bear all the costs of the engagement, provided that America shows its gratitude by calling it the Horace J Fletcher Memorial War.

The hero is Jim Townsend, a newspaperman. He is in love with the cheese magnate's daughter, Joan, and on good terms with the Fletchers, until he discovers that Fletcher's cheese is adulterated with Grade B milk. This opens his eyes to Fletcher's chicanery, and turns him into a pacifist. At which point American patriots, who have already banned *William Tell* and *The Swiss Family Robinson* from libraries and schoolrooms, discover that he is the owner of a Swiss watch. He is labelled un-American and thrown into jail. When the war begins, he is drafted and Joan, alienated by his attack on her father's cheese, transfers her affections to another. End of Act One.

Act Two opens in Switzerland, where the war is being fought (the Swiss hotels having offered favourable rates to the combatants). In the background we hear the noise of battle, but on stage American soldiers are knitting comforts for the folks back home. Jim, by yodelling, lures the Swiss Army out of hiding and they are captured. A spy among them then confesses that it was he who pumped the Grade B milk into Fletcher's cheese.

Despite Jim's protestations that he is still a pacifist, he is proclaimed a hero. The soldiers return home in triumph and there is a grand peace celebration. Everyone is happy except the soldiers, who find they have no jobs. To solve this problem, the Government puts a stiff tariff on imported caviar. Russia protests and the show ends with patriotic singing as all agree that Russia too must be taught a lesson.

George and Ira took a lot of trouble over composing a spirited and ironic march to end the first half, as the country goes to war. And to end the whole show, as it goes to war again.

Four times George wrote a march tune and played it to Ira, who each time said, "That's fine. Just right. Okay, I'll write it up." And each time George replied, "Not bad, but not yet. Don't worry, I'll remember it; but it's for an important spot and maybe I'll get something better."

In the spring, George and Ira went to Atlantic City to have detailed discussions of the show with producer Edgar Selwyn. It was the off season, so most of the rooms in their hotel were empty, which meant that George could have a piano in his room without disturbing other guests. His room was next to Ira's and, late one night, Ira was in bed reading next day's Sunday papers, when George came in in his pyjamas, saying he thought he had the march at last.

They both went next door to the piano and George played his new march. Ira liked it, but needed reassuring that George wouldn't change his mind again. George didn't and this fifth version became the title number of the show, 'Strike Up The Band!'. It was unusual in two ways – first, because the number had come to George while he was lying in bed, not while he was playing the piano; secondly, because the verse to it is in a minor key, which hardly any of his songs ever are. This helps give it its strongly ironic flavour, especially when, as reprised in the show, it is played slowly. (An even more ironic footnote is that during the Second World War the tune *was* quite often played on radio and records as a morale booster – so much for satire.)

In April 1927, needing a quiet retreat away from the Gershwin household in order to work, George and Ira took a lease on a country house called Chumleigh Farm in Ossining, on the Hudson River just north of New York. Ira's wife, Lee, went with them and they stayed there for weeks. It proved a good place to compose in, and George and Ira worked as they felt inclined, often late into the night.

The house was set in forty acres of farmland and was so peaceful and remote that soon they took to inviting guests for a day or a weekend – those who came included George S Kaufman (still polishing the book), Harry Ruby, the influential columnist Franklin P Adams and Lee's younger brother, English Strunsky.

It was here that George and Ira first got really involved in painting as a hobby. George had always enjoyed making casual drawings and Ira had once considered taking up illustration as a career. Now they both bought watercolours and spent many of the long evenings painting or sketching. Among the sketches George made there are one of his fox terrier, Jock, and one of English Strunsky.

While they were at Chumleigh Farm, both George and Ira bought cars. George's was a used Mercedes tourer. A mechanic from the company that supplied it gave him a few lessons and soon he was happily bowling along the country roads.

Ira took lessons from English, who was a good driver, but they didn't do much good. Ira was a born non-driver and soon gave up for ever, explaining that he couldn't abide the dirty looks from other drivers. Lee, who had learned to drive the summer before, took over driving her husband's car (after a short refresher course from English).

Early in June, George S Kaufman delivered his completed script to Edgar Selwyn. This script was something of an historic event in the world of musical comedy, because for the first time the book was written by an experienced and successful playwright. Along with *Show Boat*, it led the way towards musicals being organised round the book, rather than having a plot cobbled together to showcase stars and songs.

Another piece of irony is that this change should have been brought about by Kaufman, who was normally indifferent, if not hostile, to musicals. Once, when a songwriter asked to reprise a song in a show, Kaufman famously replied, "Only if you let me reprise some of the jokes."

He had only decided to use music in *Strike Up The Band* in order to soften the impact of what he always considered the most uncompromising play he ever wrote. Edgar Selwyn, although proud to be producing what he described as "a landmark play, a real work of art", admitted he was relieved that it would have songs to tone down its message.

With a richer and more thought-provoking book, George and Ira's songs had to become more subtle and varied. What *Strike Up The Band* called for was a score closer to operetta in its complexity (although not in its romantic lushness). To help themselves achieve this, they used several of the devices used by Ira's heroes, Gilbert and Sullivan (late in his life, when asked how much influence Gilbert had had on his work, Ira laughed and said Gilbert influenced *everything* he did).

One such device they used was the patter song, giving one to Horace J Fletcher entitled 'A Typical Self-Made American', and another to his Government crony, Colonel Holmes, called 'The Unofficial Spokesman'.

In order to vary the pace of the show George and Ira also inserted some lyrical numbers. One was a touching duet between Jim and Joan, 'Seventeen And Twenty-One', and another was 'The Man I Love', which had been dropped from *Lady Be Good* two years before. To this they added a masculine counterpart, calling it 'The Girl I Love'.

It wasn't until the show began rehearsal in July that George and Ira reluctantly gave up their lease on Chumleigh Farm, after a couple of weeks of having to drive into town almost every day.

Rehearsals ended and, on 29 August, the show started a one-week tryout at the Broadway Theatre in Long Branch, New Jersey. After that it moved to the Shubert Theatre in Philadelphia. It was scheduled to play there for six weeks, but after two it closed, in spite of much desperate rewriting by Kaufman. It had been greeted enthusiastically by the critics, but the public stayed away in droves.

During this dismal run in Philadelphia, Ira and the two Georges were standing on the pavement outside the Shubert one night as the trickle of customers made their way in. A cab drew up and two elderly men got out, in elegant evening dress. They bought tickets and went into the theatre. "Probably Gilbert and Sullivan," said Ira, "coming to fix the show." "Why don't you put jokes like that in your lyrics?" grumbled Kaufman.

Probably most of the trouble with *Strike Up The Band* was that its anti-war attitude was simply not in tune with public feelings. In the twenties, in spite of the horror everyone felt about the bloodbath of the Great War, civilian America had seen none of it. What most people felt was pride that the US Army had gone over there and beaten the Germans in only a year-and-a-half. And they felt even more proud that, in the peace negotiations that followed the war, America had emerged onto the international stage for the first time in history as a world power. The twenties was a time of optimism, and *Strike Up The Band* seemed sniping and negative.

Edgar Selwyn, recalling how he had described the piece as "a landmark play, a real work of art", now told Kaufman, "I still say your play is all those things, George. I guess that's why we're in trouble."

All the same, everyone involved in putting on the show was disappointed. All except Kaufman, who habitually expected everything he wrote to fail. Some little while after the show closed, he was attending the first night of another show on Broadway when the principal backer of *Strike Up The Band* came up to him in the foyer. Kaufman cringed inwardly, expecting recriminations, but the backer greeted him with pleasure and introduced his wife, saying, "My dear, here's the man you've been wanting to meet all these years, George Gershwin!"

Kaufman tried to correct this misapprehension, but the man went cheerfully on. "Tell me, Mr Gershwin, tell me one thing. With all the magnificent music you've written, with all the money your shows have made, why is it that I had to invest in a failure? Why wasn't *Strike Up The Band* a big success?" Kaufman shrugged and gave in. "Kaufman gave me a lousy book," he said.

During the tryouts of *Strike Up The Band*, the real George Gershwin (and Ira) was already at work on the score for another musical. This was again for Aarons and Freedley, again with the Astaires (*Lady Be Good* having closed in London at the beginning of the year), and again with the orchestra augmented by the pianos of Phil Ohman and Victor Arden.

Aarons and Freedley, using their profits from *Lady Be Good, Tip-Toes* and *Oh, Kay!* had built their own theatre on West Fifty-Second Street, calling it the Alvin (a combination of the first syllables of 'Aaron' and 'Vinton'). A new Astaire musical seemed just the thing to open it with.

Guy Bolton had not been available to write the book, partly because he was back in England with PG Wodehouse adapting *Oh, Kay!* for its London opening in September. They were so nervous about whether a British audience would appreciate a plot about bootleggers that "in their gloomier moments they... even felt that it might be necessary to construct a completely new story and fit the Gershwin numbers into it." No such thing proved necessary, however. *Oh, Kay!* opened with relatively little alteration and had a long and successful run.

In the absence of Bolton and Wodehouse, Aarons and Freedley cast about and decided to hire the humorist Robert Benchley, pairing him with Bolton's old collaborator, the experienced Fred Thompson.

Benchley, the great comic essayist and one of the most likeable men who ever lived, was at this time the drama critic for *Life* (not the famous photographic journal, but its predecessor, which published light essays and cartoons). He had been a theatre lover since his days at Harvard and Aarons and Freedley were aware that he had only recently abandoned an attempt to co-write a play with his friend Dorothy Parker.

Benchley was delighted to be approached and took the job, feeling that a musical comedy involving both the Gershwins and the Astaires must have so much going for it that writing the book would be a piece of cake. He soon found out that it wasn't. This sort of writing, working as part of a creative team, was a very different discipline from crafting tight, neat, humorous essays in peace and solitude.

The show, which was called *Smarty*, involved Benchley and Thompson in endless revisions, cuts, changes and inserts. Everyone offered suggestions. Eventually, as Benchley said, "Our connection with the show got more and more academic, until finally we weren't connected at all."

Benchley decided to bow out of the production. One of his last jobs was to watch the rehearsal of a scene he had rewritten four times during the previous week. This rehearsal seemed to sum up all the chaos of mounting a musical comedy.

As some of the actors in the show went through the scene, others, not involved, slurped coffee and rustled sandwich bags. At the same time, stagehands bustled about setting scenery. Ladders and furniture were moved on and off and about, men called to each other from the wings. There was a rope dangling from the flies, so that the rehearsing actors had to duck to avoid it. At first it was in the centre of the stage, then it moved to the left, then to the right. At the end of the scene, Vinton Freedley asked Benchley how he thought it went. "I liked it best with the rope in the middle," said Benchley, edging out of the theatre to return to the relatively rational world of reviewing. At George's suggestion, he was replaced by writer Paul Gerard Smith.

In *Smarty*, Adele Astaire played the heroine, Frankie, and Fred played her guardian, Jimmy Reeve, who is keeping her pearls in a safe and refuses to part with them. To try and retrieve them, Frankie seeks the help of her boyfriend, Peter, who is an intrepid young aviator (Lindbergh had made his famous solo flight across the Atlantic the previous May). Peter, trying to steal the pearls, gets involved with two inept comic crooks who are also after them.

When the out-of-town tryouts started in Atlantic City in October, nothing seemed to work. The critics panned the show, and houses were so poor that it was losing about ten-thousand dollars a week. Drastic and immediate revision was called for.

Benchley and Thompson had made one of the crooks a woman, and this character didn't seem to work. Aarons and Freedley decided it would help the show if she were changed to a male crook, so that the role could be played by the bumbling Victor Moore, who had been such a success in *Oh, Kay!*.

The writers got to work on further rewrites and came up with several effective scenes, including one where the two crooks, now named Herbert and Dugsie, find a bowl of punch and get drunk, after which the drunken Herbert (Victor Moore) decides that it will help things if he shoots his partner. Dugsie agrees to his fate with intoxicated resignation.

Aarons and Freedley further decided that most of the trouble lay with the songs. They threw out about half of them, including the outstanding 'How Long Has This Been Going On?', and George and Ira started writing replacements at top speed. Aarons and Freedley were so much inclined to blame George and Ira for sub-standard work that Aarons accused them of not trying to write a hit score, and they made George pay for the copying of the orchestrations of the new songs.

George paid up without a murmur and he and Ira, during the six weeks the show was trying out, came up with almost a whole new score. This was harder on Ira than on George, because his pace of work was slower – sometimes he would spend days perfecting a single lyric. But all their hard work paid off. By the time the show reached New York, everything had gelled. The company were relieved, and slightly surprised, to find that at last they had a hit on their hands, now that its title had changed from *Smarty* to *Funny Face*.

Funny Face opened at the Alvin on 22 November. Victor Moore almost stole the show as Herbert, and George and Ira's new songs worked perfectly. The sensuous 'How Long Has This Been Going

George aged around sixteen, shortly before managing to get his first song published

Betty Compton, Adele Astaire, Gertrude McDonald and Fred Astaire in *Funny Face*, November 1927

Jack Donahue, George, Sigmund Romberg, Marilyn Miller and Florenz Ziegfeld at a rehearsal of the hurriedly-composed *Rosalie*, December 1927

George and Ira about to segue triumphantly from the twenties into the thirties

Paul McCullough as Colonel Holmes and Bobby Clark as Horace J Fletcher in the second and successful version of *Strike Up The Band!*, January 1930

Victor Moore as Vice-President Alexander Throttlebottom and William Gaxton as President John P Wintergreen in *Of Thee I Sing*, December 1931

George at work on his self-portrait *Me*, in the living-room of his apartment at 33 Riverside Drive

Todd Duncan as Porgy and Anne Wiggins Brown as Bess, at Porgy's window, October 1935

Snapshot of Oscar Levant, taken by George in the apartment on Riverside Drive

George conducting the Los Angeles Philharmonic in rehearsal, February 1937

On?' had been replaced by the lighter 'He Loves And She Loves', which was more suited to Fred's delivery and gave him his first major romantic solo. He also had the number 'High Hat', which gave him his first ever number in top hat and tails.

As in *Lady Be Good*, there was a non-romantic duet between Fred and Adele, expressing their closeness. This was the title song, 'Funny Face'. There was a witty patter song that George and Ira wrote at the last minute, satirising conversational clichés – 'The Babbitt And The Bromide' (Fred sang and danced this in his sole screen appearance with Gene Kelly, in the 1946 film *The Ziegfeld Follies*). And above all there was the song that was the hit of the show, sung by the two lovers – 'S' Wonderful'.

George and Ira barely had time to heave a sigh of relief before they were busy contributing songs to a Florenz Ziegfeld musical, *Rosalie*. Ziegfeld had originally hired Sigmund Romberg to write the score for this, but was able to offer him only three weeks in which to produce it. Romberg, who was busy at the time writing another show, *New Moon*, said he couldn't possibly manage the job alone, and that he would need a collaborator. He suggested George and Ziegfeld agreed.

Rosalie again brought together the talents of Bolton and Wodehouse. Wodehouse wrote lyrics to Sigmund Romberg's music, and Bolton co-wrote the book with William Anthony McGuire. Their plot was inspired by the highly publicised visit to America in 1926 of Queen Marie of Rumania, although it bore no relation whatever to the real life of that worthy monarch. Instead, it told of how the princess of a fictional kingdom, visiting America, wins the love of a young West Point lieutenant. The princess, Rosalie, was played by one of the top musical comedy stars of the twenties, the charming and witty Marilyn Miller.

George, as it turned out, wrote just under half the songs for the show. Romberg wrote eight and he wrote seven, including 'Ev'rybody Knows I Love Somebody' (using the same tune as one of the songs in *Funny Face*, 'Dance Alone With You'), 'How Long Has This Been Going On?' (dropped from *Funny Face*) and so many other bits and pieces dropped from *Funny Face* that Vinton Freedley came out of the first night (10 January 1928) muttering something to the effect that if he hadn't seen the show before, he certainly felt he had heard it. (It also included 'Show Me The Town', a number dropped over a year before from Aarons and Freedley's *Oh, Kay!*.)

While working on *Rosalie*, George's thoughts again veered back to the possibility of writing an opera. On 10 October, while he had been embroiled in the out-of-town problems of *Funny Face*, the play based on *Porgy*, written by Dorothy Heyward with help from DuBose, had opened on Broadway. George went with Kay Swift to see it when he got back to town and still liked it as a subject, but there was another play he had seen that enticed him almost as much.

Oddly enough, in spite of George's usual pronouncements about his music, such as "My people are American, my time is today – music must repeat the thoughts and aspirations of the times", this play, *The Dybbuk*, written by S Anski, was based on an old Jewish folk tale, full of Khassidic mysticism and superstition.

Set in a Polish stetl, or small village, it told the story of a young couple promised to each other in marriage before they were born. They do not marry, or even meet, until they are grown up. Then they meet and fall in love. But as punishment for not marrying her, he dies and his soul, unable to rest, wanders the earth. A 'dybbuk' is just such a ghostly wandering soul and, eventually, his dybbuk enters her and possesses her.

The play had been a Broadway success in 1920 and George saw a revival of it played at a New York Jewish venue called the Neighbourhood Playhouse. Ira felt that its attraction for George was its sympathetic portrayal of a minority group, the Jews in Poland.

George began to jot down melodic phrases for possible use in an opera based on *The Dybbuk*. Some were not recognisably Jewish, some definitely were, one being a slow hypnotic rhythm resembling the chanting in a synagogue. There were notes for arias and dances, but for the time being notes was all they remained, as his thoughts moved off again to other projects.

Early in 1928, the leading French composer, Maurice Ravel, made his first visit to America (where he would hear a lot of good jazz and go back home to write the jazz-influenced 'Boléro'). His fifty-third birthday was due on 7 March and the singer, Eva Gauthier, decided to arrange a party for him in New York on that day. She asked him if there was anything in particular he would like for a birthday present, and he said, "Yes. To hear and meet George Gershwin."

George was delighted by the compliment and played at the party; Ravel in return was delighted by George's playing. As Eva Gauthier wrote: "George that night surpassed himself, achieving astounding feats in rhythmic intricacies so that even Ravel was dumbfounded." During the next few days they met several more times at New York parties (including one of Jules Glaenzer's) and a mutually respectful friendship grew up between them.

Whether it was inspired by Ravel's visit or not is unclear, but four days after the birthday party, on 11 May, George sailed for Europe, taking with him Ira, their young sister Frankie, Frankie's fiancé Leopold Godowsky Jr (son of the famous pianist) and Ira's wife Lee.

Unlike George's previous trips, this was to be simply a holiday. There was no London show for George to help nurse into life, although coincidentally there was a show in rehearsal there for which Ira had written the lyrics.

Called *That's A Good Girl*, the music for it had not been written by George but by Phil Charig, who had been rehearsal pianist on several of their shows and had become a friend. The original plan had been for the songs to be written by Jerome Kern and Oscar Hammerstein, but they got themselves so heavily involved in writing *Show Boat* that Max Dreyfus of Harms Music had to arrange for Phil and Ira to dep for them.

There was no further work for Ira to do on *That's A Good Girl*, so he and George could both concentrate on rest and relaxation. They had committed themselves to writing a new musical for Aarons and Freedley during the coming summer, again starring Gertrude Lawrence, and this was a convenient break before beginning.

The Gershwins' first port of call was London. They spent two weeks there and George renewed acquaintance with many friends, including George, Duke of Kent, and Lord and Lady Mountbatten. On a visit to New York, George had presented Lady Mountbatten with an autographed copy of 'The Man I Love'. She liked the song so much that on returning to London she had persuaded the

Berkeley Square Orchestra to play it and publicise it.

As a result, by the time of George's visit it was sweeping the country. During the first half of 1928 at least eight British dance bands made recordings of it. From England it would cross to France and American visitors, hearing it in both countries, would return home demanding to hear it again. It would become a hit on both sides of the Atlantic without ever appearing in a successful show.

One of London's most fashionable night clubs in 1928 was the Kit-Kat Club, which had taken its name from a famous eighteenth-century gentlemen's club run by a proprietor called Christopher Catt. It had an excellent resident band led by saxophonist Al Starita, and during the Gershwins' visit they were invited there for an evening of Gershwin music in George's honour.

Also, although there was no new show of theirs in preparation there, George and Ira were able to attend the last night of one of their past successes. This was Gertrude Lawrence's previous Aarons and Freedley musical, *Oh, Kay!*, which celebrated the end of its long London run on 24 March.

The next day all the Gershwins left London for Paris. They were to stay there for five weeks and, although Mabel Schirmer (née Paley) and her husband were still living there, a party of five was larger than they could accommodate in their apartment, so the Gershwin party was booked into the Hotel Majestic.

Ira's plan while in Paris was simply "to see the sights and drink beer" (Prohibition still being in force in America), but George had brought with him the incomplete score of the piece he had begun on his last visit – 'An American In Paris' – and he intended to try and finish it, while involving himself in a hectic round of parties, interviews, concert-going, and seeking out such musical luminaries as Darius Milhaud, Igor Stravinsky, Serge Prokofiev, Georges Auric, Francis Poulenc (whom he had met on his previous visit) and, of course, Maurice Ravel.

As it turned out, a lot of their concert-going turned out to be to hear Gershwin music. Parisian orchestras, aware of George's presence in their city, hastily rearranged their programmes to feature his music. On 31 March, before the Gershwins had been in Paris a week, George and Ira attended a Saturday afternoon concert at the

Théâtre Mogador, where, after pieces by César Franck, R Brunel, Arthur Honegger and JS Bach, the Pasdeloup Orchestra made a valiant attempt to play 'Rhapsody In Blue', having had only half an hour to rehearse it and, having had only a simplified dance band arrangement to work from. Two pianists, Wiener and Doucet, made a brave but somewhat misguided attempt to divide the difficult piano solo between them.

It was such a riot of dragged tempi, inaccurate rhythms, fluffed fingering and faulty intonations that George swiftly sneaked out to hide in the bar, having to be equally swiftly summoned back by Ira at the end to receive the standing ovation that the house awarded him.

George was thrilled by the ovation and it even moved him to find something of interest in the performance, which was the way the classically-trained French musicians attempted to play every note in exact true pitch, giving the piece a curiously different feel.

As an encore, Wiener and Doucet played a verse and three choruses of George and Ira's 'Do, Do, Do', evidently with more rehearsal and certainly with more confidence. The audience loved that too.

One evening in April, Mabel Schirmer took George and Frankie to a party. (It was Mabel who once remarked, "Deep down inside of all the Gershwins – George, Ira, Frankie – there's a motor, always going, always running.")

George as usual played the piano, but this time Frankie also sang. Since her entry into show business at the age of ten, she had gone on to sing in several intimate revues on Broadway, such as *Merry-Go-Round* and *Americana*. Her slightly husky voice had matured into one that was not strong, but was clear and true, and she got an enthusiastic reception. The famous hostess Elsa Maxwell, who was at the party, soon spread the word about Frankie's singing to another American songwriter then in Paris – Cole Porter.

Cole Porter and his wife Linda both adored Paris and they spent most of the twenties living there. It wasn't until later in 1928 that he would have his first big success, with the song 'Let's Do It'. In April he was still struggling to make his name (in spite of his inherited fortune, he was firmly determined to succeed in his chosen profession) and, in pursuit of success, he was mounting a revue at the Les Ambassadeurs night club.

At Elsa Maxwell's suggestion, he arranged to hear Frankie sing, was equally taken with her voice and asked if she would appear in his revue performing "a Gershwin speciality". On 10 May she did, wearing a simple but beautiful gown with a bouffant skirt and accompanied at the piano by George. Cole Porter had written a witty lyric for her to sing before she embarked on her string of Gershwin songs, explaining how it felt to be the the sister of a famous composer. Her turn was received with wild acclaim and she stayed with the show (but without George) for the next two weeks.

Meanwhile, in his spare moments, George sat in his room at the Majestic Hotel and worked away at 'An American In Paris'. As the piece progressed, he even made another expedition to the Avenue de la Grande Armée and bought a few more taxi horns.

From time to time his work was interrupted by visitors. He was now so well-known and admired in the world of music that it seemed everyone in it wanted to meet him. The young English composer, William Walton, dropped in, among many others. So did the conductor Leopold Stokowski. He looked at the score so far of 'An American In Paris' and expressed interest in presenting the finished piece. George had to explain that he had promised its first performance to Walter Damrosch and Stokowski dropped the score like a hot brick. In spite of all the interruptions, George did manage to finish another section of the work, the 'blues' section.

'Rhapsody In Blue' continued to dog the Gershwins everywhere they went. Early in April, George himself was asked to play his piano transcription of it at a party given in his honour, attended by many of the cultural elite of Paris. Among them was the choreographer and principal dancer of the famous and influential Ballet Russe, Anton Dolin. On hearing George play the 'Rhapsody', he immediately decided he must create a ballet based on it.

Within two weeks he had done this, and on 16 April, at the Théâtre des Champs-Elysées the Gershwins attended the ballet's first performance, danced by Anton Dolin himself.

On 29 May, towards the end of their Paris stay, there was a concert featuring another of George's compositions. The pianist Dmitri Tiomkin, who would later go to Hollywood and become an outstanding writer of film music, performed the European premiere of the 'Concerto In F', at the Théâtre National de l'Opéra.

As at the performance of 'Rhapsody In Blue', George's piece came at the end of a full programme by other composers. The preceding pieces were the overture from Weber's opera *Euryanthe*, Liszt's 'Piano Concerto In A Major', and 'Cortège Macabre', an early piece by George's American near-contemporary, Aaron Copland.

This was the first time George had heard his 'Concerto In F' performed by somebody else. It received a standing ovation and the Paris critics were unanimous in its praise. Some of the celebrities in the audience, however, were less sure. Prokofiev complained that it was less of a structured composition than a succession of thirty-two bar choruses, and Diaghilev, the guiding impresario of the Ballet Russe, managed to be wrong twice by describing it as "good jazz but bad Liszt".

Samuel Dushkin, George's violinist friend, for whom he had turned two of his piano 'Novelettes' into the piece 'Short Story', was living in Paris at the time, and the evening after the 'Concerto In F' the Gershwins all went to a musical party at his apartment.

After a performance of Bach's 'Concerto For Two Violins', and a piece by pianist Vladimir Horowitz, George played. After an intermission, Horowitz played his own étude based on *Carmen*, then Samuel Dushkin, accompanied by George, played 'Short Story' and another similar Gershwin piece, 'Blue Interlude'. It was all a pleasantly formal evening.

Even in Paris, Broadway seemed just round the corner. While George was there he received a telegram from Flo Ziegfeld asking him to write the music for a new play for comedian Eddie Cantor, due to start rehearsals in September. Or if not, would he commit himself to writing some other show.

George had to turn down the Eddie Cantor play, as he and Ira were already committed to the new Gertrude Lawrence musical, but he agreed to write a show for Ziegfeld when that was finished. He also began to feel that it was time he and Ira returned to New York.

This feeling grew stronger when he also received a wire from producer Edgar Selwyn. Selwyn had been brooding for months over the failure of *Strike Up The Band* and had decided that if the satire in it was toned down somewhat, it might work on Broadway after all. He wanted to know if George and Ira would be willing to have a go at rewriting some of the songs to suit a new and softened show. If they would, then he would approach George S Kaufman about applying the same treatment to the book.

George wired back that this was fine by him. He too felt that *Strike Up The Band* deserved another shot, but both he and Ira, separately and together, had commitments, and they might not be able to work on it together for a year.

Selwyn replied that that suited him fine, because the extra year would help the public forget the previous flop. He then went off and spoke to Kaufman, who wanted no part of any such revision. He was proud of *Strike Up The Band* as his strongest piece of satire, and he wanted no part of diluting its strength.

Selwyn badgered him on the phone day after day and, eventually, Kaufman said a firm and final "No". He could not and would not revise the book. However, he added, he would be perfectly willing to let Morris Ryskind do the job, if Ryskind was willing and if Selwyn was willing to use him.

Ryskind of course had in a way instigated the whole piece, so Selwyn was happy to approach him, and did. Ryskind said he was happy to take on the job, but he candidly admitted that, being less well established in his writing career than Kaufman, he was less willing to take chances, and so, in spite of his heartfelt pacifist principles, this would be a considerable watering down. Selwyn happily agreed with this approach and it was arranged that Ryskind would start work on the new book early next year, after he had finished collaborating (with Kaufman) on the Marx Brothers' play *Animal Crackers*.

The Gershwin party left Paris at the end of May, but instead of heading straight home they went first for a couple of weeks in Vienna. There, at the Hotel Bristol, George continued to work on 'An American In Paris', whenever he wasn't out experiencing the musical life of the city. He went to hear a performance of the controversial new 'jazz opera' by Krenek, *Jonny Spielt Auf*, and was invited to the apartment of the famous atonalist Alban Berg to hear Berg's 'Lyric Suite', played by an ensemble led by Rudolf Kolisch.

George enjoyed both compositions greatly. He also realised the depth of musical training and insight necessary to write such pieces and, in spite of his own genuine sense of himself as a genius, felt great reverence for their composers. At Alban Berg's, after the performance of the 'Lyric Suite', Berg asked to hear some of George's work. George played some of his songs and Berg responded to them with enthusiasm. "But how can you possibly like my music when you write the kind of music you do?" George asked in surprise. "Music is music," said Berg.

From the world of older Viennese music George was taken to meet the aged widow of the waltz king, Johann Strauss II (who tried to sell this rich American the original manuscript of *Die Fledermaus* for an exorbitant sum). From the world of operetta he met Franz Lehár, composer of *The Merry Widow* and Emmerich Kálmán, composer of *The Countess Maritza* and *Sari*. Kálmán escorted Ira, Lee and George to the famous and highly-fashionable Sacher Café, near the Opera. As they walked in the café orchestra began yet another spirited rendition of 'Rhapsody In Blue'.

The musicians of Europe had accepted George as a talent fit to stand alongside their own leading composers of light music. Unfortunately, this visit to Europe would be the last George would ever make. By 20 June he and his party were back in New York, and he would never find time to cross the Atlantic again.

Arriving back, his luggage included eight bound volumes of the works of Debussy, a Musel reed pipe organ and the still-incomplete score of 'An American In Paris'. George had promised Walter Damrosch that it would be ready in time for the New York Symphony Society to perform it in their winter programme and, as well as completing that, there was the Gertrude Lawrence musical to be written for Aarons and Freedley.

The book was being written by Fred Thompson, this time in collaboration with Vincent Lawrence, and the title that had been decided on was *Treasure Girl*.

The plot was not one of the best that George and Ira ever had to work with. A rich eccentric, Mortimer Grimes, holding a treasure hunt on his estate, buries a treasure of one-hundred-thousand dollars, which the finder can keep. The heroine, Ann, divides her time during the performance between hunting for the treasure and pursuing (and being pursued by) the hero, Neil.

They did their best and came up with several pleasant songs, including 'Oh So Nice', which was a fairly successful attempt to write a fox-trot with the feeling of a Viennese waltz, and 'Where's The Boy', one of the most tender of their romantic 'blues' numbers. But neither their score, nor the talents of Gertrude Lawrence and Clifton Webb, could do anything to save the show. After the usual out-of-town tryouts, it opened at the Alvin Theatre on 8 November and closed before the New Year, racking up only sixty-eight performances.

The show it had replaced at the Alvin, *Funny Face*, transferred to the Princes Theatre in London, still of course with the Astaires, but with the two idiot burglars now played equally well by Leslie Henson and Sydney Howard. It too opened early in November, but unlike *Treasure Girl*, it had another long and successful run.

Meanwhile, George had managed to finish 'An American In Paris'. He completed it in two-piano form on 1 August and eventually completed his full orchestration ten days after *Treasure Girl* opened, on 18 November.

George described it as "an orchestral tone poem" and, explaining what he had aimed for in writing it, he said:

> This new piece, really a rhapsodic ballet, is written very freely and is the most modern music I've yet attempted. The opening part will be developed in typical French style, in the manner of Debussy and the Six, though the themes are all original. My purpose here is to portray the impression of an American visitor in Paris, as he strolls about the city and listens to various street noises and absorbs the French atmosphere...
>
> The opening gay section is followed by a rich blues with a strong rhythmic undercurrent. Our American friend perhaps after strolling into a café and having a couple of drinks, has succumbed to a spasm of homesickness. The harmony here is both more intense and simple than in the preceding pages. This blues rises

to a climax followed by a coda in which the spirit of the music returns to the vivacity and bubbling exuberance of the opening part with its impressions of Paris.

It seems possible that George wrote 'Debussy' by mistake. Debussy and Les Six hardly share the same manner, Les Six being musical enemies of Debussy. Maybe he meant to put the name of their leader, Erik Satie. Certainly his jaunty opening to 'An American In Paris' has more of the humorous feel of one of Satie's pieces than of anything Debussy wrote, and it is significant that three years after its premiere, in 1931, one of Les Six, Francis Poulenc, singled it out as one of his favourite compositions of the twentieth century.

The premiere took place on 13 December at Carnegie Hall, with Walter Damrosch conducting the New York Symphony Society orchestra. Again it was presented among compositions by other composers. The programme ran: 'Symphony In D Minor' (Franck), 'Adagio For Strings' (Lekeu), 'An American In Paris' (Gershwin), 'Magic Fire Scene' from *Die Walküre* (Wagner).

After 'An American In Paris' finished, Otto Kahn made a brief speech to the audience, saying that George was almost a genius. "In fact," he said, "some day he will be a genius, but geniuses must suffer, and George hasn't suffered yet." Florenz Ziegfeld, who was in the audience, and who was notoriously demanding to work for, thought of the revue George had agreed to compose. He turned to Lorenz Hart sitting next to him. "He'll suffer," he said.

This time George had written a piece that did not feature the piano. Instead the jazzy tone of 'An American In Paris' (especially in the blues section) is mostly carried by the trumpet.

Overall, it is built on a number of musical themes, some occurring briefly, some being more fully developed, and it has considerable variety of mood, from the jaunty opening through the exciting chaos of Parisian traffic (complete with taxi horns), to echoes of the music hall, followed by the gentle homesick sadness of the 'blues' section, then back via a touch of the Charleston into the exuberant ending.

Again George augmented the symphony orchestra, this time with even more percussion – snare drums, bass drum, cymbals, rattle, triangle, tom-toms, xylophone, wire brush, woodblock, glockenspiel and celesta. And again the critics were divided, from those who found it cheap and inane, albeit possibly good fun, to those who enjoyed its rollicking spirit and cleverness, and recognised the further advance in George's compositional technique. As Morris Gershwin proudly told one critic at the time, "It is very important music – it takes twenty minutes to play."

CHAPTER NINE

'Strike Up The Band'

During 1928, George and Ira at last made the break from the Gershwin family home. George rented a penthouse apartment on the seventeenth floor at 33 Riverside Drive in Manhattan. At the same time, Ira and Lee moved into the penthouse alongside. The two apartments shared a terrace, looking out over the Hudson River to New Jersey, and the terrace provided a link from one to the other, so that in effect they became one.

Money, and the display of money, meant little to George, and this apartment was probably the main extravagance of his life. It was decorated and furnished in the 'modern' style of the late twenties and thirties, with severe hard outlines, white or veneered walls, parquet floors, black woodwork in the chairs and book cases, concealed lighting and the odd dash of chrome.

He had there his Steinway, his books, his music, his mementos and, as the years went by and his interest in painting and sculpture expanded into collecting, it would grow into something of an art gallery. In sculpture he liked African art and, in painting, he favoured the French moderns. Among the artists he liked were Picasso, Utrillo, Derain, Modigliani, Chagall and Rousseau, but his favourite was Rouault.

His cousin, the painter Henry Botkin, who advised him in choosing paintings, and frequently purchased them on his behalf, considered that eventually George had "one of the most significant collections of modern art in America", and among his most prized paintings were Picasso's 'Absinthe Drinker' and one of Rouault's melancholy clowns. "Oh, if I could only put Rouault to music," he once said. I am keen for dissonance. The obvious bores me. The new music and the new art are similar in rhythm, they share a sombre power and fine sentiment."

As his interest in producing his own paintings grew and he moved from watercolours to oils, Henry Botkin also advised him in buying materials. More and more, painting became his major relaxation. He turned out to have considerable skill as a draughtsman, and a strong sense of compositional rhythm.

His approach was always that of a committed artist. Painting was more to him than a mere pastime, and he became more than merely competent. Many critics considered that if he'd concentrated on art instead of music, he could have made a reputation in that field also.

At dinner one day he mentioned proudly that someone had told him he need never write another note, because he could make a fortune with his palette and brush. One of the lady guests was duly awed. "Isn't it amazing," she said, "that one man should possess a genius for two of the arts?" "Oh, I don't know," said George objectively. "Look at Leonardo da Vinci."

At first he painted portraits, mainly of family and friends and associates in the world of music. Portraiture would always be his strongest suit. As his assurance grew he extended his scope to still lifes and landscapes, but with these he was rather less successful.

Also in the apartment was a small gymnasium, with a rowing machine, a punch ball, a dartboard, and a small silver-coloured upright piano that someone had given him. All his life George liked to keep fit, almost like an athlete.

In many ways he led rather a spartan existence. He rarely drank, he smoked cigars only in moderation, and food interested him so little that he often had to be reminded to eat. Thus, unlike Ira, he never put on an ounce of fat. As Ira rather enviously said after George's death, he kept himself like a boxer. And he enjoyed all manner of sports, such as tennis, golf, ping-pong, swimming, skiing and what he continued to refer to as 'horse riding'.

When George moved into the new flat he gave a housewarming dinner, making the occasion a celebration of his career so far. Those he invited included Max Dreyfus, Eva Gauthier, Paul Whiteman, Ferde Grofé, Fred and Adele Astaire, Walter Damrosch, Bill Daly and Ira.

From then on his apartment (and Ira's) became a cross between the

Gershwin family home, with all its comings and goings, and the Paley salon. Friends and business associates came and went and, every Sunday afternoon the salon would meet in either George's flat or Ira's, staying on for a delicatessen supper and then long past midnight, in a heady atmosphere of wit and artistic discussion and music. Regular members included writers, composers and lyricists like Vernon Duke, SN Behrman, Lillian Hellman, Howard Dietz, Arthur Kober and Kay Swift, but always the centre of attention was George.

Soon after George moved into the apartment, he received a phone call from the musician who would not only become a prominent member of the Gershwin salon, but would also submerge his own career almost totally in George's music – Oscar Levant.

Oscar had been aware of George for years. Since 1918, in fact, when, as a twelve-year-old in Pittsburgh, he had been bowled over by George's accompaniment to Nora Bayes. Since then he himself had become a formidable classical pianist, and besotted with Gershwin music.

The reasons for this went back into his upbringing. In many ways his background was identical to George and Ira's. His father Max, who died when Oscar was almost fifteen, had been born in St Petersburg, and his mother's parents were also from Russia.

Unlike the Gershwins, the Levants were fiercely Orthodox and they had a genius in instilling guilt matched only by the Catholic Church. Oscar was the youngest of four sons, to the eternal disappointment of his parents, who had wanted a girl, and Max told each of his sons in turn a parable about mother-love:

A son murders his mother and cuts her heart out to present to his sweetheart. With the heart in his hand, he rushes off to present it to his fiancée. In his hurry, he stumbles, and the disembodied heart that he clutches in his hand cries out, "Did you hurt yourself, son?"

He also told his sons that "no man can be great unless he loves music". Both Oscar's father and Annie, his mother, loved music, but they differed about musicians. Max, himself a highly-skilled jeweller, thought they were little better than vagrants. Annie, whose brother, also Oscar, was a well-established Broadway conductor, thought differently.

All her four sons turned out to be talented musicians, but Oscar was outstanding as a pianist and she determined that he would be

143

groomed for a concert career. From the age of seven he would be hauled in from baseball games in the alley, howling and screaming, and made to practise the piano, often till his fingers bled.

Nonetheless, he loved music and was proud of his ability. His first day of high school happened to be the day before a widely-advertised concert to be given in Pittsburgh by the heroically famous pianist, Paderewsky. The twelve-year-old Oscar, still kept in short pants by his mother, sauntered into the class and asked, "Do you want to hear what Paderewsky is going to play tomorrow night?" The teacher, Oscar Demmler, expecting to hear a list of the pieces in the programme, said, "Yes." Young Oscar went to the piano in the corner of the room and reeled off the whole concert.

Demmler, an amiable man, became his music teacher as well as his class teacher, and Oscar's knowledge of classical music broadened enormously. But he was turning into a sullen and resentful youth. Like George, he was something of a child of the streets, passionate about baseball, fascinated by gambling and crapshooting, and a truant from school.

After his father's death, his firm and sarcastic mother decided that he should be got away from the bad influence of the streets. In February 1922 she took him to New York, rented him a furnished room, found him a highly-regarded piano tutor, Sigismond Stojowsky, and set off home to Pittsburgh, forbidding him to follow her.

Stojowsky was an excellent teacher and Oscar's playing progressed, but, at the age of fifteen he found New York terrifyingly lonely. At first he spent most of his time reading (he was already extremely widely read), but gradually he made friends, who often enough were slightly older versions of the street-wise kids his mother had wanted to get him away from. He began to explore the night life, the speakeasies and theatres and vaudeville houses, and found that he got a great kick out of show tunes and popular songs, both of which had been forbidden at home.

This bothered him. With all his background in Bach, Beethoven and Mozart, to enjoy these catchy trivia must be the musical equivalent of drinking bathtub gin. Unable to see his way to getting concert bookings, he began getting odd jobs playing for parties in hotels, or as a rehearsal pianist for shows, where he continued to enjoy the music of composers like Jerome Kern and Irving Berlin.

The problem caused him real moral agony. Then, in 1924, not long after the Aeolian Hall concert, he heard the Paul Whiteman Band perform 'Rhapsody In Blue'. It struck him with the force of a revelation. Apparently it was possible to amalgamate popular song and classical music into something musically respectable. Till then Stojowsky had been his musical guru – from then it was George.

He began angling to meet George. In 1925 he met Phil Charig, who was the rehearsal pianist on *Tell Me More* and *Tip-Toes* and had become a member of the Gershwin circle, and he badgered Phil to bring him to George's top floor apartment at the Gershwin house. Eventually Phil did, but unfortunately on that occasion George was busy orchestrating his 'Concerto In F' with Bill Daly and he barely acknowledged Oscar's presence.

Trying to get closer to George, he managed to get accepted as a member of the Paley salon, but somehow, whenever he went there, it was on a evening when George didn't. It was little consolation that he soon became accepted there as the regular pianist. In George's absence. Once at the Paleys' he was asked if he thought George's music would be played a hundred years hence. "If George is around, it will," he said.

He began getting better jobs as a pianist, first in the dance band led by Dave Bernie, then (having been poached away) in the much more famous and prestigious society band of Dave's brother, Ben Bernie. With the Ben Bernie Orchestra he was frequently featured playing 'Rhapsody In Blue'.

On 3 December 1925 Oscar called in sick, leaving the Ben Bernie Orchestra to find a substitute while he attended both the afternoon premiere and the evening performance of 'Concerto In F'. He found it far more self-assured and successful than the 'Rhapsody In Blue', a torrent of contrasting musical ideas. It stimulated his own growing urge to compose both concert pieces and shows. To be another Gershwin.

His career began to echo George's more and more. He made a fairly successful trip to London as the pianist with the Rudy Wiedoeft Orchestra, staying on for a while when the band returned to New York, and even accompanying the American singer Frank Fay at the London

Palladium.

Returning to New York himself, he began to try his hand at writing songs, and when his first song 'Keep Sweeping The Cobwebs Off The Moon' was published by Harms music, he came under the wing of Max Dreyfus. Max became so fond of this clever and abrasively witty new protege that he became almost a father to Oscar, who took to spending hours hanging around the offices of Harms Music. Where again he failed to run into George.

In 1927, what with the modest success of 'Keep Sweeping The Cobwebs Off The Moon', and with his playing of the 'Rhapsody In Blue' with Ben Bernie, Oscar was becoming known on Broadway. That year he was sought out and cast in a musical, *Burlesque*, in a small part which required piano playing. Its premise was the setting up of a musical, and its star was Frank Fay, playing a no-good drunken comic. His long-suffering wife was played by a newcomer to leading roles, Barbara Stanwyck, and the show would make her a star.

Barbara and Oscar became friends (although she would later marry Frank Fay) and he began getting invitations to high-grade parties (including Jules Glaenzer's) in the hope that he would bring her. She refused to go anywhere near such gatherings, warning him to beware of phonies, but he went, and soon became a valued guest for his playing and his wit. But he still didn't run into George.

In 1928 Oscar, who was by now totally nocturnal, was awakened at noon by the shrilling of the phone in his hotel room. It was conductor Frank Black, who was in the Brunswick recording studio with the wax warmed ready to record, an orchestra rehearsed to play the 'Rhapsody In Blue' and a missing pianist off on a bender. He needed Oscar fast.

Oscar didn't even ask about the fee. He was delighted to be asked. After playing the 'Rhapsody' for four years he knew it inside out and now, if he recorded it, at last George would hear it. He played it beautifully, with a light-hearted confidence that was almost casual, at the same time bringing out the piece's whole range of feelings. The record was released, he waited for some reaction from George and, eventually, unable to bear the suspense any longer, phoned him at his penthouse.

George politely asked him to bring the record round. Oscar did, and suffered agonies while George listened through it, waiting for the master's verdict. All George said was, "I like mine better." As Oscar said years later, "George was quite firm in his preference for his own version on Victor. He was unstinting in his declaration of the superiority of his performance over mine."

Again Oscar failed to strike up a rapport with his hero and he went away. But his record sold well, helping to build up his reputation as well as George's, and it led to frequent calls for him to perform the 'Rhapsody' on the growing medium of radio. So frequent, in fact, that whenever he played it over the air, and his mother happened to hear it, she would phone him and say aggrievedly, "Again, the 'Rhapsody'?" This amused George so much when he eventually heard the story that it became a standing joke between them.

At the beginning of 1929, on 9 January, 'An American In Paris' was given its radio premiere. It was performed by an orchestra led by Nat Shilkret, who had been a fellow student with George of Charles Hambitzer and who, by 1929, was a successful studio band conductor for both recording and radio.

Having presented 'An American In Paris' on radio, Shilkret's next move was to set up a session to record it, which he arranged at the Victor studios in February. This was the first time that a Gershwin concert piece was to be recorded in its entirety and George, excited by the occasion, brought along his French taxi horns.

He became so excited in fact that Nat Shilkret found him getting in the way during rehearsal and had to ask him to leave the studio, only allowing him back for the recording. He had to come back for the recording because he had been allotted the small musical task of playing the short bridge passages on celeste. And he was still so excited during the recording that he forgot to play one of them, as a keen listener can spot on reissues.

At around the same time, now that the Four Marx Brothers were safely launched and well into the run of *Animal Crackers*, Morris Ryskind began rewriting the book of *Strike Up The Band*. And George and Ira got down to work on their musical for Ziegfeld.

The show was to be based on a play that had been a big hit on Broadway between 1918 and 1920. Written by Sammy Shipman, it was set in a sort of fairy-tale version of China, and it was called *East Is West*. Quite why Ziegfeld wanted to base a musical on it is unclear, because

in the words of Bolton and Wodehouse, who in around 1917 wrote a
Chinese musical called *The Rose Of China*, "It is the view of competent
critics that – with the possible exception of *Abie's Irish Rose* and
Grandma's Diary – East Is West is the ghastliest mess ever put on the
American stage, but this is an opinion held only by those who did not
see *The Rose Of China*.

A large part of the problem seems to be that before you know it in
plays like this your heroine has gone cute on you, "twittering through
the evening saying 'Me Plum Blossom. Me good girl. Me love Chlistian
god velly much'." Furthermore: "All heroines of Chinese plays turn out
in the end to be the daughters of American missionaries, kidnapped by
bandits in their infancy. This is known as Shipman's Law."

It is only fair to say, however, that George and Ira were greatly
excited by the piece, seeing it as a sensitive play which would lend itself
beautifully to integrating the songs into the action. Without even
waiting to sign a contract with Ziegfeld they settled down to write.

Among the songs they produced were the unforgettable
'Embraceable You', and an elegant and thoughtful number called 'In A
Mandarin's Orchid Garden'. More poetic than any other song they ever
wrote, it was intended as the background to a ballet.

They had written about half of the score when Ziegfeld changed his
mind. He wanted them to drop work on *East Is West* and start work on
another musical, *Show Girl*, which he wanted to present that summer.
It was not only going to star Al Jolson's wife Ruby Keeler, it would also
have Eddie Foy Jr and Jimmy Durante in the cast and use the Duke
Ellington Orchestra as the pit band.

Will Vodery at this time was still Ziegfeld's musical director and,
almost certainly, it was he who suggested Ellington, whose orchestra by
then had become famous as the house band at Harlem's Cotton Club,
where it then had been appearing for over a year. Already it was an
outstanding band – if not *the* outstanding band – and Ellington's
energetic manager, Irving Mills, was known to be eager to have it play
for a Broadway show.

The curious thing about Ellington playing for a Gershwin show is
that here were these two major composers working together for the
only time in their lives, and neither one ever mentioned the other
afterwards, or took any musical influence from each other or, as far as

one can tell, ever exchanged a word. It is as though each was isolated in his own musical world.

The plot of *Show Girl* was nothing if not in-house. Based on a witty and fast moving novel by JP McEvoy, it was a fictionalised account of the life and loves of one of Ziegfeld's most famous stars, Dixie Dugan, from the time she crashed her way into an interview with him to her eventual stardom in the *Follies*.

Working for Ziegfeld was never easy for composers. George and Ira found he had a disconcerting habit of turning up unannounced to make sure they were working. As they both kept very much their own unstructured hours, it frequently happened that he found George painting and Ira reading, which did not make for an easy working relationship.

Nonetheless, they kept turning out songs at an amazing rate. All told, they wrote twenty-five songs for *Show Girl*, of which only twelve were eventually chosen for inclusion. In addition to these, Jimmy Durante, playing a props man, sang several of his own songs, including 'So I Ups To Him', 'Who Will Be With You When I'm Far Away' and 'I Can Do Without Broadway (But Can Broadway Do Without Me?)'.

Furthermore, there was to be a ballet in the show to the music of 'An American In Paris'. This was to be choreographed by the celebrated Albertina Rasch, who was the wife of Dmitri Tiomkin, and whom George and Ira had met with her husband in Paris. Both had now immigrated to America.

Apart from 'An American In Paris', the score for *Show Girl* was not one of George's most distinguished. Only one song in it turned out to be outstanding, and that was 'Liza (All the Clouds'll Roll Away)', which would be better known if *Show Girl*, which opened on 2 July, hadn't turned out to be one of Ziegfeld's greatest flops, turning a witty, fast-moving novel into a turgid, stately and over-magnificent spectacle.

It was a flop in spite of having an extra unplanned (and unwanted) attraction. On many nights, while Ruby Keeler (playing Dixie Dugan) sang and danced to 'Liza', her husband Al Jolson would leap up unbidden from the audience and run up and down the aisles singing along with her.

It was such a flop in fact that Ziegfeld refused to pay George and Ira any royalties on the show. He did his best to beef up the score by adding some additional numbers by Vincent Youmans, and began bombarding George and Ira with abusive telegrams. George, to whom money meant little, was forced for the only time in his life to threaten legal action in order to collect. Ziegfeld at first threatened a counter-suit, blaming them for not writing a hit score, but eventually he gave in and paid up.

Apart from his royalties, the best thing George got out of the show was 'Liza'. It remained one of his favourite songs all his life, one that he frequently played at parties, improvising around it endlessly.

Not surprisingly it was also a favourite piece of the great improviser Art Tatum, who would arrive in New York from his home town of Toledo in 1932. Tatum's piano playing stunned everybody, even George, who would listen to him in amazement for hours at a time.

In the month after *Show Girl* opened, George made his public debut as a conductor, at one of the summer concerts held regularly at the Lewisohn Stadium. This vast outdoor concert hall, at One-Hundred-And-Thirty-Eighth Street in Manhattan, had been given to New York City in 1915 by Adolph Lewisohn, a German-born Jew who had moved to America and made a fortune in mining.

Built entirely of concrete, and seating up to fifteen thousand, it was intended to be reminiscent of a semi-circular Roman amphitheatre, surrounded by a pillared arcade. Unfortunately, according to some critics, it more resembled a municipal sewage plant. The concrete seats were cold and hard, as well as being rough on the clothes, and the acoustics were not good. But, in spite of all this, its summer concerts were popular and well attended.

George had made his first appearance there on 27 July 1927, when he was the piano soloist for both 'Rhapsody In Blue' and 'Concerto In F', accompanied by an orchestra conducted by Willem Van Hoogestraten. This time, as well as playing the 'Rhapsody' (again), he would conduct 'An American In Paris'.

To prepare himself for this, he took lessons from his former harmony teacher, Edward Kilyeni, who taught him the basic essentials of baton technique, then had him practise at home, conducting to Nat Shilkret's recording of the piece.

His practising turned out to be effective. At the performance, on 26 August, his beating time was accurate and clear, his enthusiasm for the piece was evident, and it was obvious that he was the one in charge. From this time on he would conduct frequently.

At around this time Morris Ryskind delivered to Edgar Selwyn the revised book of *Strike Up The Band*. It was now a much gentler satire than it had been before. For instance, Ryskind, who naturally had been discussing the project with his friend Ira, had adopted Ira's suggestion of exchanging one Swiss product – cheese – for another – chocolate – the idea being that chocolate presents 'a sweeter image'. As Ira said when making the suggestion, "What's the difference? They're both made with milk."

Other changes were even more drastic. The war with Switzerland was turned into a dream of Horace J Fletcher (upset that Washington will not put a tariff on Swiss chocolate, he is given a sedative by his doctor and falls asleep). In his dream he sees himself leading the American Army against the Swiss. So instead of saying about the tariff war "This is the sort of thing that happens", the show was weakened into saying "This is the sort of thing you dream might happen".

In addition, Edgar Selwyn cast two strong comic leads as Horace J Fletcher and his government crony, Colonel Holmes. They were the popular and energetic comedy team of Clark and McCullough.

Bobby Clark and Paul McCullough had been at school together, back in their home town of Springfield, Ohio. McCullough, born in 1884, was four years the older. In his early teens he had found he enjoyed attending tumbling classes at the local YMCA and when he made friends with young Robert Edwin Clark in around 1898, he encouraged him to come along as well.

Clark was a natural-born performer, who had already sung in a local choir and played the bugle in a boys' band and, after the pair of them had practised tumbling for a couple of years, they entered show business, working their way up through minstrel shows and circuses to vaudeville to burlesque to Broadway.

Along the line their tumbling had gradually metamorphosed into comedy. Bobby Clark turned out to have a natural talent for off-beat humour, which mingled well with their physical slapstick, and Paul McCullough became a sort of eccentric straight man. Clark's trademark, developed at around the same time as Groucho's painted-on moustache, was a pair of painted-on black spectacles.

In *Strike Up The Band*, taking full advantage of the fact that most of it was supposed to be a dream, they spent much of the time rushing madly round, inserting bits of their own routines where they felt like it. A few years earlier, when they were in a 1926 Broadway show called *Here Goes The Bride* (written by *New Yorker* cartoonist Peter Arno), their performance was described by critic Brooks Atkinson: "With the Marx Brothers gone [*they were between shows*], Clark and McCullough are the logical First Actors for the Stage... Their genius rises to its greatest magnificence when they are running in circles round the stage, now and then emitting a staggering bellow of song."

Making most of the action a dream took a great deal of the strength out of the satire. But it allowed George and Ira more freedom in their songs and their revised score was a definite improvement. They continued to use a great range of song-styles – ballads, patter numbers, rhythm numbers, marches – as well as parodies of the styles of operetta to mock the grandiose self-importance of big business and government.

They discarded almost half the original score and, among the songs that were dropped, was 'The Man I Love'. It had to be dropped because by 1929 it had become so popular and well-known that to insert it in a new show was impossible. It would have sounded like an old song revived. George and Ira replaced it with a song called 'Soon', which had a similar feel but was better suited to being sung as a duet.

They also added a whimsical comedy number – 'I Want To Be A War Bride' – and one of their best patter songs, 'If I Became The President'. A lively and light-hearted finale now recapitulated the plot and the song 'I've Got A Crush On You' was resurrected from the previous year's ill-fated *Treasure Girl*.

By October the score was almost done and George's mind returned to *The Dybbuk*. By now he had a whole file of musical ideas for an opera based on it and was even considering going to Europe to study Jewish music. On 11 October he wrote to a friend saying that he had spoken to Otto Kahn about the project, and that Kahn was enthusiastic.

Performances of his other work also continued. On 10 November, in a concert at the Blackstone Theatre in Chicago, the singer Eleanor

Marum performed George and Ira's poetic song 'In A Mandarin's Secret Garden', which they had published separately after the show it was written for – *East Is West* – was aborted.

On that same evening George made his first indoor appearance as a conductor, taking the baton during a concert by the Manhattan Symphony to take them through 'An American In Paris'.

Two weeks earlier, on Tuesday, 28 October, an event had occurred that shook the whole of America and would change the carefree and irresponsible twenties into the depressed thirties. Wall Street had crashed.

The crash did not affect the mood of the country all at once. It took maybe a year for the financial collapse to create the conditions of the Depression, and at least two for public attitudes to sink from elation to despair. But happening when it did, the sobering effect of the crash put people into a frame of mind where the cynical outlook of *Strike Up The Band* seemed more appropriate than it had in 1927. This time the show was a success.

It was also helped by the fact that for the first time a Gershwin show had a pit band of first-class jazz musicians. Led by the famous cornetist Red Nichols, it included four future band leaders – trombonist Glenn Miller, drummer Gene Krupa, and clarinettist Benny Goodman, who left part way through the run and was replaced by clarinettist and altoist Jimmy Dorsey. They did not, of course, improvise, but it is hard to imagine a band better suited to playing George's arrangements.

The tryouts started at the Shubert Theatre in Boston on the evening of Christmas Day 1929. At the first performance, George conducted and, when the show moved to New York, opening at the Times Square Theatre on 14 January, he did so again, this time humming and whistling and singing along to himself so enthusiastically that one reviewer referred to him as "the star of the show".

Aided, perhaps more than anything, by the energetic performances of Clark and McCullough, the show became a hit, running for the then respectable total of one-hundred-and-ninety-one performances. George frequently attended throughout the run, occasionally conducting, and continuing to sing along. Kaufman told him sourly that he should have his name printed in the cast list, but this enthusiastic singing along indicated a change in George. In addition to his joy in creating music he was beginning to get real enjoyment from hearing his music played and sung by others.

CHAPTER TEN

'Of Thee I Sing'

In 1929, with the advent of the talkies, it dawned on the Hollywood studios that in future they were going to need a lot of music. Descending on Tin Pan Alley, they bought every music publishing house they could lay their hands on. Metro-Goldwyn-Mayer, for instance, bought Miller Music and Feist. Warner Brothers bought Remick's, Witmark and Harms Music. Tin Pan Alley, as George had first known it, disappeared, becoming a branch of the film industry.

Max Dreyfus sold the Harms catalogue to Warner Brothers for nine million dollars, agreeing, as part of the contract, to publish no music himself for several years to come. Just before he closed the deal, he put his pet protege Oscar Levant on the Harms payroll as a songwriter, much as he had hired George eleven years before.

Part of the reason he did this was because he knew that Oscar had been approached by Paramount to go to Hollywood, to repeat his stage role in the screen version of *Burlesque,* and he hoped that Oscar's Harms salary would keep him in New York a while longer. It didn't. Almost at once he took a train for California.

Oscar enjoyed Hollywood. For the screen, *Burlesque* had been retitled *The Dance Of Life* (originally the name of a 1923 treatise on sex, written by Havelock Ellis and bought by Paramount simply so they could use the title). By being hired to appear in it, he was lucky enough to be on the spot for the birth of the movie musical. After his part in the filming was over, he phoned Max Dreyfus and said he wanted to find him work writing music for the movies.

Max Dreyfus got him a job at the new studio, RKO, the only major studio of the thirties which had not been around in the silent movie days. At the age of twenty-two Oscar virtually became its music department. In addition, being far more knowledgeable about literature than most of RKO's budding executives, he also became involved in selecting books and scripts for the studio to film.

Still in 1929, while engaged in all this activity (and in a torrid affair with Nancy Carroll, who had replaced Broadway's Barbara Stanwyck as star of the film version of *Burlesque*), he also found time to write the score for a Broadway musical. This was a whimsical fairytale piece, based on the Rip Van Winkle story and called *Ripples*.

It was produced by Charles Dillingham, with lyrics to Oscar's songs by Graham John and Irving Caesar. None of the songs was outstanding, but one, to which Irving wrote the lyrics, became a considerable hit. It was called 'Lady, Play Your Mandolin' and Max Dreyfus was duly proud of his young favourite's success.

Ripples opened at the New Amsterdam Theatre on Broadway in February 1930. It starred the famous ventriloquist-comedian, Fred Stone, but in spite of his presence it was obvious from the first night that it would be a flop. Mostly this was because it was too old-fashioned and wholesome for the time. Its main appeal was to families with children, and there simply weren't enough of those among the sophisticated Broadway clientele to keep it running.

Oscar, who had returned to New York to work on the show, was uneasily aware that across the street, at the Times Square Theatre, there was a far superior musical – *Strike Up The Band*. He took to drifting across the street during performances of *Ripples* to listen to George's exciting new score – from a show that was old-fashioned to one that was breaking new ground.

One afternoon in March 1930, when he was standing at the back of the Times Square Theatre listening enviously to George's score, a slim woman tapped him on the shoulder and asked, "How's your show doing?" Oscar recognised her at once. It was Ira's wife, Lee.

He took her across the street to hear something of *Ripples* and, as he later recalled, "After she had seen a few numbers... she developed in me a scorn for my own music almost equal to hers." Oscar apologised for the poor quality of his songs, explaining that fairytales had no real appeal for him, and Lee, rather agreeing, not only took him back across the street to watch the ending of *Strike Up The Band*, but followed up by inviting him to come back to Riverside Drive with her and spend the evening at Ira's apartment. At last he had the chance of becoming part of George's inner circle.

Which was probably not the best thing that could have happened to him, because for the whole of the next eight years he almost totally submerged his own life in the Gershwins'. Ira and Lee, who were (and would remain) childless, almost adopted him. Lee became his friend and confidante, and Oscar once said gratefully, "Leonore was a gracious hostess and the first person to tolerate my social dissonances." Spending time in their apartment, he naturally took to wandering along the terrace that linked it to George's.

Although he hung onto his room at the Park Central Hotel, where he had been living in 1928 when he recorded 'Rhapsody In Blue', he started spending so much time at the twin apartments, eating meals, helping George and Ira with their work, and socialising, that it was almost as if he lived there. Letting his own work and income slide, he became, in his own words "a penthouse beachcomber".

To Oscar, the double household resembled the one he had grown up in. Once again he was the youngest in a household of talented brothers, presided over by an assertive strong-willed woman (it was Lee's assertiveness as much as anything that had attracted the reclusive Ira). She even resembled Oscar's mother in having a talent for being at once loving and undermining, although her technique was subtler. The line she is given in the biographical film *Rhapsody In Blue*, although fictional, is reputedly well in character: "Do me a favour, Ira – don't ever turn out to be a genius like your brother."

To the insecure Oscar, George seemed glowingly self-confident. "There was nothing frustrated about George," he once wrote. "There was no gap between his dream and his doing." Having now met George, he worshipped him in person as much as he had worshipped his music.

They became friends, although George, as in all his relationships, remained somewhat remote. Seen together, they presented an interesting contrast. Both were from similar backgrounds, but George had worked hard to develop a cultured manner and appearance – tall and good-looking, he had learnt to move with well-bred elegance, wearing tailored suits and sometimes even spats.

Oscar, on the other hand, with tousled hair and clothing, was awkward, clumsy and knock-kneed, retaining all the graceless abrasiveness of the street kid he had once been. George enjoyed sports, and kept himself fit like an athlete. Oscar disliked physical exercise. "My favourite exercises," he once said, "are grovelling, brooding and mulling."

He was, however, the better pianist. George's playing, no matter how fluent it was and how much real enjoyment he gave people (and himself) by playing, always remained somewhat unexpressive. Nor did he have Oscar's technique. Composer David Diamond once pointed out that "Gershwin couldn't run through a Chopin 'Prelude'", whereas Oscar knew by heart and could play the whole of Chopin. All his pianistic ability he now put at George's service.

George came to enjoy both Oscar's playing and his wit, and Oscar became the court jester of the Gershwin salon, his own musical ambitions withering in the light of George's energy and success. He wrote little music of his own from 1930 until after George was dead, and never another musical.

Oscar had barely become part of the Gershwin circle when Hollywood summoned George and Ira. The studios, in addition to buying up all the music publishers, were also approaching all the established Broadway composers. The studio that approached the Gershwins was Twentieth Century Fox, who wanted them to write the score for a musical called *Delicious*. They signed the contract in April 1930.

George admitted to the press that, not being much of a moviegoer, he was inexperienced with films and was "approaching them in a humble state of mind". Humble he may have been, but both he and Ira would have some familiar ground beneath their feet because the screenplay for the film was being written by their old colleague Guy Bolton, in collaboration with Sonya Levien.

They looked forward to their trip to Hollywood with some eagerness, but although they had signed the contract in April they were not due to go there until November. Meanwhile there was another musical to be written for Aarons and Freedley. And at the same time as they began work on that, George happened to get a job that would give him a chance to do a bit of movie-going.

Paul Whiteman and his Band had made one of the earliest musicals, *King Of Jazz*. This film, which was so prestigious that Universal had even made it in a primitive form of Technicolor, was due to have its world premiere at the Roxy Theatre in New York on Monday, 5 May. As was frequent at major cinemas in those days, there was to be a stage show between performances, and the Whiteman Band was to head it. George was hired to perform 'Rhapsody In Blue' with the Band at every performance during the first week. As things turned out, this would be his last-ever appearance with Paul Whiteman.

The Aarons and Freedley musical, *Girl Crazy*, would also see the end of an era in George's life. It would be the last of his twenties-style lightweight musicals. Again Guy Bolton had written the book, this time in collaboration with Jack MacGowan.

Its plot concerned the adventures of a young New York playboy, Danny Churchill, whose parents, fearing that their son is growing up effete and dissipated, send him out west to the masculine cow town of Custerville, Arizona, where he can learn to be a man, away from the distracting fleshpots of the big city, especially women.

Arriving there, having come all the way from New York in Giefer Goldfarb's taxicab, he falls in love with postmistress Molly Gray, who is practically the only woman in town. He is followed to Custerville by many of his New York friends (a necessary piece of plot to provide girls for the production numbers) and a lot of comedy mileage is got out of the clash of cultures, especially when Danny opens a dude ranch staffed with Broadway chorines. Eventually, through the love of a good woman (Molly), Danny becomes a reformed character.

For *Girl Crazy* George and Ira turned out one of their best-ever scores. In addition to 'Embraceable You' (salvaged from the aborted *East Is West*), it had 'But Not For Me', 'I Got Rhythm' and a delightful laid-back number sung in the show from time to time by a quartet of rustics drifting across the stage during scene-changes, 'Bidin' My Time'.

The part of Danny was played by the singer and dancer Allen Kearns, who had played the hero in *Tip-Toes*, while Molly was played by Ginger Rogers. Although she was then only nineteen, Ginger, who had a formidably ambitious mother, had been working in Hollywood from the age of six, as well as touring in vaudeville. This was her Broadway debut.

The lead comedian, playing the part of Giefer Golfarb, was Willie Howard. A likeable comic, whose real name was Lefkowitz, Willie was a small, slender man with a big hooter. He could sing surprisingly well, in a high, piercing alto, one of his set pieces being a burlesque of the sextet from *Lucia*, but his basic act was to impersonate various unlikely nationalities. Among his most popular were a French professor and a Mexican president in a big hat, and the humour sprang from the entire unconvincingness of these impersonations. His Jewish vocabulary continually leaked through, causing him alarm and bewilderment when the audience laughed. Naturally, in *Girl Crazy*, he eventually found himself in cowboy costume, having become the town's sheriff.

George and Ira wrote a speciality number for him called 'Goldfarb, That's I'm'. He also sang a series of imitations of singers of the day using the song 'But Not For Me'. Not, however, until after it had been sung tenderly and straight by Ginger Rogers.

Good as Willie Howard was, he and everyone else in the show were eclipsed by an almost unknown newcomer. One of the characters in the show was Frisco Kate, wife of the man running the gambling room at the dude ranch. Vinton Freedley was having trouble casting the role when his attention was drawn to a young woman singing at the Brooklyn Paramount Theatre. She had, for some years, been making poorly paid appearances at parties, weddings and small seedy night clubs and the Paramount Theatre job was her first small break. Her name was Ethel Merman.

Ethel's voice in those days had not developed the tendency to brassy self-parody it would have in later years. It had lift and lightness, while still having driving rhythm and the trumpet-like power that could fill a theatre. Vinton Freedley, as soon as he heard her, brought her round to audition for George at his penthouse.

She sang several swing numbers for him, including 'Exactly Like You' and 'Little White Lies', and George, impressed, said, "Don't ever go near a teacher. He'll ruin you." He then played her the three numbers she would sing in the show: 'I Got Rhythm', 'Boy! What Love Has Done To Me!' and a New York Jewish satire on 'Frankie And Johnny' called 'Sam And Delilah', about a man who betrays his lover by going back to his wife.

In her first autobiography, called *Who Could Ask For Anything More?*

in America and *Don't Call Me Madam* in Britain, Ethel told of her reaction:

Imagine the great Gershwin sitting down and playing his songs for [me]... I was tongue-tied. When he played 'I Got Rhythm', he told me, "If there's anything about this you don't like, I'll be happy to change it." There was nothing about that song I didn't like. But that's the kind of guy he was. I'll never forget it. I smiled and nodded, but I didn't say anything. I was too busy thinking how to phrase the music. Gershwin seemed puzzled at my silence. Finally he said again, "If there's anything you don't like about these songs, Miss Merman, I'll be happy to make changes." It wasn't like that; it was only that I was so flabbergasted. Through the fog that had wrapped itself round me, I heard myself say, "That'll do very nicely, Mr Gershwin."

Good as the cast was, the pit band for the show was equally outstanding. Once more led by Red Nichols, who had done the same job for *Strike Up The Band*, it again included Glenn Miller, Gene Krupa and Benny Goodman, who would again leave part way through the run and again be replaced by Jimmy Dorsey. And this time it included a fifth future band leader, the outstanding trombonist Jack Teagarden.

In the autumn of 1930, once *Girl Crazy* was cast and in rehearsal, George turned his attention once more back to *The Dybbuk*. Through Otto Kahn, the Metropolitan Opera had heard of George's project and, they were so keen to mount the proposed opera, that they offered him a contract. At which point everything fell through. George set about obtaining the opera rights to the play and learned that they were not available, having already been bought by an Italian composer, Lodovico Rocca. If he was going to write an opera, it looked more and more as if it would have to be based on *Porgy*.

After the usual out-of-town tryouts, *Girl Crazy* opened at the Alvin Theatre on 14 October, again with George conducting the opening night. It was a smash. The verve of the music kept it triumphantly alive, in spite of the fact that the storyline was now old-fashioned and over-familiar, complete with love-gone-wrong at the end of the first act and a happy reconciliation at the end of the second.

Embraceable You was the hit song and the effective star of the show was Ethel Merman. Not only did she have a stunning voice, she was a new kind of singer. Previous sexy singers tended to be mournful, singing of love-gone-wrong as the wages of sensuality. Ethel gave the impression of knowing all about everything and approaching life with total control.

Naturally her stand-out number was 'I Got Rhythm'. Four years later George still remembered the thrill he'd got from the audience's reaction to her singing it, and Ethel herself, years later, wrote:

> As I went into the second chorus of 'I Got Rhythm', I held a note for sixteen bars while the orchestra played the melodic line – a big tooty thing – against the note I was holding. By the time I'd held that note for four bars the audience was applauding. They applauded through the whole chorus and I did several encores. It seemed to do something to them. Not because it was sweet or beautiful but because it was exciting.

There was the usual opening night party after the show, and Ethel went to bed after it so late that she barely managed to get up in time to meet George for a lunch date they had arranged next day. George asked her had she seen the reviews. No, she said, she hadn't had time. "They're raves, all of them," he said. "You're in with both feet."

Two weeks later, on Sunday, 2 November, there was another celebration in the Gershwin household, when sister Frankie married her fiancé, Leopold Godowsky Jr. Leopold, son of the famous pianist of the same name, was himself an excellent violinist, but his real claim to fame was as an inventor. In collaboration with another Leopold, Leopold Mannes, he invented the Kodachrome process for colour photography.

The next few days were full of upheaval for the Gershwins. On the afternoon of the day that Frances got married, Morris and Rose set off to Florida for a holiday. Three days later, on 5 November, George, Ira and Lee took a trans-continental train for Hollywood to start work on the film *Delicious*.

Also on the train were Guy Bolton, who had written the book, as well as movie executive Nick Schenk and stage producer Edgar Selwyn, who happened to be Schenk's brother-in-law. Schenk and Selwyn were nothing to do with *Delicious*, and nor were the various film personalities also aboard, but the movie people had their own private car, and every evening the Gershwins joined them as they played poker and partied across America.

In Hollywood, George and Ira and Lee rented a two-storey Spanish-style house, previously tenanted by Greta Garbo, at 1027 Chevy Chase, in Beverly Hills. They would do most of their work for *Delicious* in this house, although on the Fox lot they also had a cottage set aside for them, one normally used by DeSylva, Brown and Henderson.

George settled easily into the athletic side of California life, playing tennis, going for golfing and swimming weekends at Palm Springs and taking daily hikes up Franklin Canyon with a trainer he had added to his retinue.

It was at around this time that he gave up smoking cigars, hoping that this would help alleviate the 'composer's stomach' he still suffered from. This ailment also increasingly affected his eating habits – food had never greatly interested him and his meals became an unenticing procession of cereals, rusks, dry toast, sour cream, and fruit, both fresh and cooked. Nothing helped.

Meanwhile, he worked. *Delicious* was to star Janet Gaynor and Charles Farrell, who had made three films together and were well-established in the public mind as a romantic duo, despite the fact that off-screen she was reputed to be more butch than he was.

Gaynor by 1931 was just slipping off the top of her then-immense popularity. Usually she played simply an innocent victim, a role for which her big round eyes and wholesome beauty completely suited her. But in 1927 and 1928 she made three films – *Seventh Heaven*, *Street Angel* and *Sunrise*, the first two with Farrell and the last two directed by the great FW Murnau – that offered her the opportunity to do much more with that characterisation. Between them they won her the first-ever Oscar for best actress. Unfortunately, in 1930 she quarrelled with Fox, to whom she was contracted, wanting better scripts than they were giving her. The studio suspended her until she backed down, then reinstated her in a long succession of innocuous 'sweetheart' roles, one of the better ones being in *Delicious*.

Its plot concerned Heather (Janet Gaynor), a poor Scottish immigrant, who falls for a rich polo-playing Long Islander (Charles Farrell) on board ship during her voyage to America. In spite of the usual love-triumphs-over-adversity routine (most of the adversity springing from their social and cultural differences) it did attempt to express the darker side of a newly-arrived immigrant's life – the descent from notions of America being a fairytale promised land to the reality of grinding big city poverty and loneliness.

George and Ira pieced together their songs for the score largely from unused bits and pieces, sometimes with Ira writing new words, and sometimes not. The witty 'Blah, Blah, Blah' was another song rescued from the wreck of *East Is West*, and another song, 'Delishious', George had been playing to visiting journalists as far back as the previous April. From a long way further back, and with the script specially contrived by Bolton and Levien, they even included their 1919 party piece, 'Mischa, Jascha, Toscha, Sascha', although it was edited out of the completed film.

After six weeks in Hollywood they had the songs almost completed, and George began work on his other music for the film. There were to be two main pieces. The first, a mixture of song and music some eight minutes long, was called 'Welcome To The Melting Pot' and was to accompany a humorous dream sequence in which Heather imagines the delights of the New World.

In her dream she is welcomed at the gangplank by a horde of reporters, eight Uncle Sams, Mr Ellis of Ellis Island, the Statue of Liberty and the Mayor of New York, offering her the key to the city as dollar bills rain from the skies. Ira's lyrics contain several in-jokes, such as when Heather is asked for her impression of America and replies "S'Wonderful, S'Marvelous", and much of George's music resembles uplifting, patriotic songs distorted by blue-notes.

The other extended piece, placed at the climax of the picture, was to accompany Heather's terror as she finds herself on the run from the police in the nightmare of the real city, with its docks and skyscrapers and subways, continually finding herself confronted by unnerving strangers. It was to be totally orchestral, re-creating the sounds and bustle of New York and, in the script, it was labelled 'New York Rhapsody'.

One of the rhythmic effects that George made use of was the sound of riveting and, after considering the title 'Manhattan Rhapsody', he soon began to think of his composition as 'Rhapsody In Rivets'. As he originally wrote it for the film, the piece was six minutes long and he felt pleased with it.

Capturing the spirit of his native city in music appealed to him deeply, and the piece became more ambitious than the studio had asked for. George felt it deserved a life of its own and, in his spare time, set about developing it for concert performance. As he wrote in a long letter to his first biographer, Isaac Goldberg, a few months later: "Nearly everybody comes back from California with a Western tan and a pocketful of moving picture money. I decided to come back with these things – and a serious composition besides, if the climate would let me. I was under no obligation to the Fox Company to do this. But, you know, the old artistic soul must be appeased every so often."

Towards the end of 1930, while still in Hollywood, he received a phone call from George S Kaufman, who was planning to write another musical, this time in total collaboration with Morris Ryskind.

Now that the country was entering the Depression, with more and more people out of work and going hungry, it seemed to Kaufman that the theatre-going public might be ready to accept a show satirising the essential similarity between the two major political parties in America, with particular reference to the idiocies of presidential campaigns. His tentative title for the show was *Tweedledee.*

When he had suggested the idea to Ryskind, Ryskind was at first dubious. "Well," he said thoughtfully, "before we go into this thing seriously, we might as well make up our minds that no one will produce it. But we'll have a lot of fun writing it." Kaufman told him he was wrong. He, Kaufman, was prepared to put up the money for the show himself (in the event he put up half of it), and he would get Sam Harris to produce it.

Sam Harris was a successful Broadway producer who had once been in partnership with George M Cohan. A small, undistinguished looking man, endlessly amiable and soft spoken, he had little education but impeccable taste, which was immediately obvious in his well-tailored appearance. He had humour, as well as a clear, sharp mind, and everyone in the theatre world, from the highest to the lowest, adored him. He had happily agreed to produce *Tweedledee,* and now Kaufman wanted George and Ira to write the songs.

George was delighted to agree. One of Kaufman's ideas was for the two parties to compete in providing a new national anthem, ending up with two that were almost identical, and the idea immediately took George's fancy. "We'll sing each item against the other for a first act finale," he said. "We'll handle it contrapuntally." "I'll take your word for it," said the unmusical Kaufman.

Meanwhile, social life in Hollywood continued. On New Year's Day 1931, George and Ira and Lee drove to the fashionable resort of Caliente, in Mexico, to attend a party given by movie mogul Joe Schenck (brother of Nick and the head of Twentieth Century Fox). Again there was a performance of 'Rhapsody In Blue', augmented by the performance of two Spanish dancers. It has been suggested that one of these was the young Margarita Carmen Cansino, a cousin of Ginger Rogers, who later went on to stardom as Rita Hayworth, but as she was only twelve at the time this seems improbable, even though Rita came of a Spanish-dancing family.

During January, with his work on *Delicious* completed, George continued developing 'Rhapsody In Rivets', which he had by now decided to give the less definite title 'Second Rhapsody'. He also received from Kaufman and Ryskind the first outline of *Tweedledee*. Already there had been two major changes. It was now called *Of Thee I Sing* (a line borrowed from Samuel Francis Smith's stirring patriotic song, 'America') and the idea of the two parties competing to produce an anthem had been dropped.

What had happened was that Kaufman and Ryskind, when they got down to actual work on the original idea, had discovered that simply using the two political parties as protagonists was far too impersonal. What was needed was a leading character for the audience to identify with. "Come to think of it," said Kaufman, "we could also use a heroine."

The new idea they came up with was to start the show during the run-up to a presidential election, with the leaders of a party sitting round discussing strategy in the proverbial smoke-filled room. They are trying to select a candidate, and are so devoid of genuine policies that in desperation they finally ask a chambermaid what interests her most in life. "Money," she says. After some discussion they reject this as an issue, on the grounds that money is too controversial. "What else?" they ask her. "Love," she says.

Adopting love as the central plank in their platform, they choose a bachelor, John P Wintergreen, as their candidate, and plan to hold a beauty contest (in Atlantic City) at which the winner will receive his hand in marriage, thus not only becoming Miss America but also Miss White House. This will not only secure for Wintergreen the respectability of marriage, but will also ensure his election as he woos her, because he will propose to her in every state, and all the world loves a lover.

The plan is carried out and Wintergreen is duly elected, but things start to go seriously wrong when he refuses to marry the winner of the contest, a Southern beauty called Diana Devereux, on the grounds that he has meanwhile fallen in love with his secretary, Mary Turner, smitten by her housewifely ability to make corn muffins. Miss Devereux being of French descent, this almost causes a war with France.

He marries his secretary and the situation gets worse and worse. He is on the brink of impeachment when his wife announces he is about to become the father of twins. Suddenly the situation is saved, since parenthood has even greater appeal to the public than love, and America has never impeached an expectant president. In a cynically happy ending, the duty of marrying Miss Devereux devolves on the vice president, Alexander Throttlebottom.

When Kaufman and Ryskind sent a synopsis of this plot to Sam Harris, explaining why they had modified their original idea, he replied with a wire saying, "WELL IT'S CERTAINLY DIFFERENT." Ryskind, who had doubts about the box office appeal of the story, said unhappily, "Didn't I tell you it was no use?" Kaufman, who rarely smiled, smiled. "Listen," he said, "you don't know Harris. He's a low-pressure type. That's the equivalent of wild enthusiasm from another producer. You know what it means? It means 'Great – try and have it ready for rehearsal in August'."

When George and Ira got their copy of the outline, they swiftly produced two songs. One was called 'Who Cares?' and the other, based on the new title, was 'Of Thee I Sing'. In writing the lyric, Ira gleefully sent up the sentimental patriotism of the original by extending "Of thee I sing" into "Of thee I sing, baby", making that the first line of the song, and thus mocking both campaign-songs and the love songs of Tin Pan Alley.

George began playing the two songs they had written at parties, and soon Kaufman, in New York, was alarmed when a friend he met in the street told him how much he liked the songs for the new show. Kaufman, previously unaware that any songs had been written, said, "I'm going to patent an invention which will keep composers away from pianos at parties. It might be expensive, though; eight strong men would probably be needed to make it work. Maybe I'd better come up with something which'll keep pianos away from composers."

In spite of Kaufman's protests, George, when he got back to New York, continued to play all his new songs at parties as soon as they were written, causing Kaufman eventually to say in irritation, "If you play that score one more time before we open, people are going to think it's a revival."

The two new songs weren't the only Gershwin compositions to be heard in California that January. On the fifteenth, George attended a concert of American music given by Artur Rodzinski and the Los Angeles Philharmonic. In it 'An American In Paris' was given its West Coast premiere. It got such an enthusiastic reception that George was forced to go up on stage and take a bow.

During that same week, a show called *Lightnin'*, starring Will Rogers and Louise Dresser, opened at the Carthay Circle Theatre. Every night, the house orchestra (Abe Lyman and his International Band) opened the performance with a short concert that included both 'I Got Rhythm' and a 1930 song with a lyric co-written by Ira and Billy Rose (to music by Harry Warren). It had been featured in a Broadway show called *Sweet And Low* and was called 'Cheerful Little Earful'.

George's last job on *Delicious* was to supervise the recording of rough versions of all the songs for the film at the correct tempos, so that there would be no mistake when the final versions were done. As a favour, he hired one of the singers from Paul Whiteman's vocal trio, The Rhythm Boys, to sing the words, so the then little-known Bing Crosby earned an unexpected fifty dollars.

Although the Gershwins were due to set off back to New York on 22 February, George, used to the working practices of Broadway, expected to return to the studio to see the music through its final stages. But Hollywood doesn't work that way. He was there to write music, and once the music was written and delivered, he was off the picture. The studio had plenty of lower-paid people around who could do any necessary arranging or editing.

When George and Ira (and Lee) arrived back in New York they had a meeting with Kaufman, Ryskind and Sam Harris. George and Ira performed the two new songs, and Ira's first line to 'Of Thee I Sing' aroused some strong objections, especially from Kaufman, who felt that its irreverence might be too much for the public to take. George and Ira fell back on the well-tried ploy of saying that of course if the public didn't take to it they'd be only too happy to write a replacement. Both feeling confident that no such action would be necessary.

Also at the meeting, Kaufman and Ryskind announced that they were going off to Atlantic City to work on the book, and expected to have a first draft of Act One finished in sixteen days. They were as good as their word. George received it in the mail on the seventeenth day.

When he received it, in the middle of March, he was busy orchestrating the 'Second Rhapsody', and his work on that would continue to dominate his thoughts for the next couple of months. He played a piano version of it at one of Jules Glaenzer's parties, where it was heard by Bill Paley, who owned the Columbia Broadcasting System. Afterwards George wrote to a friend: "He was so crazy about it that he called me several days later and asked me if I would like to have Toscanini conduct it next season. I said I would like it very much if Toscanini would like to do it."

Arturo Toscanini was then the principal conductor of the New York Philharmonic-Symphony Orchestra, and the music critic Samuel Chotzinoff, who knew both him and George, had been trying to arrange a meeting between the two for some time. As luck would have it, not long afterwards, on an evening in April, Toscanini came to Chotzinoff's house for dinner. After the meal, Chotzinoff suggested, as he had on several previous occasions, that he and George should meet. Toscanini seemed happy with the idea, and Chotzinoff dashed to the phone and told George to hurry over.

George, now full of the hope that Toscanini might give the 'Second Rhapsody' its New York premiere, was there like a shot, bringing with him several friends, including Oscar Levant. He was happy that Oscar was there, partly because he felt Oscar's credentials were stronger than his own in the classical music world, but mainly so that they could play the 'Second Rhapsody' for Toscanini in its two-piano version.

Almost as soon as he and his entourage arrived, George was seriously thrown when he learned that Toscanini had never heard the 'Rhapsody In Blue'. He could hardly believe his ears. Afterwards he wrote indignantly to a friend: "Can you imagine a man living in the last seven years – being connected with music – and never hearing the 'Rhapsody In Blue'?"

That evening George made sure Toscanini did hear it. He and Oscar played that and several other Gershwin pieces, including the 'Second Rhapsody'. Toscanini commented kindly on both pieces, but made no offer to conduct the premiere of the 'Second Rhapsody'.

Chotzinoff tried again about eighteen months later, arranging for George to come round again and play some of his works as part of a little variety show he was giving for Toscanini. Again Toscanini seemed pleased with what he heard, but again he expressed no interest in conducting any of it. And he never did conduct any Gershwin piece as long as George was alive.

On 23 May, George completed the orchestration of the 'Second Rhapsody', all except for two piano cadenzas still to be written. Its running time was around fifteen-and-a-half minutes.

A little over a month later, on 26 June, he hired a studio at the National Broadcasting Company, and fifty-five musicians, and tried out his orchestration by getting them to play it. He was pleased with the way it sounded, and felt it was the best concert piece he had written so far, especially in its orchestration and structure. Also he was pleased that NBC had used their direct wire to the Victor Recording Studios to make him a private recording of the performance.

With that out of the way he put the 'Second Rhapsody' aside for the moment and, in July, began work with Ira on the songs for *Of Thee I Sing*. Kaufman and Ryskind were still polishing the book, and Kaufman was still worrying about Ira's lyric to the title song.

Because the plot, as outlined by Kaufman and Ryskind, was still fairly conventional, most of the satire had to come in the treatment of it. This made the songs more important than ever, and for the first time Ira began originating some of them, coming up with witty and malicious ideas for which George had to compose appropriate music.

The score he created was full of imagination and humour. The song 'Of Thee I Sing', which in the plot was John P Wintergreen's campaign song, starts out with the feeling of a solemn hymn then, on the word 'baby', collapses into mushy love song sentiment. Solemnity is mocked by pastiches of grand opera, such as in the Senate scene, where the mockery is heightened by beginning with lightweight vamp-till-ready chords. The sentimentality of the Viennese waltz is used to underline the climactic song 'I'm About To Become A Mother (Who Could Ask For Anything More?)', and there is a flavour of the Salvation Army in the bogus morale-booster, "Posterity is just around the corner".

Overall, the show as it became has more sung scenes than spoken ones, with music and lyrics of varying styles and lengths flowing from one piece into the next as the action progresses. Plot and character are expressed in both music and lyrics. An excellent example is the song 'Who Cares?', which near the beginning of the show is sung "brightly, even glibly". Towards the end of the show, as Wintergreen holds in his arms the wife he refuses to give up, the stage is darkened and the song is reprised movingly and gently.

At around the time George and Ira completed their songs, George was involved in another Concert Of American Music at Lewisohn Stadium. He was to play 'Rhapsody In Blue', with an orchestra conducted by his friend and musical colleague Bill Daly. To Oscar Levant's delight, he was also to appear on the bill, performing Robert Russell Bennett's 'March For Two Pianos And Orchestra'. Bennett was a young composer who had at times helped arrange George's songs for the theatre and who, like George, was inspired by Broadway themes. He was to play one piano while Oscar played the other. It was to be the twenty-four-year-old Oscar's performing debut in New York.

The performance was scheduled for 10 August and, on that night, George and Oscar, already in their tuxedos, had an early dinner with Lee and Ira. During the afternoon a light, steady rain had begun to fall and, just before the four of them were due to leave, it turned to a heavy summer downpour. The seats in the stadium were drenched, and a phone call came to say that the concert had been postponed until tomorrow.

Oscar phoned Barbara Wooddell, a dancer in the *Follies Of 1931* who would become his first wife. He asked her to bring a friend for George and, instead of the concert, he and George and the two girls went out on the town.

The same thing happened on the next night. And on the next. And on the next. Each night George and Oscar and Barbara and another girl went out on the town instead of performing.

On the fourteenth, the skies miraculously stayed clear. Both George and Oscar played well, although Oscar had a stomach-churning attack of stage fright before going on, and it became clear from the reviews that George still had some way to go before totally convincing the more serious critics.

One of them, Olin Downes, wrote in the *New York Times*: "Mr Gershwin is a city composer. His music comes from the bricks, the cabaret, the theatre. It is music of which it could be said that like Topsy it has 'just growed'... It is still short, from the symphonic angle, on the technical side..." Of course, Olin Downes had not yet heard the 'Second Rhapsody'.

Shortly after the Lewisohn Stadium concert, rehearsals began for *Of Thee I Sing*, which was directed as well as co-written by Kaufman. Lois Moran played the heroine, Mary Turner, and the hero, John P Wintergreen, was played by William Gaxton, a handsome actor who was good but rather weakened his performance by tending to pad his part with cheap gags. He also began mimicking the mannerisms of New York's mayor, Jimmy Walker, instead of playing the intended fictional character. This marred the tightness of the show, and it annoyed Kaufman and Ryskind, but audiences never seemed to mind.

It was the third principal, however, who stole the show. The part of the ignored and functionless vice president, Alexander Throttlebottom, went to Victor Moore, who turned in the performance of his career, adding a touch of pathos to this forlorn, unrecognised character who could only gain admission to the White House by joining a conducted tour, and couldn't join the Washington Public Library because he couldn't provide two references.

The show was due to begin its first tryout at the Majestic Theatre in Boston on 8 December, but five days before that George and Ira had another premiere when the film *Delicious* was released. Fox had re-orchestrated the songs and cut George's 'New York Rhapsody' from six minutes down to one. As one critic wrote, in the magazine *Outlook And Independent*: "George Gershwin is said to have written the music involved, but you'd never know it."

The Boston tryout made up for all that. The show was already in fine shape, George conducted the orchestra for the first night, and the audience greeted the show with enthusiasm. The title song offended nobody. On the contrary, its first line became a catchphrase, with members of the audience greeting each other in the corridors and foyer by saying, "Of thee I sing, baby!"

Boston's toughest critic, HT Parker of the *Transcript*, gave it what was possibly the most favourable review of his life, saying:

> From half-past eight to a quarter to twelve the first audience rejoiced unflaggingly in what was set before it. We who are fond and foolish, and so ambitious for the American theatre, went home with the warming sense that a new play had enlarged it. Hitherto our theatre has produced nothing like Mr Kaufman's and Mr Gershwin's musical play. It is a long, brave step upward in the progress of such pieces from characterless, threadbare convention to lively reflection of our life and comment upon it. For once, in its modest way, Boston is the seat of a theatre event.

Kaufman, who up to the first performance had been convinced, as usual, that they had a flop on their hands, heaved a sigh of relief. He became so grateful to all concerned that after the second or third night of the tryout he offered to sell Ira a share in the show (George and Morris Ryskind already had stakes in it). Ira borrowed two-and-a-half thousand dollars from George and bought a five per cent share (the show had cost eighty-eight thousand dollars to mount – fifty thousand cash, the rest credit). Within a few months Ira was able to repay the loan, and eventually he made an additional profit of around eleven thousand dollars.

The show opened at the Music Box in New York on 26 December. Again George conducted for the first night, and again all the critics were unanimous in its praise. With one curious and solitary exception – Kaufman's old friend Robert Benchley, by now reviewing plays for the *New Yorker*, wrote: "The whole thing, during great stretches, was reminiscent of an old Hasty Pudding 'scoop' in which lese majesty was considered funny enough in itself without straining for any more mature elements of comedy." ('Hasty Pudding' refers to the Harvard student society's annual revue).

Benchley's attitude is interesting in that it is the exact equivalent in comedy to the heavyweight music critics' attitude to George. Benchley was a major humorist, well grounded in the humour of the past, and it is hard for someone who has read Swift or Voltaire to take *Of Thee I Sing* very seriously as trenchant satire. In the last analysis, it was simply very good entertainment, and much of its success rested on the old truth 'If you make people think, they'll hate you, but if you make them think they're thinking, they'll love you'.

Even in the midst of the Depression, *Of Thee I Sing* did amazingly well. It had the longest New York run of any Gershwin show and, in spite of all Kaufman's hits it was the first of his shows to run for over a year – for four-hundred-and-forty-one performances. By the time it had been running a year it had been seen by four-hundred-and-fifty-thousand people and had grossed over one million, four-hundred-thousand dollars. Not bad for a show costing eighty-eight thousand dollars to mount.

After the New York run the company went on tour, then returned to reopen on Broadway on 15 May 1933. During the original Broadway run a second touring company had also been formed. Beginning in Chicago, it toured successfully for eight months. No other Gershwin show ever had two productions running concurrently.

One night, during the first Broadway run, George and Kaufman were standing at the back of the stalls watching the show, and during the gentle reprise of 'Who Cares?' Kaufman was surprised to see that some of the audience had tears in their eyes. "What's the matter with them?" he whispered to George. "Don't they know we're kidding love?"

"You're doing nothing of the kind," said George. "You may think you're kidding love, but when Wintergreen faces impeachment to stand by the girl he loves, that's championing love. And the audience realises it even if you don't." To his horror he saw a shadow of real pain pass across Kaufman's face. It was gone almost at once, but George, always sensitive to the feelings of others and aware that Kaufman was trapped in an unsatisfactory marriage, realised that, as he later told a friend, he'd touched a nerve that he hadn't intended to touch at all. Swiftly he changed the subject by complaining that the music in the next scene was being played too fast.

Once *Of Thee I Sing* was triumphantly launched, George was able to turn his attention back to the 'Second Rhapsody', and a month after the opening, on 29 January 1932, he gave it its world premiere in Boston, with the Boston Symphony Orchestra, conducted by Serge Koussevitsky.

Writing about the genesis of the piece, he said: "I had seven weeks in California. The amount of music which the picture required was small and quickly written. The parties and night life of Hollywood did not interest me in the least. They bored me in fact. Here was my chance to do some serious work. Seven weeks of almost uninterrupted opportunity to write the best music I could possibly think of! What a chance!"

Describing it to biographer Isaac Goldberg at the time he was composing the original version for *Delicious*, he had written: "There is no programme to the 'Rhapsody'. As the part of the picture where it is to be played takes place in many streets of New York, I used as a starting-point what I called 'a rivet theme' but, after that, I just wrote a piece of music without a programme."

The Boston premiere went well. The audience received the piece with enthusiasm, and after the performance Koussevitsky met George backstage in the artists' room and told him he was a genius. The critics, however, were not so sure. The stern HT Parker wrote: "The 'Second Rhapsody' seemed tempered and in degree denatured by reflections and manipulation. It sounded over-often from the study table and the piano rack... The motives... lack the arresting and driving qualities of the First, but the rhythmic, melodic, harmonic, and instrumental expansion is more inventive and skilful... Mr Gershwin waxes in craftsmanship but at the cost of earlier and irresistible élan." Another critic wrote: "Humdrum, with emphasis on the last syllable."

A week later, on 5 February, and still with Serge Koussevitsky and the Boston Symphony Orchestra, George premiered the 'Second Rhapsody' in New York.

In January, Oscar Levant, after some dithering, had married Barbara Wooddell, and thus was spending less time around George. Nonetheless, he came with him to the New York premiere to lend moral support. After the reactions of most of the Boston critics, George was apprehensive about the reception the piece would get in his native city.

Alone with Oscar in the green room before the performance, George became so nervous, his 'composer's stomach' plaguing him, that Oscar suggested he relax by playing some of the tunes they both liked on the green room piano. George at the piano, he knew, was George happy.

Sitting down, George began to play, and for the next half hour he lost himself in a parade of his songs. Then the call-boy knocked on the door shouting, "Ready, Mr Gershwin!"

George, in his nervousness, rounded on Oscar. "Now look what you've done!" he shouted. "I haven't had time to warm up!" Oscar was both hurt and amused.

The New York critics were kinder than those in Boston had been. One of them, Lawrence Gilman, wrote: "Jazzarella, undiminished in gusto and vitality, dances here... The happy few will recognise and value the skill of her evolutions and the subtlety of her guile... Music's most enlivened daughter is, as usual, bringing down the house."

That was better, but George was moving on from Jazzarella. At last, at the beginning of 1932, he felt he was almost ready to begin work on an opera.

CHAPTER ELEVEN

'Let 'Em Eat Cake'

A t the beginning of 1932, George resumed his correspondence with DuBose Heyward. In a letter dated 29 March, he said that, after considering various ideas for compositions, his mind kept coming back to *Porgy*, which had made the most outstanding play he knew about black Americans. He was setting off for Europe in just over a week, but would like to discuss the idea of setting *Porgy* to music before he went, if DuBose would phone him.

DuBose did phone. He was glad to hear from George on two counts. First, because he welcomed the idea of collaborating with him on an opera, and second, because he was suffering financially from the Depression and would be glad of the chance to make some money. He reassured George that the operatic rights to *Porgy* were still free and clear.

George, with all his usual commitments, didn't set off for Europe as planned. Nor did he immediately get round to working on *Porgy*. But what he did do in preparation was to start taking a series of lessons in composition from a well-known New York music tutor called Dr Joseph Schillinger. What he wanted was to improve his ability at manipulating musical themes and rhythms, so that he could keep musical continuity while sustaining interest over a longer work.

Schillinger was a musical theorist. His theory was basically that all great works were composed in accordance with discoverable mathematical principles. By analysing the melodies, harmonies, rhythms, orchestrations and forms of great compositions of the past, covering all styles and eras, he had evolved a set of such principles.

In his tuition he made use of formulas and slide-rules, and his exercises, laid out on graph-paper, had forbidding titles like 'Rhythmic Groups Resulting From The Interference Of Several Synchronised Periodicities'. Composition, using the Schillinger method, became largely a matter of calculation.

George became fascinated by the intricate mathematical patterns that Schillinger found in music, and he became as enthusiastic about the system as a boy with a new toy, extolling Schillinger's theories to anyone who would listen. Including Oscar Levant, who consistently made fun of them.

In Oscar's opinion, Schillinger's highly-systemised tuition consisted of the "reduction of all musical procedures, from the most formidable to the least imposing, to a mathematical system... [it was the] compositional equivalent of playing the piano in six easy lessons."

Composer Vernon Duke was also sceptical. "You don't understand," George told him. "I used to do all kinds of things – harmony and counterpoint, I mean – I thought they were just parlour tricks. They always went great at parties. Now they'll go right into my music."

In spite of his friends' reservations about the Schillinger method, which it is only fair to say has been taught in several major universities and conservatories, George was stimulated by the intellectual effort involved in learning it, and delighted to find that for him it worked. He started going to Dr Schillinger for three ninety-minute lessons a week, and would continue to keep in touch with him and seek his advice throughout the next four years.

He began going to more and more concerts and recitals, and he began reading up on musical history and theory. Ever since he became obsessed by music in his teens he had enjoyed reading about it, and with his retentive memory would often amaze his friends with obscure facts about pieces or performances or the lives of composers, but now he began to buy up every book he could lay his hands on. It was all part of his continual urge to improve.

On 2 May 1932, at around the time he started his lessons, it was announced that the Pulitzer Prize committee at Columbia University would award that year's drama award to the writers of *Of Thee I Sing*.

There had been rumours that the show was being considered for this prestigious writing award since the day it had opened, but everybody, especially Kaufman, had dismissed the idea. As he pointed out, the award had never been given to a musical, only to straight plays, and that season's crop also included Philip Barry's *The Animal Kingdom*, Robert E Sherwood's *Reunion In Vienna*, Elmer Rice's *Counsellor-at-Law* and Eugene O'Neill's *Mourning Becomes Electra*.

Fortunately for *Of Thee I Sing*, the Pulitzer committee had for some years been dissatisfied with the narrow rules, established in Pulitzer's will, that governed the award (such as insisting that dramas should be those "raising the standards of good morals, good taste, and good manners").

The previous year they had awarded it to Eugene O'Neill's stark play about incest, *Strange Interlude*, and this year they bent the rules again by announcing that musicals were plays. They did, however, remain sufficiently respectful of tradition to restrict the award to the words of the piece, not its music. After all, the Pulitzer awards were all supposed to be for 'Letters'. Thus Kaufman and Ryskind and Ira won it, not George.

As a result of the award, the text and songs of *Of Thee I Sing* were published in book form, in a series edited by the critic George Jean Nathan and called *The Theatre Of Today Dramatic Library*. It was the first American musical comedy to be published in book form, and it outsold all the other titles in the series.

George may not have had his music published in that book, but in the same month as the Pulitzer Prize announcement, May 1932, eighteen of his songs were published by Random House in a limited edition of three hundred copies, under the title *George Gershwin's Song Book*.

This was actually a project of another firm of publishers, Simon & Schuster, who would publish it in an open edition the following September. They had been after George since 1929 to assemble such a book, urging him to get down on paper some of the wonderful variations he played. Gradually, during 1931 and the first part of 1932, he had written out improvisations on eighteen of his favourite songs.

These were 'Swanee', 'Nobody But You', 'I'll Build A Stairway To Paradise', 'Do It Again', 'Fascinating Rhythm', 'Oh, Lady Be Good', 'Somebody Loves Me', 'Sweet And Low Down', 'That Certain Feeling', 'The Man I Love', 'Clap Yo' Hands', 'Do, Do, Do', 'My One And Only', "S'Wonderful', 'Strike Up The Band!', 'Liza', 'I Got Rhythm' and 'Who Cares?'. The songs were printed in their original sheet music arrangements as well as in the more complex piano variations, which were dedicated to his friend Kay Swift.

George was still planning to make a trip to Europe, but his plans had to be cancelled when, on 14 May, Morris Gershwin suddenly died. George, always emotionally reticent, never expressed any grief. His letters and public utterances at the time speak only of his work and future plans. Whatever bereavement he felt at losing a father for whom he always had great affection remained securely locked within.

A week later, on the twentieth, George wrote again to DuBose Heyward, disappointing him by saying he wouldn't be able to start work on *Porgy* until he'd completed another musical for Aarons & Freedley, which was scheduled to open the following January. After that, however, he'd be free.

This musical had come about in rather a hurry. Alex Aarons had rather precipitately signed exclusive contracts with Jack Buchanan (at three thousand dollars a week) and Lyda Roberti (at one thousand dollars a week), guaranteeing each of them at least eight weeks' work in a show. So, as he told Vinton Freedley, they needed a show in a hurry. Together they hired writer Herbert Fields to provide one.

At the beginning of June, while waiting for Fields to come up with a plot, George made up for missing his trip to Europe by taking a short holiday in Cuba. His companions on the trip were three friends – Ev Jacobs, Emil Mosbacher and the writer Bennett Cerf. They were staying at the old Almedares Hotel in Havana and, at four on their first morning, they were wakened by a sixteen-piece rumba band, which had heard of George's arrival and come to serenade outside his bedroom window. Not only George and his friends were wakened. Several other guests were too, and checked out of the hotel next day in outrage. But George was flattered, and decided he'd write a rumba of his own.

He was less flattered by an attractive young Cuban woman he met during his stay and made a date with for luncheon. She didn't show up, but that afternoon he went to the Yacht Club and there she was on the terrace. "Hey," he said, "you stood me up today." The girl was pleased to see him, but apologetic. "Oh," she said, "I meant to phone and tell you I couldn't meet you, but I simply couldn't think of your name." This depressed George for days.

He listened to a lot of Cuban music, fascinated by the rhythms of the bands and the dancers and by the native percussion instruments. Like the taxi horns, he took a selection of these back to New York with him, and immediately set about composing his rumba. As usual he started by writing a two-piano version. This took him three weeks, finishing on 9 July.

It was at around this time that the second company of *Of Thee I Sing* was due to open in Chicago. In this production, Wintergreen was played by Oscar Shaw, Throttlebottom by Donald Meek and Mary Turner by a young actress called Harriet Lake, who later became more famous as Ann Sothern.

Oscar Levant's brother Harry had been hired to conduct the orchestra, and when George and Ira went there to look over the production before the opening, they invited Oscar to go with them. Oscar, who was finding that marriage to Barbara Wooddell was less effective at lifting him out of his natural gloom than hanging around with the Gershwins, swiftly accepted. Barbara, who had a small part in the Broadway production, stayed behind in New York.

The Chicago production presented no problems and George, after taking over the conductor's baton from Harry Levant for the opening night, returned to New York and began orchestrating his rumba. He began on 1 August and had the whole job completed on the ninth.

The work is in three sections. It opens with a rhythm that is part rumba and part habanera, and then a Cuban-style theme appears in the strings. There follows a section in three-part counterpoint (probably resulting, like much of the piece, from George's studies with Schillinger). This soon combines, still in counterpoint, with fragments of the first theme.

A clarinet cadenza leads into the sad and reflective second section, which is mostly a two-part canon played over a harmonic background. After this builds to a climax, the third section begins, suddenly faster again and with phrases from the previous sections overlapping each other, finally leading back into the first theme. As a coda, the piece builds into an exciting rumba, for which George used the percussion instruments he had picked up in Havana – the cuban stick, the bondo, the gourd, and the maracas.

A week after he had finished the orchestration, on 15 August, the piece was given its premiere at the Lewisohn Stadium, as part of the first-ever all-

Gershwin concert, given by the New York Philharmonic Orchestra.

The concert was to begin with 'Strike Up The Band!', conducted by Bill Daly. This would be followed by the 'Concerto In F', also conducted by Daly, after which Albert Coates was to take over the baton for 'An American In Paris'. Daly would conduct the 'Rhapsody In Blue', Coates the 'Second Rhapsody' and 'Rumba', and then Daly would return to conduct a medley of four of George's songs as a finale – 'Fascinating Rhythm', 'The Man I Love', 'Liza' and 'I Got Rhythm'.

George, already down to play the solo piano for 'Rhapsody In Blue' and 'Second Rhapsody', did not think he could also manage the 'Concerto In F', so he asked Oscar to play it. There would be no pay, but to Oscar that was irrelevant. He felt overwhelmed by the honour. And although he knew the invitation arose from necessity, at last he felt he was accepted by George as a colleague.

The concert went off well. George was elated. Next day he wrote to a friend, saying: "I really believe that last night was the most exciting I ever had. First, because the Philharmonic Orchestra played an entire evening of my music and, second, because the all-time record for the Stadium Concerts was broken. I have just gotten the figures: seventeen-thousand-eight-hundred-and-forty-five people paid to get in, and just five thousand were at the closed gates trying to fight their way in – unsuccessfully."

Among the five thousand trying to get in, Oscar spotted an old friend, unrecognisable without his stage costume of curly wig, battered topper, trench coat and motor horn, who was trying to sneak in through a back entrance. It was Adolph Marx, more widely known as Harpo. Somehow Oscar managed to provide him with a ticket.

The audience of over seventeen thousand, however, Oscar found unnerving. As usual in his life, none of his family was among them, not even his wife Barbara, with whom he was having one of their all-too-frequent arguments. Clearly it was an audience entirely composed of Gershwin fans, because they greeted every number and every performer with loud and prolonged applause. Oscar had never played for an audience of that size before, and he found out he didn't like it. He had eaten a meal that afternoon with George and Bill Daly and, in the not-very private dressing room backstage, he threw it up.

Although nearly crippled with stage-fright, he played well. So well that, as soon as he finished, George's mother, Rose, came up to him and looked him straight in the eye and said, "Promise me you won't get any better." The 'Concerto In F' would become his favourite Gershwin piece and, once the ordeal of playing it was over, he found himself thoroughly enjoying the evening.

A few days later, when he next visited the Gershwins', he was still glowing with elation. George greeted him with what Oscar described as "a small boy smile ... his hands clasped behind his back".

"What would you rather have," he asked, "money or a watch?" As he spoke, he handed Oscar a handsome art deco watch with a rectangular face. On its back was inscribed:

From George to Oscar
Lewisohn Stadium
August 15, 1932

"It is by this watch," Oscar liked to say, "that I have been late for every important appointment since then. But I'm grateful now that I didn't get what I would have preferred then – the money." He wore it till its numbers became an indecipherable blur. But the stage-fright he had felt at the Lewisohn Stadium would prevent him going anywhere near the concert platform for the next five years.

The 'Rumba' had been well-received. George didn't think it had been heard to good advantage, its tone colours and percussive effects being muddied and dissipated by the poor acoustics of the open-air stadium, but several critics had liked it. One of them, Pitts Sanborn, considered it fresh and spontaneous, and superior in rhythmic inventiveness to Ravel's 'Boléro' (written four years earlier).

Not long after the concert, Herbert Fields came up with the book for the Aarons and Freedley musical. It was to be called *Pardon My English* and, as well as starring Jack Buchanan, who was English, and Lyda Roberti, who was Hungarian, it now also included actor George Givot, who was Greek, and Jack Pearl, who was a German-American comic, his catch-phrase being "Vas you dere, Sharlie?".

The plot that Herbert Fields had concocted involved a pair of actors being mistaken for swindlers, and a kleptomaniac who marries the daughter of the chief of police. The ill-assorted collection of accents in the cast had been difficult for him to fit into a plot, and it was now going to do no favours for the crisp delivery of Ira's lyrics. When George and Ira began work on the score, which they did in September 1933, it was with some reluctance. Both agreed that they were only involved in this as a favour to Aarons and Freedley.

Among the twenty numbers they wrote, sixteen would end up in the show, among them one that again showed the influence of Dr Schillinger. This was a piano piece, 'Two Waltzes In C', in which George tried the experiment of introducing counterpoint and countermelody to the Broadway stage.

Early in September, while George was still writing the score for *Pardon My English*, he received a letter from DuBose Heyward, telling him that the Theatre Guild, which had presented the play *Porgy*, was anxious to mount a musical based on it, and that Al Jolson had for a long time been keen to play the title role (in blackface). He had even, a couple of years before, performed an excerpt from the play on his radio programme. DuBose assumed that George would already have been discussing the opera project with some producer, and wondered whether this would conflict with the Guild's interest.

The Theatre Guild, which had a distinguished reputation, had grown out of the Washington Square Players, a semi-amateur group of aspiring playwrights, actors, directors and producers who had got together in 1915, many of them working for nothing, to present plays they considered to be of artistic merit, regardless of their commercial potential.

After America entered the Great War in 1917, they soon had to disband, because many of their key members entered the armed forces. After the war, in 1919, they re-formed, under the title 'The Theatre Guild'. Now things were on a more business-like basis. Their shows were mounted to professional standards and, as their basic audience they had a group of Guild members who subscribed enough to guarantee each production a four-week run.

They were helped to get going by Otto Kahn, who lent them the Garrick Theatre rent-free to mount their first production, a play by Jacinto Benavente called *The Bonds Of Interest*. This did outstandingly well because during its run there was a strike by Actors' Equity, which closed down all the companies playing on Broadway except the Theatre Guild. This, being a co-operative, was deemed exempt.

The money the Guild made from *The Bonds Of Interest* established it fairly firmly and it settled down to a run of highly-regarded plays, by the likes of Shaw and Strindberg. It was an impressive list of plays, except for the fact that the Guild was able to find almost none good enough that had been written by an American. This was why they had been so pleased to present *Porgy*.

George wrote back to DuBose, saying that he found it "very interesting that Al Jolson would like to play the part of Porgy, but I really don't know how he would be in it. Of course he is a very big star, who certainly knows how to put over a song, and it might mean more to you financially if he were to do it – provided the rest of the production were well done. The sort of thing I had in mind for *Porgy* is a much more serious thing than Jolson could ever do."

He went on to express his continuing interest in basing an opera on *Porgy*, but that writing it as well as he wanted to would take time, and "be more a labour of love than anything else". Bearing this in mind, he continued: "If you can see your way to making some ready money from Jolson's version I don't know that it would hurt a later version done by an all-coloured cast."

He finished by saying that he had not so far discussed the proposed opera with any producer, his idea being to "write the work first and then see who would be the best one to do it".

DuBose's literary agent, Audrey Wood, was also pressing George. A few weeks later, on 14 October, she phoned him to say that she was being harassed by Al Jolson, who was more anxious than ever to play Porgy, and she wanted to know what George's interest was in the piece.

As a result of this conversation, George again wrote to DuBose, reaffirming his previous view that "if Jolson wanted to do the play and that it meant more money for you I saw no objection to it in view of the fact that Jolson couldn't do an operatic version of it anyway. His version would undoubtedly be the play as you wrote it with the addition of perhaps a few songs... I don't want to stand in the way of your making some money with your property at the present time, and... I don't believe that it would hurt a serious operatic version in any way."

There was one thing George didn't know at that time, which was as well for his peace of mind. This was that the Theatre Guild, urged by Jolson, had now approached Jerome Kern and Oscar Hammerstein II, both fresh from *Show Boat*, to write the score for their proposed production. A version of *Porgy* with a score by Kern and Hammerstein might well turn out too close to George's proposed opera for comfort.

DuBose replied to George almost at once, saying that he had just learned that he was "in a fairly tight spot financially" (not only did he and his wife now have a daughter, he had also lodged much of his savings in a New York bank and the bank had been closed by the Depression). He said he was grateful for George's attitude, which he thought was splendid. It made him more eager than ever for the two of them to collaborate sometime, as planned, but at present he was releasing the rights in *Porgy* to Jolson. It was possible that any plans for an opera might have to be postponed indefinitely.

George's thoughts of writing an opera went on hold. He carried on working on the score for *Pardon My English*, taking time out to involve himself in a benefit concert, given by the Musicians' Symphony Orchestra at the Metropolitan Opera House, on 1 November.

The first half of this concert was given over to César Franck's 'Symphony In D Minor', conducted by Sandor Harmati. The second half was all Gershwin. It began with Bill Daly conducting the 'Concerto In F', this time with George at the piano. Then Daly conducted the medley of four Gershwin songs that had been used to end the concert at the Lewisohn Stadium.

After that, George took over the baton to conduct 'An American In Paris' and 'Rumba', to which he had now given the title 'Cuban Overture'. His reason for this was that "When people read 'Rumba' they expect the 'Peanut Vendor' or a like piece of music. 'Cuban Overture' gives a more just idea of the character and intent of the music."

This concert gave rise to an unfortunate incident. Bill Daly had helped George with writing the orchestrations for the four songs in the medley, and the short passages linking them. During rehearsal, a trumpeter played something during one of these passages that puzzled him. "Did I write that there?" he said. This remark led one of the viola players in the orchestra, Allan Langley, to believe that Bill had had a hand in all of George's compositions. As a result, he wrote an article for the *American Spectator*, a four-page monthly founded and edited by George Jean Nathan.

The article was entitled "The Gershwin Myth", and in it Langley heavily criticised George's concert work, saying rather mysteriously that it was full of "blatant orchestrations" and "transparent anachronisms". He said the

'Concerto In F' was "disgusting", and ended by suggesting that men like Ferde Grofé and Bill Daly did much of George's composing.

"As for 'An American In Paris'," he wrote, "the genial Daly was constantly in rehearsal attendance, both as repétiteur and adviser, and any member of the orchestra could testify that he knew far more about the score than Gershwin. The point is that no previous claimant to honours in symphonic composition has ever presented so much argument and controversy as to whether his work was his own or not."

George seemed unmoved by this attack, but Bill Daly was furious on his behalf. He wrote a long letter to the New York *Times*, which it published in the following January.

> I thank Mr Langley for the compliment, but I neither wrote nor orchestrated the 'American'. My only contribution consisted of a few suggestions about reinforcing the score here and there, and I'm not sure that Gershwin, probably with good reason, accepted them. But then, Gershwin receives many such suggestions from his many friends to whom he always plays his various compositions, light or symphonic, while they are in the process of being written. Possibly Mr Langley feels we all get together (and we'd have to meet in the Yankee Stadium) and write Mr Gershwin's music for him.
>
> In fine," it went on, "I have never written one note of any of his compositions, or so much as orchestrated one whole bar of his symphonic works.

George, while Bill was composing this angry rebuttal, was involved in *Pardon My English*, which was turning out to be a disaster, mainly because of its feeble plot. By the time it opened at the Alvin Theatre, on 20 January 1933, it was without Jack Buchanan, who had walked out after the Boston tryout (George's 'Two Waltzes In C' left the production then too).

It lasted on Broadway for just forty-six performances, then closed, leaving Aarons and Freedley with debts totalling seventy-five thousand dollars. Freedley swiftly fled to Panama to escape their creditors, and lay low there for several months. The whole episode caused such bitterness between the two partners that they split up. *Pardon My English* was the end of Aarons and Freedley.

For Aarons, it was also the end of his career on Broadway. He went to Hollywood, involving himself as Associate Producer on such musicals as *Broadway Melody Of 1936* and died in 1943.

George did find some good in *Pardon My English*. He became emotionally involved with one of the girls in the chorus, an affair that, while brief, was sufficiently serious for him to consider marrying her. He dropped the idea after hearing her play some of his tunes on the piano, knowing that there was no way he could live with that kind of piano playing.

The failure of *Pardon My English* meant that several good songs in it by George and Ira went unremembered. There was 'My Cousin From Milwaukee', 'Lorelei' and a witty conversational ballad called 'Isn't It A Pity?'.

George was always fiercely defensive of these songs. A few months afterwards, he and a group of friends were holidaying at a country house and sunbathing nude in the garden. Bennett Cerf, who was among the party, said in the course of conversation that he thought the score for *Pardon My English* had been below par. Immediately George leapt up and insisted everybody come inside while he proved different. As Cerf later wrote: "I can still see him sitting at the piano, stark naked, playing the songs and singing them, too, at the top of his voice. George belonged at the piano. I have never seen a man happier, more bursting with the joy of living, than George when he was playing his songs."

Early in 1933, at around the time of *Pardon My English*, George moved house, giving up Riverside Drive and moving into a more spacious penthouse apartment at 132 East Seventy-Second Street. Ira and Lee moved into an apartment across the street, at number 125. These apartments were naturally not connected by a terrace, so, in order to work together more efficiently, the brothers had a private telephone line installed, linking them.

George, in spite of the fact that his main motivation was music and not money, was now considerably well-off, and this new apartment, a duplex, was impressive. George was proud of it, and enjoyed showing it off. It had fourteen rooms, one of them being a huge panelled reception hall, and another having in it the biggest bar anyone had ever seen, made of glass (Prohibition would be repealed in December that year).

There was a work room, a gymnasium, an art studio, an English-style den, a box room, a sleeping porch with jalousies and a high-ceilinged living room hung with the paintings he had collected (although at around the time he moved many of these took a leave of absence, when the Chicago Art Club honoured his collection by presenting much of it in a show). Also on the walls of the apartment, both in the living room and the work room, were hung examples of his own work, prominent among them a portrait of his father.

The work room contained a desk that had been designed specially to suit his requirements. It was wide enough to support large manuscript paper, and it had all sorts of racks and compartments for pens, pencils, rulers, erasers, etc. Also in the room were two Steinway pianos, standing side by side.

George's taste had developed since he moved into Riverside Drive five years before, and this apartment was not decorated in such a severe and uncompromising modern style. It was still modern, but the lines and colours were more restrained, and the furniture was of more traditional design.

It was also unlike Riverside Drive in that, in spite of having fourteen rooms, not one of them was a guest room. Oscar Levant, who by now was divorced from Barbara Wooddell, was one of the few of George's friends who was given a key.

After moving, George and Ira got back to work. The team that had created *Of Thee I Sing* had been reassembled to make a sequel. This time, Kaufman and Ryskind had decided to attack the world of politics even more fiercely, satirising the attitudes of the Left and the Right, and the dangerous foolishness of political enthusiasm in general.

The show they wrote was called *Let 'Em Eat Cake*, and its plot involved many of the characters from *Of Thee I Sing*. In a torchlit opening, John P Wintergreen and his sidekicks, who got into the White House by staging beauty contests and invoking parental love, are contesting the next election against the candidate of the other party, John P Tweedledee.

Tweedledee wins and becomes president. Wintergreen and a former cabinet colleague, Louis Lippman, find themselves unemployed. Being unskilled in any way of earning a living, they use the savings of Alexander Throttlebottom to set up a business manufacturing 'Maryblue' shirts. Because of the Depression, the business does poorly and, in order to boost sales, Wintergreen goes down to Union Square, where soapbox agitators harangue the public. There, allying himself with one of the agitators, named Kruger, he starts a Blue Shirt movement, preaching revolution.

The movement catches on, its members buying a lot of blue shirts and forming themselves into an army. The army marches on Washington and, in a *coup d'état*, Tweedledee is evicted from office and dictatorship of the proletariat is established, under the leadership of Wintergreen. He has promised the Blue Shirt troops that if they evict Tweedledee he will collect America's foreign war debts for them. He tries, but the nations that owe these debts refuse to pay. To settle the matter, a baseball game is organised between nine representatives of the League of Nations and nine members of the Supreme Court.

Throttlebottom is appointed umpire and, when he makes a decision in favour of the League of Nations, he is hauled before a military tribunal and sentenced to be guillotined (as good revolutionaries, the Blue Shirts have imported a guillotine from France, just in case). Then Kruger takes over the reins of government, making America a military dictatorship, and sentences Wintergreen to be guillotined as well. His wife Mary comes to comfort him, and Kruger tells her cynically that announcing a pregnancy "may have worked four years ago, but it won't work now".

Throttlebottom is about to be beheaded when Mary saves the day by leading on stage a fashion show. This proves so fascinating to the Blue Shirts that it disrupts the proceedings. With the Blue Shirts in disarray, Wintergreen restores democracy to government, then decides to return to the shirt business. Thus the ineffective Throttlebottom becomes president.

This script was written when Hitler's brown shirts had just come to power in Germany. It is a long way from the light-hearted musicals of only a few years before, and even a considerable step forward from *Of Thee I Sing*. That had satirised an aspect of American politics as it was; *Let 'Em Eat Cake* was like a nightmare vision of a possible future.

In the thirties, the two perceived political nightmares to Americans were communism and fascism. *Let 'Em Eat Cake* attacks both, with additional sideswipes at the right-wing Daughters of the American Revolution and the left-wing Union League. All seriously committed politics is suspect.

The songs that George and Ira produced for the show rose to the occasion. George at last managed to use the idea of counterpointing two anthems, beginning the show (as before) with 'Wintergreen For President', but this time behind it rises the competing theme 'Tweedledee For President'.

That was not the only such piece. As George said, writing about *Let 'Em Eat Cake*: "I've written most of the show contrapuntally, and it is that very insistence on the sharpness of a form that gives my music the acid touch it has – which points the words of the lyrics, and is in keeping with the satire of the piece."

The show's one ballad, 'Mine', sung by John and Mary Wintergreen (and the chorus), is a notable example of counterpoint, having both a melody and a counter-melody (and a counter-lyric). George had originally written the music as an exercise for one of his lessons with Schillinger.

Other outstanding songs included Kruger's rabble-rousing number 'Down With Everything That's Up'. This was preceded, for contrast, by a calm ensemble number sung by the summer-afternoon strollers in Union Square (which is what it was called).

Once the Blue Shirt movement begins, it has its rallying-song, which of course is 'Let 'Em Eat Cake'. Even Throttlebottom has a song, 'Comes The Revolution', and the songs associated with the various major characters and movements recur throughout the show in a counterpoint of their own.

At the beginning of Act Two, after the Blue Shirt movement has taken over the country (and the set and costumes are all in shades of blue), there is a sweet but slightly threatening ballad, 'Blue, Blue, Blue'. Interestingly, the tune for this had been written by George some time before, and was reposing in his files when Ira remembered it. It was a strain that George was fond of. He felt that some day he might make more of it, and at first was reluctant to donate it to the show. Eventually he gave in gracefully, and Ira used it well.

All in all, their score for *Let 'Em Eat Cake* is arguably the best that George and Ira ever wrote. Certainly it is their best-integrated. Which makes it all the sadder that *Let 'Em Eat Cake* was another flop. It started its tryouts on 2 October 1933, at the Shubert Theatre in Boston, and had its New York premiere on 21 October at the Imperial Theatre, running there for only ninety performances.

It was a flop even though it had many of the same ingredients as the massively successful *Of Thee I Sing*. Produced by Sam Harris, with a book by Kaufman and Ryskind, and songs by George and Ira, it had a cast including William Gaxton as Wintergreen, Lois Moran as Mary, and Victor Moore as Alexander Throttlebottom.

Several things prevented it from being a success. First, it was a sequel. This so disposed the glittering first night audience of invitees to be critical, even before the curtain went up, that the usually benign Sam Harris told *Variety* afterwards that, in future, first nights for his shows would be for "critics plus a paying audience, the receipts going to charity".

Another factor against its success was that many elements in it were dark and downbeat. Act Two, where everything was in shades of blue, was depressing to look at, even though dramatically effective. And to bring a guillotine on stage and threaten to behead the beloved Alexander Throttlebottom disconcerted the audience and alienated them.

Worst of all, the show was too topical. There had been revolutionary activity in Cuba, leading to US headlines such as "TOO CLOSE FOR COMFORT", and a show featuring a successful proletarian revolution was indeed that. And of course there was Hitler in Germany.

Dramatically, the main weakness in the show was its ending, where the flight from reality towards a fashion show on the part of the characters seemed to reflect a similar flight from reality by the writers. They had written themselves into a dark corner from which light-heartedness was no escape.

George and Ira put a lot into the three satirical musicals, *Strike Up The Band*, *Of Thee I Sing* and *Let 'Em Eat Cake*. They worked and re-worked their songs so carefully that they were no longer able to turn out musicals at the rate of three or four a year, as they had in the twenties.

The misfortune, so far as keeping George and Ira's work alive goes, is that the songs they wrote for those three shows are tightly integrated into their fabric. Almost none of them is remembered today because, unless the songs are seen in the context of the shows, they lose a lot of their strength and resonance. And none of the shows seems likely ever to be re-staged. Which is a pity, because they contain much of the Gershwins' best work.

CHAPTER TWELVE

'Porgy And Bess'

D uBose Heyward was still keen on collaborating with George on an opera based on his book and play. The Jolson-Kern-Hammerstein production was still in abeyance, due to the many commitments of Kern and Hammerstein, whose success with *Show Boat* had led to them being inundated with work. So, late in 1933, DuBose wrote again to George, saying that he wanted *Porgy* to become a folk opera, not a musical comedy. "I want you to tell me if you are really going to write that opera – and *soon*," he wrote. "If you are, I'm going to turn the [Theatre] Guild down definitely."

George replied that he was clearing his desk of all future projects, and intended to begin work on the opera early in 1934. Otto Kahn, still aware that George was likely to write it, at around the same time offered him a bonus of five thousand dollars if he signed a contract with the Metropolitan Opera to mount the production.

George considered this proposal seriously, but eventually rejected it. "The reason I did not submit this work to the usual sponsors of opera in America," he wrote at the time, "was that I hoped to develop something in American music that would appeal to the many rather than to the cultured few." He wanted his opera presented in a theatre, not in an opera house.

The Theatre Guild, now seeing the prospect of Al Jolson playing Porgy receding, were if anything even more keen on mounting a Gershwin opera. They had never produced an opera before, but in DuBose Heyward's words, "They had gambled once on *Porgy* and won... most certainly they did not want anyone else to do it, and so contracts were signed."

Jolson, Kern and Hammerstein withdrew, and George signed his contract with the Theatre Guild on 26 October 1933, five days after the New York opening of *Let 'Em Eat Cake*. On 3 November the Guild announced the planned production to the press, saying they hoped to have the opening the following autumn, which was a bit optimistic as George had not yet written a note. He warned them not to set any definite date.

In preparation for getting down to work, George installed a third Steinway at his apartment. A problem that still had to be resolved was how he and DuBose Heyward, who was writing both the book and the lyrics, were to work together. DuBose refused to leave Charleston and live in the North, and George could not for the time being leave New York, because he had just signed a radio contract to broadcast twice a week on station WJZ, mainly in order to support himself while he wrote *Porgy*.

His half-hour programme, called *Music By Gershwin*, earned him two thousand dollars a week. It was not scheduled to begin until Wednesday, 14 February, but after that it would appear every Wednesday and Friday until Friday, 1 June.

Its theme was 'The Man I Love', and on the programme George was the host, playing the piano, conducting the orchestra, and introducing not only his own music but that of younger composers and lyricists he admired, such as Harold Arlen, Dorothy Fields, Morton Gould, Richard Rodgers, Rube Bloom and Oscar Levant. There were live interviews and informal chat and, once, George even played a song by his younger brother, Arthur.

Although Arthur from time to time in his life was a salesman of motion picture films (with some success) and, later, a stockbroker, his heart, like George's, was in music. He once described himself as "a leading composer of unpublished songs", having written well over one-hundred-and-fifty. But not all went unpublished. Eventually he wrote the score for a musical comedy called *The Lady Says Yes*, which appeared on Broadway in 1945, running for eighty-seven performances.

George found his twice-weekly radio programme harder work than he had expected, what with having to select and rehearse (and often arrange) a dozen songs a week, as well as choosing guests and overseeing the scripts. He grew to detest the job, and matters weren't helped by the fact that the programme's sponsor was Feenamint, a popular laxative.

George's friends, aware of his 'composer's stomach', felt that he himself was hardly a great advertisement.

The solution to George and DuBose's collaboration difficulties turned out to be Ira. A system was evolved whereby George and DuBose would make occasional trips to visit each other, but that most of the time DuBose would post completed scenes and songs to George, who would sit down with Ira, writing the music while Ira polished the lyrics.

DuBose was keen to get going. On 12 November 1933, only two weeks after the Theatre Guild contract was signed, he posted to George two copies of his proposed first scene.

When they arrived, George was about to make a concert appearance with the Pittsburgh Symphony, so it took him over a week to reply. When he did, on 23 November, he wrote: "Think you have done a swell job, especially with the new lyrics," but went on to warn DuBose, who had suggested putting in more dialogue, that "there may be too much talk". He also admitted that, "On account of many things I have to do at present I haven't actually started composing."

The appearance with the Pittsburgh Symphony was to celebrate the tenth anniversary of 'Rhapsody In Blue'. George was to play both the 'Rhapsody' and the 'Concerto In F', and the orchestra was to be conducted by Bill Daly.

Unfortunately, Bill Daly was not free to attend the rehearsals, so George invited Oscar Levant to come with him and play the piano parts while he conducted and rehearsed the orchestra. They went by overnight train, sharing a drawing room. When the time came to go to bed, Gershwin, as if by right, got into the more comfortable lower berth. Levant clambered into the upper, and as he later wrote:

> I adjusted myself to the inconveniences of the upper berth, reflecting on the artistic-economic progression by which Paderewski has a private car, Gershwin a drawing room and Levant a sleepless night. At this moment my light must have disturbed George's doze, for he opened his eyes, looked up at me and said drowsily, "Upper berth – lower berth. That's the difference between talent and genius."

There was always this slight needle in the friendship between

195

George and Oscar. Oscar was envious of George's success and self-confidence, while George, who craved the acceptance of such serious-minded fellow composers as Aaron Copland, was well aware that whereas they tended to dismiss him as a mere composer of show-tunes, they greeted Oscar's few compositions with approval.

The Pittsburgh concert was only part of the tenth anniversary celebrations for 'Rhapsody In Blue'. As well as guesting with several other major orchestras, George himself, with the help of his manager, had organised a one-month tour that would cover twelve thousand miles, playing one-nighters in more than forty cities all over America, plus a short excursion into Canada. It was due to begin in Boston on 14 January, and he would be accompanied by the forty-piece Leo Reisman Band, one very similar in style and instrumentation to Paul Whiteman's. Charles Previn was to be the conductor and James Melton would tour as second pianist.

As preparation for the gruelling tour, George decided to take a short holiday in Florida, where he would stay with his friend Emil Mosbacher, who had gone with him to Havana, and who had now rented a house in Palm Beach. He also arranged to call in at Charleston on his way there, confer with DuBose Heyward and, if possible "see the town and hear some spirituals and perhaps go to a coloured cafe or two if there are any".

This was George's first visit to Charleston, the setting for *Porgy*. It was only for a day or so, and he knew he would need to be there longer if he was to get to know the town and its black population. He arranged to call on DuBose again for an overnight stop on his way back to New York, and suggested that once his radio series ended, in June, he would find somewhere to stay in Charleston and come down for a month or so to explore the area properly.

Once he got to Palm Beach, where he found Emil Mosbacher's rented house "charming", he did not entirely rest. He had decided that his forthcoming tour with the Leo Reisman Band, although it was in celebration of 'Rhapsody In Blue', should also have a new showpiece. One of his favourites among his songs had always been 'I Got Rhythm', and he settled down to create a set of variations on it for piano and orchestra. It says something for what he had already learned from Dr Schillinger that he composed much of this quite complex piece without getting anywhere near a piano.

On 2 January 1934, after spending New Year's Day with Emil Mosbacher, he set off to make his second flying visit to DuBose Heyward. There he did a bit more work on the 'Variations on "I Got Rhythm"' and, after he got back to New York he polished it off, completing it on 6 January and dedicating it to Ira.

It is scored for a full symphony orchestra, plus alto and tenor saxophones, banjo and Chinese gong. It opens with a four-note ascending phrase on the clarinet, taken from the first measure of the song. This theme is repeated by the piano, then by the full orchestra. The piano plays the complete chorus of the song, then the orchestra is used to develop a scintillating series of variations.

George had come a long way in his ability to develop a theme. His variations change the tune not only in structure, melody and rhythm, but also in mood. The first variation is full of animal energy, the second slow and sad. Others following are firm and aggressive, poignant and sonorous, or whirling and sparkling with festivity. The whole thing is a confident *tour-de-force*.

On 14 January, in Boston, the tour began. To make it, George had hired a special train to transport the more-than-fifty people involved, plus their instruments, equipment and luggage. Among George's equipment was his practice keyboard, a heavy instrument designed to rest on a table top. This, for the tour, he entrusted to a newcomer among his entourage, Paul Mueller.

Paul was a good looking and amiable young man who had been found by Kay Swift and hired by George as a general factotum. He would remain in that capacity for the rest of George's life. On the tour, his main jobs were to see that all the instruments arrived undamaged wherever they were due, to give George a daily massage to keep him in shape (seeing that on tour he would have to forgo his habitual tennis and golf), and to fend off the hordes of groupies, mainly members of local music clubs, who at every city made a bee-line for both George and the other featured pianist, James Melton.

"The tour," George wrote, "was a fine artistic success for me and would have been splendid financially if my foolish manager hadn't booked me into seven towns that were too small to support such an expensive organisation as I carried. Nevertheless, it was a very worthwhile thing for me to have done and I have many pleasant memories of cities I had not visited before."

Among the cities were Boston, Syracuse, Omaha, Detroit and Toronto, and the tour finished at the Academy of Music in Brooklyn, on Saturday, 10 February. By which time DuBose Heyward had sent George his first drafts of two more scenes – Act 2, Scene 1 and Act 2, Scene 2.

George, on his return to New York, got down to preparing his first radio broadcast, due to be transmitted on 14 February. It was at around this time that Kay Swift also got him to go into analysis. The analyst he went to, Dr Gregory Zilboorg, was one of the most fashionable in New York at the time. George went to him for a complex variety of reasons.

The main reason was his hope that perhaps his constipation had a mental cause, and that analysis could cure it. Another was that he was endlessly curious – analysis was enormously fashionable in America by 1934, everyone in society seemed to have at least one analyst, and George wanted to know what it was all about, if only to join in the conversation. There may also have been a nagging feeling deep inside him that he should be better able to relate to other people, to be less detached and inhibited.

Dr Zilboorg's eventual opinion, while keeping the details private, was that George's ailment was indeed rooted in a chronic neurosis. He was also able to tell George that it was an ailment not uncommon among musicians. And his analysis did help George to become a little less self-centred.

He continued going to Dr Zilboorg for about a year. They became friendly, and George once drew a pencil sketch of him, lying on a couch. Oscar Levant, as usual, scoffed. "Does it help your constipation, George?" he asked. "No," said George, "but now I understand why I have it."

It is ironic that Oscar himself eventually became addicted to analysis, having several analysts at a time for the rest of his life and preaching vehemently and knowledgeably to anyone who would listen (and many who wouldn't) on the benefits of psychiatry to the human race. Naturally, he had first entered psychotherapy in emulation of George. George, when he found out, was furious, accusing Oscar of imitating him.

Towards the end of February 1935, George at last began work on *Porgy*. DuBose Heyward's original novel was set among the black community of the port of Charleston. Charleston is a historic southern city (the first shot of the Civil War was fired there, at Fort Sumter), which in DuBose's youth was somewhat down on its luck, having suffered not only war, but also fire, earthquakes, hurricanes and declining trade.

Although DuBose himself came of white southern aristocracy, albeit somewhat impoverished, he knew the city's black community well. In the Charleston of his youth there were streets where both black and white families lived (black servants found it convenient to live close to the houses where they worked) and, as a boy, he had lived in one of these mixed-race streets.

It was near a wharf and many of the residents were stevedores. The neighbourhood was fairly calm during the week, but on Saturdays there were frequent whisky-soaked fights, often violent, and on Sundays there was sacred singing and boisterous adult baptisms.

The black population were Gullahs, a social group peculiar to South Carolina and Georgia. The word derives from 'Angola', whence many of them came (but not all – many also came from Sierra Leone) and they spoke in a patois of their own which had striking affinities with the languages of West Africa (it is still spoken today, but mainly on islands off the Carolina coast).

DuBose's mother, Jane, had been brought up on a plantation, surrounded by Gullah servants and their language and folklore fascinated her. So much so that in adult life she gave lectures to tourists visiting Charleston on the subject. One of the tales she told was of her childhood nurse Chloë, who had been brought from West Africa into slavery as a child. All that Chloë had to remind her of her African origins were a deeply-treasured string of beads and a little wooden doll she called 'Porgo'.

DuBose had heard about Chloë and her doll from childhood, and when he started his novel, he decided to call his central character 'Porgo'. His mother, Jane, who was still lecturing at this time and did not wish to seem to be cashing in on any success his novel might have, changed the name of the doll in her lectures to 'Gabo'. DuBose, with true southern gallantry, felt he could not usurp the name 'Porgo' all to himself. So he altered the name of his character to Porgy.

The character Porgy, as opposed to the name, was based on a local character named Sammy Smalls. One day, early in March 1924, DuBose happened on the following item in the Charleston *News And Courier*:

> Samuel Smalls, who is a cripple and is familiar to King Street, with his goat and cart, was held for the June term of Court of Sessions on an aggravated assault charge. It is alleged that on Saturday night he attempted to shoot Maggie Barnes at number four Romney Street. His shots went wide of the mark. Smalls was up on a similar charge some months ago and was given a suspended sentence. Smalls had attempted to escape in his wagon and was run down and captured by the police patrol.

"Just think of that old wreck having enough manhood to do a thing like that," DuBose said to his sister. He clipped out the item and kept it.

"Sammy was neither very virtuous nor very villainous," a Charleston resident who remembered him recalled. On the odd occasions he was arrested, he was a problem to the police. They had to arrest not just him, but also his cart and his goat. It was an extremely smelly goat, as everyone who remembered him remembered, and once the police had jailed Sammy they usually just let him go again quite soon.

Wherever he lived, it was probably not in Cabbage Row, which DuBose chose for the setting of his book and renamed 'Catfish Row', relocating it on the waterfront. Architecturally this was a decaying pair of buildings, not far from where DuBose himself lived. Inhabited entirely by blacks, and with an equally decaying courtyard behind, it was noisy, overcrowded, and troublesome to the police, who frequently had to deal with violent altercations.

'Cabbage Row' was only its unofficial name, acquired from the vegetable stalls that its shopkeepers set out on the street. Its actual address was 89-91 Church Street, and the reason why it was built the way it was, as two narrow tenement houses with an archway between, leading to a courtyard behind, was that at the time it was built, in the 1700s, houses in Charleston were taxed according to their street frontage. It had been built as a tenement from the start, and was not, as some have believed, a big house that had seen better days.

The plot of DuBose Heyward's novel, which has changed very little through its various transformations into a play, an opera and a film, is set in the early years of the twentieth century and tells of the crippled beggar, Porgy, and his love for the woman Bess.

Porgy, though crippled in the legs, has an upper body as strong as the stevedore he might have been. When, after he has become involved with Bess and the brutish character, Crown, comes to kill Porgy and reclaim her, Porgy is powerful enough to kill Crown instead.

The whole novel is crammed with colour and suspense. There is a brawl over a dice game in which Crown kills one of the other players. There is sex when, at a picnic, Crown reasserts his sexual hold over Bess and seduces her. There is 'happy dust', brought to Catfish Row by the dapper and dangerous Sportin' Life, who lures Bess away from Porgy, back to her old life of drink and drugs. And all the way through the book there are poetic images, like the buzzard that hovers over Catfish Row, presaging death, and a vicious hurricane that terrifies the inhabitants.

The book is set down in sharp and accurate detail, and one of the aspects of it that appealed to George, from the first moment he read it, is its constant awareness of music, of the music of spirituals, of sea shanties, of street sellers, of dances, of the blues.

One of the few changes made as the book mutated into a play and then into an opera was that it became Bess's story as well as Porgy's. The book was mostly told through Porgy's eyes. In the play, Bess grew into a more complex and tragic character.

In the play, too, the plausible bootlegger and drug-dealer, Sportin' Life, who barely appeared in the book, became a disturbing influence on Bess right from the start.

Most altered was the ending. In the book, Porgy's life is shattered when Bess leaves to go back to her old dissipated life in Savannah; in the opera it is the bright lights of New York she leaves for, and the story ends on a note of faint hope as Porgy sets out determinedly in his goat cart to find her.

DuBose Heyward's job, in turning the play into a libretto, was to further cut down the dialogue, to suggest which passages might be turned into songs, and to rewrite those passages as draft lyrics. He and George initially had a disagreement over the dialogue between the songs. DuBose thought it should simply be spoken; George wanted almost all of it set to music, like grand opera. George prevailed.

When he began work on *Porgy*, on around 25 February 1934, he set about writing the songs first. But writing these songs demanded a new way of working. He was used to either writing the music first, or to writing words and music together. Now he was presented with the problem of writing music for lyrics that were already written. Even though these lyrics could be changed somewhat, this was a challenge, and he rose to it gleefully.

Beginning at the start of Act One, the first song he composed for *Porgy* was the lullaby 'Summertime'. He was now working more single-mindedly on *Porgy* than he ever had on any project he had been involved in. The only other work he had in hand was his twice-weekly radio show. This was two weeks into its run when DuBose, who was doing everything he could to hurry things along, wrote to him, enclosing the draft libretto for Act Two, Scene Three.

He wrote: "I have been hearing you on the radio and the reception was so good it seemed as though you were in the room. In fact, the illusion was so perfect I could hardly keep from shouting at you, 'Swell show, George, but what the hell is the news about *PORGY*!!!'" He couldn't wait for George to come and spend some time in Charleston absorbing the local music, as he still felt there was a lot that George remained unaware of, and which should be in the score.

He also still hoped, for financial reasons, that the production might be mounted during the following autumn. If it wasn't going to happen, he would need to get some other work to tide him over.

Two-and-a-half weeks after that letter, on 19 March, and in spite of having a ten-day bout of flu, DuBose sent George Act Two, Scene Four. This contained what he considered would be George's biggest musical opportunity in the opera, when the inhabitants of Catfish Row are singing a sad spiritual, and the villain, Crown, sings a raunchy blues in counterpoint. He suggested that George worked closely with Ira on this, because by now he had realised that writing lyrics was a highly specialised skill, which he, poet though he was, did not have.

Ira at the time was co-writing lyrics with his friend Yip Harburg, to the music of Harold Arlen, for a show called *Life Begins At Eight-Forty*, but he was also keeping an eye on what George was doing, and gradually becoming more involved.

Life Begins At Eight-Forty was in effect a *Ziegfeld Follies*. Florenz Ziegfeld himself had died in 1932, but his widow, Billie Burke Ziegfeld, in association with the Shubert brothers, had decided to continue presenting the annual shows. Unfortunately, for this one they had trouble getting clearance to use the *Ziegfeld Follies* title, hence *Life Begins At Eight-Forty*. The sets and costumes for it were designed by future film-director Vincente Minnelli, then twenty-four and the hottest new designer and director in New York. Introduced socially to Ira by Yip Harburg, and sharing Yip and Ira's love of word games and light verse, he and Ira and Lee became close friends.

At the end of the month, on the twenty-seventh, DuBose sent George his draft of the last act, and a couple of weeks later he made a quick visit to New York so that he and George and Ira could confer. Their conference, held at George's apartment, went smoothly, and it was during it that George suggested that there was a spot in Act One that needed lightening. He improvised a little theme on the piano as he spoke, to show the sort of thing he had in mind. Both DuBose and Ira liked it so much they insisted he use it, and Ira at once suggested a title – 'I Got Plenty O' Nuttin''.

George worked incessantly on his score as April moved into May, and on 23 May he completed the piano-and-vocal version of his first scene. A week later, on 1 June, his radio series ended and he immediately started making plans to go to South Carolina.

DuBose had recommended to him the resort of Folly Island, which was roughly ten square miles in area and just off the coast, about ten miles from Charleston. DuBose and his wife Dorothy had a summer home there and George rented a four-room beach cottage near it, to use both as living-quarters and workshop.

He planned to stay there for five weeks, and with him for company went his cousin, the painter Harry Botkin. Going to Folly Island suited Harry perfectly, because he was at the time painting negro subjects, and hoped to find useful faces and places there.

He and George assembled quite a load of paints and canvases and easels, as well as the manuscripts and materials that George would need for working on *Porgy*. It was all loaded into a touring car, and George's man, Paul Mueller, set off ahead of them to drive it to the cottage. George and Harry travelled south by train.

The cottage was fairly primitive. It was a light, frame-built wooden structure (a few years later it would be blown into the sea by a storm), and it had no phone (there was none on Folly Island) and no running water. Water had to be brought the ten miles from Charleston, in five-gallon crocks. Fortunately the island was linked to the mainland by a bridge.

Each bedroom had a small iron-frame bed, nails and hooks in the unpainted wooden walls to hang clothes on and a small washbasin. George's also had an upright piano, also brought from Charleston.

Their screened-in porch looked out over the beach to the Atlantic Ocean. In the sea they saw porpoises and sharks and giant turtles, who would come out of the sea to sleep or bury their eggs on the beach. Sand crabs, the colour of sand, crawled on the sand around the cottage, and from the nearby swamps they could hear the roaring of bull-alligators.

There was also the insect life. There were crickets whose chirping kept George awake at nights, and when the wind blew from the swamps it brought clouds of biting mosquitoes. 'Fortunately, the cottage had mosquito screens, but even they had a disadvantage, which was the incessant noise in the night of bugs banging into them.

George had never in his life been so far from civilisation. He gleefully accepted the trip as an adventure, but wrote to his mother Rose suggesting that she would be wise not to come there, saying: "I know you like your comfort," and that he was glad he hadn't brought his dog, Tony, because it would be far too hot for him. It was so hot that he and Harry wore nothing but bathing suits or shorts all day, and their exposed skin became deeply tanned.

He also wrote to Ira saying: "This is the place for a complete rest as there isn't even a movie on the island. But – believe it or not – there is a Jewish delicatessen store."

Shortly after George and Harry and Paul arrived, DuBose and Dorothy joined them, the Heywards staying in their beach house, which they had named 'Follywood'. DuBose, wanting George to hear the sort of music that would have been around in the period when *Porgy* was set, took the whole group on several expeditions to the larger James Island, nearby. This had an isolated Gullah population, where older customs and styles of singing lingered on.

DuBose described George's reaction to some of what he heard:

> The Gullah Negro prides himself on what he calls 'shouting'. This is a complicated rhythmic pattern beaten out by feet and hands as an accompaniment to the spirituals, and is undoubtedly of African survival. I shall never forget the night when, at a Negro meeting on a remote sea island, George started 'shouting' with them. And, eventually to their huge delight stole the show from their champion 'shouter'. I think he is probably the only white man in America who could have done that.

On another night, at a little church in Hendersonville, George drew DuBose's attention to the singing of a group of Holy Rollers, where half a dozen voices were raised in a rhythmic prayer. Although each started at a different time and sang a different theme, the whole thing merged into a single pounding rhythm, "almost terrifying in its primitive intensity". George was to use his version of this effect in *Porgy*, as the prayers of six singers to God to save them from a hurricane merged into one.

Ideas came pouring out of George on Folly Island, and he worked fast to get them down on paper. He worked so hard that cousin Harry felt George was beginning to envy his freedom to paint. From time to time though, George did take some time off to paint, and he enjoyed a certain amount of social life. Once he and Harry went to a party in Charleston. There George again began to envy Harry, who seemed to be getting more attention than he was. George, seeking a reason for this, eventually put it down to Harry's painterly goatee beard. He decided that he would grow a beard himself, but his decision didn't last. After only a week or so he decided he didn't like himself with an inch of beachcomberly whiskers and started shaving again.

In August, George and Harry and Paul returned to New York, and George devoted all his attention to *Porgy*. Oscar Levant came to the apartment to work with him through the hot summer, manning the second Steinway as George polished his score. George continued to refer to the benefits he was getting from studying with Dr Schillinger, and eventually Oscar's curiosity was sufficiently piqued to overcome the reservations he had about the system. He, too, started taking lessons from Schillinger.

One afternoon, he casually mentioned to George that he was doing this. Again George was furious, accusing Oscar of imitating him out of jealousy. Oscar soon dropped the lessons, feeling they had neither helped nor harmed him as a composer.

Soon after George's return, on 27 August, Ira's show *Life Begins At Eight-Forty* had its New York opening, and he was now completely free to join in the work on *Porgy*. Others, too were roped in to help with such jobs as copying scores or playing the second, or third, piano. Kay Swift, Bill Daly, and even Dr Schillinger himself were among them.

In September, George finished the music for Act One, Scene Two, composing the songs first and then writing the rest of the music round them (still, at this stage, in two-piano form). Then, on Sunday 30 September, he had to begin his second series of *Music By Gershwin* broadcasts. This time they went out on WABC radio, and his schedule was less demanding, because the half-hours were weekly, instead of bi-weekly.

As usual, George played pieces of his composition to anyone who was around his apartment to listen. Early in November the great film director Ernst Lubitsch came there and George played him several of the songs that he, DuBose and Ira had written. Lubitsch was encouraging and made several useful suggestions about how the opera should be staged, such as having the scenery "just a bit off realism, with very free use of lighting to enhance dramatic events".

At around this time Ira wrote the lyric to the touching melody George had composed as Porgy's first duet with Bess – 'Bess, You Is My Woman Now'. George played this for an old friend and colleague, Dr Albert Sirmay, who was his editor at his music publishers, Chappell's (the house that Max Dreyfus was now running).

Dr Sirmay was moved to tears, and George picked up his private phone to Ira to tell him to come over quickly. The indolent Ira was reluctant to make his way across the street, with an elevator ride at either end, and eventually George gave up trying to surprise him and said gleefully, "I just played the duet for the Doc, and he's crying."

By this time the songs were almost completed, and 5 November found George writing to DuBose saying he would like to set tentative dates for rehearsals, and that auditions ought to begin the following January and February.

By December, the Theatre Guild, who had been considering possible directors for some time, had more or less definitely decided that they should approach the man who had directed the play *Porgy* for them – Reuben Mamoulian.

Mamoulian was the same age as George. Part Armenian and part Russian, he was born in Tiflis, the capital of the republic of Georgia, in 1898. His father was a bank president and his mother was the president of the Armenian Theatre. Young Reuben spent much of his early boyhood backstage, but when he later seemed set on a career in the theatre, his father tried to dissuade him by sending him to Moscow University to study criminal law.

It didn't work. While a student, he joined the Studio Theatre of the Moscow Art Theatre. Then, returning to Tiflis, he became a newspaper drama critic and founded his own drama studio.

When the Revolution came, in 1917, he went to London on the pretext of visiting his sister there, and stayed in England, organising a number of emigré Russian actors into a group calling itself the Russian Repertory Theatre, and touring the country with it. He went on to direct a play called *The Beating On The Door* in London's West End, then accepted an offer from George Eastman (of Kodak) to come to America and direct his new American Opera Company, in Kodak's home town of Rochester, in New York State.

He stayed there three years, directing operas and operettas of all types, including *Tannhäuser*, *The Merry Widow*, *Boris Godunov* and several of the comic operas of Gilbert and Sullivan. There he developed his theory that stage productions, even spoken plays, should have an overall rhythmic pattern, like music, with the speech and movement and sound effects and music (if there was any) all being carefully choreographed to carry the sense of the drama.

In 1927 he fell out with Eastman (Mamoulian wanted to establish a theatre for important drama, as well as opera, but Eastman didn't), but fortunately, at around the same time, managed to talk the Theatre Guild into hiring him to direct the play *Porgy*. Which he did with enormous success, before going off to Hollywood (stage directors who could handle dialogue were snapped up in the early days of talkies as fast as songwriters were). There he embarked on a long career as a director, while also continuing to work for the stage.

When Mamoulian had cast the play *Porgy* in 1927, he had great difficulty in assembling an all-black cast. While there were many black performers in New York – black musicals had been popular all through the twenties – they were mostly vaudeville actors. The craft of straight acting was foreign to them. They tended to address the audience directly, and when asked to express, for instance, joy, their reaction was to break into a few steps of Charleston.

By the beginning of 1935, the range of black actors available was greater, but the difficulty of casting George's opera was made worse by the shortage of suitable black singers. Even before Mamoulian was formally given the job of director, George had been aware of the problem, and had been keeping his eyes open for likely performers, especially for a baritone to undertake the role of Porgy. He was helped in his search by a young radio producer called Robert Wachsman, whom he had met at the studios while doing his own show.

Wachsman was producing a programme called *John Henry*, which George admired. Seeking out Wachsman, he said, "What are you doing for the next year-and-a-half?" He then invited him back to the apartment to hear what had so far been composed of *Porgy*. Wachsman was impressed by what he heard, and agreed to take on the job of talent spotting.

One of the singers that Wachsman unearthed was a tall, good-looking, black baritone. His name was Todd Duncan, and he was a teacher of music at Howard University, Washington. George had already heard his name from the music critic Olin Downes, who had heard him sing in an all-black production of Mascagni's *Cavalleria Rusticana* at the Mecca Temple on Fifty-Fifth Street in New York.

When Wachsman also suggested him to George, early in December 1934, George was a bit dubious about whether a university professor could play Porgy. Nonetheless, he phoned Todd Duncan at his home in Washington and asked him to come and give an audition at the apartment next Sunday. Duncan said he couldn't – he was singing in church that day – but he agreed to come the Sunday after.

If George was dubious about Todd Duncan, Duncan was equally dubious about George. "I wasn't very interested," he once admitted. "I thought of George Gershwin as being Tin Pan Alley and something beneath me." However, he duly arrived at the apartment at the agreed hour of one pm. "Where's your accompanist?" asked George.

Duncan hadn't realised that in New York it was usual to bring your own accompanist. "Can't you play?" he asked. George blinked. Duncan offered to try being his own accompanist, but George said, no, he'd try himself.

Duncan hunted through the sheaf of music he had brought, and selected a little known piece, 'Lungi Dal Caro Bene', by the Italian composer, Secchi. He then carefully explained to George that it was a classic, and translated the Italian so that George would know what he was singing about. George was impressed. He told Duncan that every other singer he'd auditioned had sung 'Glory Road' or 'Gwine To Heaven' or 'Ol' Man River'.

Duncan sang a few bars, with George at the piano, then George asked him if he could sing without accompaniment, as he wanted to view him full-face as he sang. Duncan could, and did, and after eight bars George stopped him and said, "Will you be my Porgy?" "I don't know," said Duncan. "I'd have to hear your music."

George laughed and told Duncan that if he came back the following Sunday he could hear some of the opera; also that Lawrence Langer and Theresa Helburn of the Theatre Guild could be there to hear him sing. Duncan came, bringing his wife (George having paid their train fares) and George had him sing some thirty songs (he had expected to sing three or four) for Langer and Helburn.

Then they went upstairs to George's work room, where George and Ira played and sang the songs for *Porgy*. They both sang, in fact, and Duncan was appalled by their voices, but in spite of them he was overwhelmed by the music. "I was in heaven," he said. "Those beautiful melodies in this new idiom – it was something I had never heard." By the time they got through Porgy's final song, 'I'm On My Way', he was weeping.

It was agreed by all present that Todd Duncan, with his rich fluid baritone, should be Porgy. His delivery was slightly stiff, but it projected well, and the stiffness could be worked on. The Guild took out an option on his services.

By 1934 there were many theatrical agencies handling black performers and, as soon as news of the intended opera began to leak out, they besieged the Guild casting office. During the first months of 1935 the office auditioned thousands of singers.

One singer approached George directly. Her name was Anne Wiggins Brown. The daughter of a Baltimore physician, she was twenty and studying singing at New York's Juilliard School of Music. Normally shy and retiring, she was sufficiently excited by the idea of a Gershwin opera to step out of character and write George a letter, asking if he would hear her sing.

He did. She came to the apartment and sang, and he chose her to play Bess – in spite of her complete lack of acting experience – because of her good vocal range. Once she was cast, as he continued to write his score, he would phone her to come round to the apartment and sing what he had written. On duets, he sang with her in his "small, but disagreeable" voice.

In order to give her some stage experience, he also arranged for her to spend some time in London, where producer Lew Leslie, as a favour to George, gave her a small part in the 1935 edition of his long-running revue, *Blackbirds*.

Another leading actress was suggested by DuBose Heyward. DuBose, being hard up, and with the opening night of the opera still some way off, had got himself hired to write two screenplays for MGM. One was based on Pearl S Buck's epic, *The Good Earth*, the other on Eugene O'Neill's *The Emperor Jones*. In a small part in *The Emperor Jones* he saw another Juilliard graduate, Ruby Elzy, and was sufficiently impressed to recommend her for the role of Serena, whose husband is knifed by Crown in the dice game.

The second series of *Music By Gershwin* came to an end on 30 December 1934 and, in January, George at last completed the piano-and-vocal version of his score. The last song he composed was a last-act trio between Porgy, Serena and Maria, entitled 'Oh, Where Is My Bess?'.

With the score written, but with the orchestration yet to begin, George decided to take a short break. He would go and spend a month with Emil Mosbacher in Palm Beach, and again would stop off en route to confer with DuBose, this time showing him all the songs. He set off from New York on 25 January.

When DuBose saw the completed songs, he was so pleased with the way Ira had developed his lyrics that he suggested it was only fair that he and Ira should split the lyric royalties between them.

At Emil Mosbacher's house in Palm Beach, George began orchestrating. The work went slowly, there being, as he wrote to Ira, "millions of notes to write". While there, he was also getting worried about the financial side of the production. The Guild was becoming increasingly concerned that the budget might get too high. It had been estimated at forty thousand dollars, but there were now fears that it might run to seventy-five thousand, or even one-hundred thousand, either of which would be beyond their resources. One day George told Emil, "I'm afraid the Guild might not go through with *Porgy*."

Emil was shrewd. He said, "George, handle it my way. Go to the telephone and tell the Theatre Guild that I, Emil Mosbacher, will put up half the money for the show. George, I bet you one hundred dollars I won't get any part of it, because as soon as they hear I'm ready to come in on that scale, they'll go ahead with the show and do anything to keep me out."

George didn't quite do that, but he did something similar. He wrote to the Guild offering to invest a quarter of the estimated forty thousand dollars. The investment would be split into four thousand from George, two thousand from Ira, and four thousand from Emil Mosbacher. The Guild replied that they'd just as soon not have any outside money in the production, and there was no further talk of abandoning the project. As it turned out, the show cost seventy thousand dollars to put on. Of this, George and Ira subscribed fifteen per cent, and DuBose five per cent.

By the time George arrived back in New York, at the end of April, pre-production was beginning to roll. Reuben Mamoulian, who was still in Hollywood, and then directing the first-ever Technicolor movie, *Becky Sharp*, was formally hired to be the director. He had not heard a note of George's music, but he had sufficient respect for George to accept the job anyway. In fact, it had taken George's name to resign him to the fact of an operatic version of *Porgy* at all, so paternally protective did he feel about the play version he had brought into being.

The Theatre Guild gave George considerable freedom in choosing his production ensemble. For his musical director he chose the Russian-born Alexander Smallens, an associate conductor of the Philadelphia Orchestra, even though Smallens admitted he was not enthusiastic about recitatives.

An opera that Smallens had recently conducted was Virgil Thomson's *Four Saints In Three Acts*. In it had been a group of twenty black singers with extremely high musical standards. Named after their leader, they were called the Eva Jessye Choir.

Normally they toured from state to state, barely making ends meet. It was while resting between tours that Eva Jessye saw a notice placed by the Guild in a show business newspaper, advertising for a black choir. She took the choir to audition at the Guild Theatre and, as she remembered it, "People from the Theatre Guild were there. We did the shout 'Plenty Good Room' and danced all over the stage. George Gershwin jumped up and shouted, 'That's it! That's what I want!' The Eva Jessye choir became the residents of Catfish Row."

Another Russian-American co-opted was Alexander Steinert. He had been coaching the singers for the Russian Opera Company when George tapped him on the shoulder at a reception for Igor Stravinsky at New York Town Hall, and asked him if he wanted to do the same job for *Porgy*. Steinert did. He signed a contract with the Guild next day.

All during the spring and summer George worked at his orchestrations. As well as doing some of this at Emil Mosbacher's rented house in Palm Beach, he also spent some time with Emil at his home in White Plains, as well as staying in a cottage on Fire Island (off Long Island), that Ira and Lee and Moss Hart had rented for the summer. But mostly he worked at the apartment, where relays of friends and colleagues laboured away at the chore of copying out the parts for the various instruments of the orchestra.

Oscar Levant was no longer among them. He had torn himself away from George to go to California and study composition with Arnold Schoenberg (and to write popular tunes for several films at Fox and RKO).

In June, before completing his orchestration, George hired an orchestra for a day to play key sections of the work, so that he could judge them. As well as the orchestra, four of the chosen singers came to the session to sing their parts – Todd Duncan as Porgy, Anne Brown as Bess, Ruby Elzy as Serena, and Abbie Mitchell as Clara, the young girl who sings 'Summertime' to her baby at the beginning. George himself conducted the tryout and, again, as with 'Second Rhapsody', he had it recorded.

Even before he finished the orchestration, the score for *Porgy* was published, by the Gershwin Publishing Company. This company was an idea of Max Dreyfus. It was a subsidiary of Chappell's, with whom he was now working, and it was to be entirely devoted to publishing George's works.

Because the orchestration was not complete, the score that was published was of George's original piano-and-vocal version. It ran to five-hundred-and-sixty pages, and it was edited by Dr Albert Sirmay. George insisted that it be published as it stood, difficult as it was to play, and not in any popular arrangement. It was only later, after some of the songs from the opera became popular, that he would permit them to be published in a simplified form.

Rehearsals for *Porgy* were scheduled to begin at the end of August, but before then the Guild began to worry about the title. They were afraid that, as the opera had the same title as the play they had presented in 1927, the public might confuse the two. George and DuBose Heyward discussed the problem, and DuBose came up with the solution. There had been, he said, "*Pelléas And Melisande*, *Samson And Delilah*, *Tristan And Isolde*. And so why not *Porgy And Bess?*"

In August, when Reuben Mamoulian eventually arrived in New York, he was invited to George's apartment to hear the score, still not completely orchestrated. He was shown to a comfortable leather armchair, and handed a highball, and Ira went and stood by George at the piano. George played, and Ira sang the words, while George joined in and sang an approximation of the orchestra parts.

"It was touching," wrote Mamoulian later, "to see how Ira, while singing, would become so overwhelmed with admiration for his brother that he would look from him to me with half-open eyes and pantomime with a soft gesture of his hand, as if saying, '*He* did it. Isn't it wonderful? Isn't *he* wonderful?'"

George finished orchestrating his complete opera, apart from its opening music, on 23 August 1935. Three days later rehearsals began.

The most difficult artist by far that Mamoulian and the musical director, Alexander Smallens, had to deal with in rehearsal was the actor John William Sublett. In his revue and night club work he was half of a team called Buck And Bubbles. 'Buck' was pianist Buck Washington, and singer and dancer John became known as 'John Bubbles', which is how he was billed in *Porgy And Bess*.

He played the part of the drug pusher, Sportin' Life, and was George's discovery. Bubbles was an elegant dancer, much admired by Fred Astaire, and George had wanted him in the part from the beginning, even though his voice was not as classically trained as those of the other singers in the cast.

But Bubbles' voice wasn't the problem. It was his vaudeville background. He had never seen a score in his life and, when the seven hundred pages that George had written were shipped to him in Texas, where he was touring, he nearly had a fit, believing that all of it was his part.

Unable to read music at all, he had to be taught his part by having it played to him and, even then, had trouble with pitch, tempo and rhythm. The slow triplets in his first big number, 'It Ain't Necessarily So', caused him endless difficulty. He couldn't seem to get them right at all, until choral director Alexander Steinert had the bright idea of tap-dancing the rhythm for him. After that, he could do it.

At one rehearsal, after numerous breakdowns of the same piece, conductor Alexander Smallens lost his temper. He slammed his fist on the score, shouted out the correction and told Bubbles how often he'd already corrected him, asking if perhaps there was something wrong with his conducting. Bubbles disarmed him completely by saying contritely, "Mr Smallens, if I had the money of the way you conduct I'd be a millionaire."

While Alexander Smallens rehearsed the orchestra, using Carnegie Hall, Mamoulian rehearsed the cast at the Guild Theatre. George was always at one place or the other, and Mamoulian was fascinated by George's complete delight in what he had created. He felt it was his greatest work and he loved every note of it. Indeed, after the first full rehearsal (which had been considerably unsatisfactory) he phoned Mamoulian and said, "I always knew that *Porgy And Bess* was wonderful, but I never thought I'd feel the way I feel now. I tell you, after listening to that rehearsal today I think the music is so marvellous I really don't believe I wrote it."

Absorbed in *Porgy* as he was, he expected everybody else to feel the same and was disconcerted when they weren't. After a later rehearsal, he and Mamoulian went for a meal at Lindy's restaurant. While there, Mamoulian absent-mindedly whistled a snatch of Rimsky-Korsakov. George was at once upset. "How can you be humming some Russian melody when you have just been rehearsing *my* music all day?" he demanded. He brooded for a while, then had a happy thought. "I know why you hummed that Russian music," he said to Mamoulian. "It's because *my* parents came from Russia."

At a later stage during rehearsals, when everybody was getting a bit stale, having heard all the music just that much too often, George suggested that he and Mamoulian and several others involved in the production go for a weekend break on Long Island "to forget completely about *Porgy And Bess*". When they got back, somebody asked Mamoulian how the weekend went. "Can't you guess?" he said. "From morning to night, for three days, George was at the piano, playing the music from *Porgy*."

The show was due to start its tryout at the Colonial Theatre in Boston on 30 September, but a week before that, on the twenty-third, the cast and orchestra performed the whole score as a concert, at Carnegie Hall. This concert, remembered by many people as the most memorable performance of *Porgy And Bess* ever given, contained every note that George had written, and it ran for over four hours. Mamoulian warned George, "If you want to have success with your opera you may have to make some harsh cuts."

George, in spite of his love for his work, proved surprisingly amenable to cutting. His professionalism overrode his creative pride and, even before the show opened in Boston, several songs were removed.

One was called 'Jasbo Brown Blues'. Suggested by DuBose, it had been placed right at the start of the show, as the overture ended, when some slow jazz-like chords from the orchestra are taken over by an on stage pianist. It is night on Catfish Row, and the pianist is playing at a dance party. Ira wrote scat-singing to accompany the piano, and the idea of the scene was to suggest urban influences from the north seeping into the more primitive southern setting, making it a society in a state of change.

Part of the reason why it was dropped so early was that it needed an extra set, and costs, as well as running-time needed to be cut. "Okay," said George, thinking of the next song, 'Summertime', "that means we start with the lullaby, and that's some lullaby."

Another song that was dropped was Porgy's 'Buzzard Song', a tragic aria about the buzzard hovering over Catfish Row, a portent of death. To include it meant Porgy singing three songs in a row (it came between 'I Got Plenty O' Nuttin'' and 'Bess, You Is My Woman Now') and George himself cut it because he realised there was a real danger that Todd Duncan, who had no understudy, might find his voice giving out if he had to sing so much eight times a week.

The Boston opening was greeted with wild enthusiasm by the audience, and the critics were united in praise, using phrases like "a great advance in American opera" and "Gershwin must now be accepted as a serious composer". The only criticism came from Theatre Guild subscribers in Boston who were unable to get tickets because the one-week run was sold out.

After the first performance, George, Mamoulian, Alexander Steinert and Kay Swift walked on Boston Common until three in the morning, arguing over further cuts. George was reluctant to lose his last-act trio, 'Oh, Where Is My Bess?', but eventually he was talked into at least changing and shortening it. Its title also slightly shortened, it became Porgy's solo, 'Where's My Bess?'.

With less reluctance, George agreed to drop the song he had been inspired to write by the church singers in Hendersonville, where a sextet pray to God to be saved from the hurricane. After all the cuts were made, the opera was some forty-five minutes shorter than it had originally been.

On Thursday 10 October, four days after the end of the Boston run, *Porgy And Bess* had its New York premiere at the Alvin Theatre. The audience, as for 'Rhapsody In Blue' nearly twelve years before, was crammed with celebrities from classical music, popular music, Broadway and high society (although this time there were fewer flappers and cake-eaters).

Again, as in Boston, the audience greeted the production with enthusiasm, although, unlike the Boston audience, some of them had reservations. Bennett Cerf later recorded that he felt this first production was too over-reverent ("stuffy and pretentious" were his words), pointing out that it wasn't until seven years later, when the opera was revived, that it really came into its own.

Oscar Levant, back from studying with Schoenberg in Los Angeles, found himself squirming in his seat. Too many of the songs had what he felt were 'Broadway endings'. Turning to a friend at the final curtain he said, "It's a right step in the wrong direction." This and other remarks he made at the time, such as calling the show "a glorious paean to American Jewish music", later haunted him, causing him real anguish. He desperately wanted to love and admire his friend's work, which had cost him so many months of his life, but somehow he couldn't.

He was right, though, about there being a lot of Broadway in the music, and about its essential Jewishness. This bothered a number of eminent black musicians, who had been hoping for something closer to the music of their race. Duke Ellington, for instance, felt that it was "grand music and a swell play, but the two didn't go together", and he was disappointed that Gershwin had elected to use elements of very primitive black music as his source, rather than the more subtle black music that was by then well-developed.

But that wasn't what George was after. He wasn't attempting to show the latest and best in black music. What he was trying to do was depict the joys and sorrows of a small isolated community, using the music of that community as the basis for music of his own. After all, he would have been quite happy to take the Polish-Jewish play *The Dybbuk* as his starting-point.

Certainly *Porgy And Bess* is too conventionally operatic (with an admixture of Broadway), but for a first opera it was a considerable achievement, especially when you consider that George had never before attempted to write music conveying deeply-felt emotions. He succeeded, and had every right to be as proud of *Porgy And Bess* as he was.

After the New York premiere, there was the usual first-night party, this time given at his huge penthouse apartment on Fifth Avenue by publisher Condé Nast. It was planned to be the grandest party of the season. Kay Swift had arranged everything and music was provided by Enric Madriguera's Latin Band although, as it happened, Paul Whiteman, who was one of the guests, also brought along twelve members of his own band. None of which made much difference, because when George arrived he headed for the piano and obligingly reprised almost the whole opera. The party went on until seven in the morning.

CHAPTER THIRTEEN

Hollywood

O n the day after the Boston premiere of *Porgy And Bess*, George went walking with a woman friend, Lois Jacoby. Tense and preoccupied, he walked faster and faster, so Miss Jacoby, in high heels, had a hard time keeping up with him. She was sure that his excitement was due to the previous night's success, but suddenly he stopped dead and turned to her, his face full of concern. "But what will I do next, Lois?" he asked.

For a moment she thought he was joking. Well, she said, there was the New York opening to come, and then maybe one in London. Then perhaps the big European cities like Paris and Vienna.

"A symphony maybe," mused George. "I wonder if I can do it. I'll have to learn all about the form. Perhaps if I work hard for a couple of years." Lois still wasn't sure he was serious. "What fun it would be," she persisted, "for you to go round the world with *Porgy And Bess*! What a kick you'd get out of it!"

"If it's that good," said George, "it'll go without me. In the meantime I've got to think about the future." He went back to talking about possibly writing a symphony.

Bored and unsettled by having no new project, in November 1935 he decided to take a four-week holiday in Mexico. He travelled there by boat, and with him went Edward Warburg, who was then the director of the American Ballet at the Metropolitan, his analyst Dr Zilboorg, and Marshall Field, the department store owner.

His hope had been to hear some music, either Indian or Mexican, which might inspire him, as the music of Cuba had done. But during his stay he heard no Indian music, and what he heard of Mexican music did nothing for him. In fact he found more interest in meeting Mexican painters.

One was the young David Siqueiros, some of whose work George bought for his collection. Siqueiros would later paint a portrait of George on stage at the piano, with the first two rows of the audience filled with portraits of his friends. George took a photograph of him, having recently developed an enthusiasm for photography. He had bought a Leica, and started taking both posed portraits and candid snapshots of friends and colleagues everywhere he went.

Another painter he met in Mexico was Diego Rivera, famous for his vast public murals on revolutionary themes. George drew a pencil portrait of him and, in his restless mental state, announced on his return, "I am going to interest myself in politics, and it is true I talked a great deal with Diego Rivera, and with his radical friends, who discussed at length their doctrines and their intentions... I'm going to try to develop my brains more in music to match my emotional development."

But George was not a political animal and this proved to be a passing fancy. He had enjoyed meeting the revolutionary painters and seeing the sights of Mexico, but he had been bored there for most of the time, and couldn't wait to get back home and back to work.

When his ship docked back in New York, he found himself being serenaded down the gangplank by the cast of *Porgy And Bess*, singing with musical accompaniment by the Charleston Orphan Band (there was a big tradition in America of training black orphans to play instruments, and many famous musicians came out of orphanage bands).

The first thing he found to occupy himself with was writing an orchestral suite based on his opera, calling it simply 'Suite from *Porgy And Bess*' (when it was recorded, thirty years later, Ira retitled it 'Catfish Row'). It has five movements – 1 'Catfish Row'; 2 'Porgy Sings'; 3 'Fugue'; 4 'Hurricane'; and 5 'Good Morning, Brother'. It had its world premiere on Wednesday 21 January, 1936, in Philadelphia, when it was played by the orchestra from the opera, and conducted by its conductor, Alexander Smallens.

The reason why the orchestra was in Philadelphia was that the opera was to begin a short season there the following Tuesday, as the first stop on a national tour. It had stayed on Broadway for a disappointingly short run of one-hundred-and-twenty-four performances. It never had a chance of recouping the seventy thousand dollars invested in it.

The few thousand dollars George earned in royalties went on paying his copyists. DuBose Heyward, who had planned on buying a house for himself and his wife with his share, had to abandon the idea. Ira made two thousand dollars, but made a lot more from *The Ziegfeld Follies Of 1936* (Billie Burke Ziegfeld and the Shuberts had by now obtained the rights to use the title). For this show, which opened on 30 January, Ira had written the lyrics to Vernon Duke's music. Among their songs was one number which became a standard: 'I Can't Get Started'.

In the *Follies* it was sung by a rising young comedian, Bob Hope (while pursuing Eve Arden) and it was played splendidly from the orchestra pit by trumpeter Bunny Berigan. Bunny would go on to become one of the outstanding musicians of the Swing Era, and so closely associated with 'I Can't Get Started' that people came to believe it had been specially written for him.

Shortly after the *Follies* opened, Ira, exhausted from both it and *Porgy*, went for a three-week cruise to the West Indies. Lee of course went with him, and so did their young friend who again had designed both scenery and costumes for the *Follies* – Vincente Minnelli. His designs continued to cause a sensation. In the New York *Times*, critic Brooks Atkinson wrote: "Vincente Minnelli has burst into the Winter Garden with a whole portfolio of original splendours. Without being in the least sensational, he has managed this season to reanimate the art of scenic display and costumery. Although he is lavish enough to satisfy any producer's thirst for opulence, his taste is unerring and the *Follies* that comes off his drawing-board is a civilised institution. Even the mediocre numbers, of which there are the usual number, look well when Mr Minnelli dresses them."

Minnelli was so exhausted from his work on the show that for the first twenty-four hours aboard the SS Britannica, he slept. All three went on to enjoy the first week of their cruise, visiting Barbados, Martinique and Curaáao, looking forward immensely to the two weeks they were to spend in Trinidad. Unfortunately, their arrival there coincided with the first day of Lent, and all merrymaking on the island

221

ceased for forty days and forty nights.

Also it rained. The high spot of their time in Trinidad turned out to be a Warner Brothers musical, based on a Jerome Kern operetta, showing at a local cinema. Ira had seen it in New York (and not liked it), but nonetheless they went to it on four consecutive nights. "You know," said Ira, "it looks pretty good here." They too were glad to get back to New York.

While Ira was away, George, bored, diverted himself by writing a song. A new sort of music was being heard in the dance halls of New York – a smoother, more driving style of popular jazz, with four beats in a bar – and the name it was acquiring was 'swing'. George, with lyricist Albert Stillman, wrote a song they called 'King Of Swing'.

It never did much. After *Porgy And Bess* came to the end of its brief tour, in Washington DC on 21 March, John Bubbles reunited with his partner, Buck Washington. In May they began performing the song in a revue called *Swing Is King*, which played at Radio City Music Hall in support of a movie musical written by Fritz Kreisler called *The King Steps Out*, starring Grace Moore and Franchot Tone.

Things had changed rapidly on Broadway during the two years George had been involved in his opera. A new generation of songwriters, treading in his and Ira's footsteps, had arrived to compete for the work – writers like Rodgers and Hart and Cole Porter – all of whom wrote witty, sophisticated songs very much in the Gershwin tradition.

At the same time, Broadway audiences had fallen off considerably since the great days of the late twenties. One of the two main reasons for this was the Depression, the other was the arrival of the talkies.

Film musicals competed much more directly with Broadway than silent movies had been able to do, and this reduced box office takings. Furthermore, Hollywood was able to pay such high wages that many of the best playwrights and performers were now spending much of their time there, thus robbing the stage of essential talent. In the nine months following the opening of *Porgy And Bess*, George and Ira were offered eleven shows to write songs for, most of them terrible and the best only fair.

In February 1936, they themselves were sought again by Hollywood. On the seventeenth they were sent a letter by Sam

Howard, of the Phil Berg-Bert Allenberg Agency, asking if the agency could represent them for film work and what their conditions might be.

George, although pleased to perhaps have the chance of working again on a musical, still had his mind on more serious composition, and regarded film work as something to subsidise that. He replied that he and Ira would want one-hundred thousand dollars per picture, plus a percentage.

This was more than he and Ira had got in Hollywood in 1931, when they worked on *Delicious*, but in 1931 they had just written a hit show – *Girl Crazy*. Now they were the authors of a show that was not only commercially unsuccessful, but also an opera, which in the film world was regarded as highbrow. As a result, the studios turned out to be slightly apprehensive. However, George's response to Sam Howard's letter did let Hollywood know that the Gershwins would be prepared to work in films, and various negotiations, through various agents, began.

On 26 June, through agent Archie Selwyn (brother of Edgar Selwyn, who had produced *Strike Up The Band*), George and Ira closed a deal with Pandro S Berman, the head of production at RKO, to work for sixteen weeks on one picture for fifty-five thousand dollars, with an option to do sixteen weeks on a second for seventy thousand dollars. This was something of a climbdown from what they had been asking, but as Pan Berman had wired them during the negotiations, "I think you are letting a few thousand dollars keep you from having a lot of fun and when you figure the government gets eighty per cent of it, do you think it's nice to make me suffer this way?"

The first picture they were hired to score was an Astaire-Rogers musical. After Adele Astaire retired, in 1932, Fred had gone to Hollywood. After making one film for MGM – *Dancing Lady*, in which his partner was Joan Crawford – he moved to RKO, who partnered him with Ginger Rogers. Together they began their highly successful series of musicals, and the one George and Ira were to work on would be their seventh, tentatively titled *Watch Your Step*.

In spite of his love of writing musicals, the prospect made George somewhat nervous. The previous six Astaire-Rogers films had had scores by composers like Jerome Kern (once) and Irving Berlin (twice), and all had been smashes at the box office. Apart from 'Swanee',

George had never composed a hit in the way Irving Berlin repeatedly did and, he knew that hits were what the studios wanted. He would have to demonstrate to them that he was not just a highbrow composer.

He and Ira were not due to go to Hollywood until August. In the few months before going there he kept himself occupied in various ways. With the help of Max Dreyfus, he attempted to organise a European tour of *Porgy And Bess*, but the show was too expensive to mount for anyone to show much interest. Eventually it was decided that such a tour might be possible if the cast took a cut in salary, but this the cast resolutely refused to do, and no tour ever took place. George would continue to brood about this all the time he was in Hollywood.

On 21 April another exhibition of his still-growing collection of paintings opened, this time in New York, at the Society of Independent Artists. Included in the exhibition were a couple of his own canvases, but they caused little interest. Harry Botkin told him not to worry, but to remember he was still improving, and that it wouldn't be long before he had produced enough good pictures to give a one-man show. Then people would start regarding him as an artist in his own right, not as a composer who dabbled in art.

He arranged performances of his 'Suite From *Porgy And Bess*' at concerts in St Louis, Washington, Boston and Chicago, appearing himself to play 'Rhapsody In Blue' and the 'Concerto In F'. On 9 and 10 July he played them again at two all-Gershwin concerts at the Lewisohn Stadium. At these concerts selections from *Porgy And Bess* were also performed, sung by Anne Brown, Todd Duncan, Ruby Elzy and the Eva Jessye Choir .

All these concerts were sufficiently successful for George to receive offers to do more. The San Francisco Symphony, learning he would be coming to Hollywood, asked him to appear as soloist with them in 1937 at their "new six-million-dollar opera house". An English impresario invited him to make a European tour in the winter of 1937-38. And a concert he gave at Ravinia on 25 July pleased the promoters so much they asked if they could commission a new work to present in 1937.

As well as the two RKO pictures George and Ira were contracted to work on, they had also heard from Archie Selwyn that the famous independent producer, Samuel Goldwyn, was interested in using them on a picture. Thus they could reasonably expect to be in Hollywood for a full year and, accordingly, decided to close down their two apartments on Seventy-Second Street (while continuing to rent them) and put all their furniture and books (and paintings) in storage while they were away.

The last night before starting to do this, in August 1936, George gave a farewell party at his apartment. But Hollywood was already on his case. While the party was still in progress, a messenger delivered the outline script of *Watch Your Step*, written by the screenwriters Allan Scott and Ernest Pagano. George and Ira dutifully retired to another room to inspect it.

In the story, which opens in Paris, Fred Astaire plays Peter F Peters, who is a ballet master for the Russian Ballet, working under the name of Petroff. He falls in love from afar with an American ballroom dancer, Linda Keene (played by Ginger Rogers) and this impels him to wonder whether he shouldn't change his style, saying, "Suppose we could combine the technique of the ballet with the warmth and passion of jazz!"

In his pursuit of Linda, who is returning to America, he arranges that they take the same boat there. They duly fall in love, but their affair is made complicated by the reporters who meet the boat and assume they are already married. Eventually everything is straightened out – Petroff does invent a new style of dancing, and they do get married.

It didn't take long for George and Ira to read the first draft of this story. As they returned to their farewell party, George said to everyone, "Gosh, but I wish I was back in New York." This was not so much a comment on the plot as on Hollywood's way of working.

On 20 August, George and Ira and Lee went west. This time they took a plane, flying from Newark, New Jersey, on TWA (then advertising itself as 'the Lindbergh line' because of Charles Lindbergh's involvement in it as an adviser and stockholder). Among those seeing George off at Newark was Kay Swift.

George had probably been closer to Kay and for longer, than any other woman in his life. Their friendship had in fact become so close that it had contributed to the break-up of her marriage. But still it was more of a friendship than a love affair, at least on George's side. They had discussed the possibility of Kay coming to California with him, but eventually both had decided that perhaps it was best to be apart from each other for a while. When George got back, in a year's time, they could see whether they felt they had a real future together.

Arriving in Los Angeles, George and Ira and Lee checked into the Beverly Wilshire Hotel. This was only to be temporary. The plan was for George and Ira to begin work, while Lee hunted round for a suitable house to rent.

Seeing that the script they had been sent was still only an outline, George and Ira decided to write a fairly long and ambitious number for Fred Astaire, on the supposition that room could be found for it in the finished scenario. The piece they came up with, entitled 'HiHo!', was a mixture of lyrics and song and commentary. When the picture's assigned director, Mark Sandrich, saw it, he was delighted. "This is real four-dollars-forty stuff," he said. The studio liked it, too. That is, until they costed it and found out it would add forty-four thousand dollars to the budget, and dropped the idea like a hot brick.

While still at the Beverly Wilshire they were contacted by Vincente Minnelli, still in New York and now directing a revue called *The Show Is On*, starring Beatrice Lillie and Bert Lahr. He wanted George and Ira to contribute a song, and they gladly turned their minds back to New York for a while and wrote a cheerful number called 'By Strauss'. This would reappear in 1951 in Minnelli's all-Gershwin film 'An American In Paris'.

On 18 August they attended a meeting of ASCAP, the all-powerful songwriters' union. The meeting was being held to discuss various current copyright questions, such as the contract binding Warner Brothers music holdings to ASCAP, but the importance of it to George and Ira was that there they met many old friends. Among those present were Yip Harburg, Harold Arlen, Vincent Youmans, Harry Warren, Bert Kalmar, Harry Ruby and Buddy DeSylva. It made the two expatriate New Yorkers feel a bit more at home in Hollywood.

Four days later they moved into a spacious Spanish-style house that Lee had found for them. Decorated in cream-coloured stucco, it stood at 1019 North Roxbury Drive, in Beverly Hills, and the rent was eight hundred dollars a month. It had a swimming pool and a tennis court and, on a lawn behind it, grew orange and lemon trees. It even had a Steinway already installed.

Early in September, Paul Mueller arrived at the house, having set off in George's Buick, laden with eight hundred pounds of personal possessions plus George's dog, Tony, to drive across America. The journey had been a nightmare. The car kept breaking down, and Tony got so sick that eventually he had to be left with a vet en route. (He showed up six weeks after Paul, full of life and ready to fight every dog in Beverly Hills.)

George soon got rid of the Buick. He sold it and bought one of the new Cord roadsters. From the moment it was put on the market, in 1935, the Cord (named after its designer) was obviously destined to be a classic. It was a long, bulbous, soft-top convertible, of which only about five hundred were ever made, and it contained many advanced features that pushed the technology of the time to its limits. It had front wheel drive, no radiator and an electrically-operated pre-selector gear box. George loved gadgets, and the Cord might have been designed to appeal to him.

Shortly after joining the household, Paul Mueller noticed another gadget of George's, which worried him. George had become concerned that his hairline was receding, so had bought a strange machine that was supposed to stimulate the scalp and arrest hair loss. Its main component was a pump the size of a refrigerator. This was connected by a hose to a sort of metal helmet, which was to be clamped around his head. When the machine was switched on, the helmet massaged his scalp with a pulsating suction, so powerful that at the end of each daily treatment his scalp was too numb to feel anything if a pin were stuck into it.

Paul gave George a lecture about the dangers of cutting off the blood supply to the brain. "You are doing yourself harm," he said. "You don't know what you're talking about," replied George curtly. He continued using the machine for half-an-hour every day.

As well as attempting to keep a full head of hair, George had also continued keeping fit. He swam, he played tennis, he played golf, and every day he went for a six-mile hike, accompanied by his dog Tony (once he got there).

As soon as they were settled in the house, the three Gershwins set about creating a replica of their New York social circle. Sunday brunches became a tradition and regular visitors included Yip Harburg,

Harold Arlen, Reuben Mamoulian, Lillian Hellman, Dashiell Hammett, Moss Hart, Edward G Robinson and Arnold Schoenberg, who was so keen on table tennis that he always brought his own bat and, who, when not playing table tennis, was usually to be found on the lawn tennis court. The most regular visitor, however, was of course Oscar Levant, then studying composition with Schoenberg, as well as writing music for Twentieth Century Fox. It was Oscar who had introduced Schoenberg to George, and they became good friends.

Schoenberg was teaching at UCLA and George became keenly interested in his complex and harmonically advanced music. Furthermore, the fact that Oscar was studying with Schoenberg, and appreciated by him, made George rather more interested in what Oscar was writing. Oscar was rather shy about showing his work to George, but once did show him a piano concerto he was composing under Schoenberg's tuition. George studied it for some moments, then said, "It looks so confused..." Oscar, always easily hurt, snapped out, "Didn't you know? I've been offered the chair of confusion at UCLA."

One musical activity they did manage to share. During George's months in Hollywood, he and Oscar would frequently stay up all night, away from all the social hubbub, listening to Brahms' quartets together.

At first George quite enjoyed Hollywood. He felt that the studios were now a lot better at making musicals than they had been in 1931, and he enjoyed much of the social life. There were dinners and poker parties with Irving Berlin and Jerome Kern, and often he visited Harold Arlen and his wife, Anya. Always, as a sort of self-mocking game, he rushed in as soon as they opened the front door, dashed to the piano and played something he had just written, then said "Hello".

George and Ira did most of their writing for *Watch Your Step* at the house, only going in to the studio when there was a problem to be sorted out (the work room they had been allotted there had previously been the dressing room of the diminutive Lily Pons, and accordingly it was not large).

The songs they wrote for Fred Astaire were not in quite the same style as the ones they had written for him in the twenties, partly because he was now less boyish, more suave and assured, and partly because George and Ira's style had developed.

George no longer tended to use repeated short phrases over a shifting harmonic background. His melodic phrases were now longer and more flowing and their rhythms were easier and more conversational, while at the same time being more built into the songs. His earlier songs could be swung – these new ones tended to swing by themselves. And Ira's lyrics were acquiring a touch of darkness, which made them all the stronger. Instead of extolling rhythm as a joyful celebration of life, it now seems to be being encouraged as an antidote to life's darkness, to lighten a time when people were concerned by the Depression and the rise of fascism in Europe.

In spite of having spent so much time over the previous two years writing an opera, their ability to write memorable songs had, if anything, improved. Among those they wrote for *Watch Your Step* were 'Let's Call The Whole Thing Off', 'Slap That Bass', 'They All Laughed' and 'They Can't Take That Away From Me'.

When they had first gone in to the studio towards the end of August and performed the first songs they had written, producer Pandro Berman and director Mark Sandrich were delighted, as was Fred Astaire, giving George and Ira the pleasant feeling that they were working with people who spoke the same language. But within a couple of weeks this amiable feeling had worn off slightly, mainly because the studio had not yet managed to come up with a final script, which prevented George and Ira from working as hard as they were used to.

One underlying thing that disturbed George about Hollywood was that, compared to New York, the pace of life was too laid-back and relaxed. Ira enjoyed this (he would live in Beverly Hills for the rest of his life), but it made George fidget.

Early in September, in an attempt to slow himself down, he went for a weekend break at Lake Arrowhead. That helped. As he wrote to his friend Emil Mosbacher: "A more beautiful place and climate I have never seen or felt. I had a grand time." Inspired by its beauty, as soon as he got back to the house he wired to his secretary in New York to ship out fifteen of his favourite paintings. Two days later he wired her to ship out his paints and brushes and canvases as well.

As the studio worked its way towards a final script, and then progressed through shooting and editing, the title of the film changed from *Watch Your Step* to *Stepping Toes* to *Stepping Stones* to *Stepping High*, but still nobody was happy with it. Eventually, early in 1937, Vincente Minnelli, who had been offered a directing contract by Paramount, arrived in Hollywood. Naturally joining the Gershwins' social circle, he heard of the problem, and gallantly offered George and Ira a title he had rather been keeping to use on some project of his own. It was *Shall We Dance?*. The studio gratefully adopted it, and George and Ira sat down and wrote their song of that name.

George was becoming increasingly unhappy in Hollywood. Another problem was that he was used to being a celebrity, and Hollywood had its own hierarchy of celebrities. To most of the movie colony, George was simply another composer. Also, he was still unsure of which direction to head in next. Discussing things with Minnelli, he suggested that perhaps he might write a Spanish opera for Minnelli to direct, or perhaps one based on *The Dybbuk*. He was also considering turning to the classics for his subjects, perhaps basing orchestral pieces on them.

Other ideas he had during his time in Hollywood were for writing a string quartet, or for making a concert tour of Europe. He considered writing a cowboy opera ("Indians," he said however, "are taboo"), and another opera based on a book he had liked, by Lynn Riggs, whose novel *Green Grow The Lilacs* was later adapted into *Oklahoma!*. The book was called *The Lights Of Lamy* and it dealt with the clash between American and Mexican cultures.

He thought of collaborating with writer Robert E Sherwood on a Broadway show that would be a cavalcade of great moments of American history, linked by Rip Van Winkle, who would periodically waken to experience them. He wanted to write a ballet. He thought of setting Lincoln's Gettysburg address to music. There was a quite definite plan to collaborate with George S Kaufman and Moss Hart (and Ira) on a musical about the setting up of a musical. This was not the newest idea, even in 1936, but this production would be different in that all four of them would appear in it, playing themselves (except Ira, who was too shy, and was to be permitted to remain an off stage voice).

As a step towards creating serious work, he wrote to Dr Schillinger in New York, asking for advice about continuing his studies. Schillinger suggested he study four-part fugues with Schoenberg and symphonic composition with composer Ernst Toch.

He never did study with Schoenberg or Toch, but the musical world of Los Angeles was to him its one bright spot. He heard and appreciated music by Stravinsky and Schoenberg, Copland and Toch, and in October 1936, he himself received a letter from a West Coast concert and opera manager called Merle Armitage.

Armitage was a keen admirer of George's work, especially *Porgy And Bess*, and he wanted to present two concerts of Gershwin music using the Los Angeles Philharmonic. George agreed. Armitage came to the house to discuss things, and eventually it was decided that the concerts would consist of 'Rhapsody In Blue', the 'Concerto In F', and instead of the 'Suite', some vocal selections from *Porgy And Bess*.

It was also decided that the concerts should be held the following February, so they began holding auditions for singers. Eventually thirty black singers with good voices were found and, at George's invitation, Todd Duncan also agreed to take part.

At the beginning of December, *Shall We Dance?* was almost completed. George by now was considerably disillusioned with the studio's attitude to music. An interview with him, reported by the Los Angeles *Evening News* at around this time, said: "One thing he won't bother to write is the background music. He suggests the theme for staff writers at RKO, but refuses to be bothered with work which 'hacks' can do." It went on to say: "He doesn't work very much with the script, because the studio, he says, doesn't like the music to be all of one tone, contrary to the plan followed by a stage production. Just as long as it keeps the general tone, it satisfies film producers."

All of which sounds very much like George being diplomatic. Not working much with the script, and not bothering to write the background music, are so far from his usual habits and appetite for work that he can't have been comfortable with this way of working. It was a far cry from the sort of integrated score he had been proud of producing for shows like *Of Thee I Sing* and *Let 'Em Eat Cake*.

Nonetheless, RKO were happy enough. Early in December they took up George and Ira's option to make a second film. Again it was to star Astaire, but this time he was to have a new co-star. There had been tensions between Fred and Ginger. He wanted to prove he could make a film without her, and she was anxious to prove she could act as well as dance, so the studio gave her a good part in their 1937 production *Stage Door*. After which she and Fred would reunite for two more films.

At one point it was announced to the press that Fred's new partner was to be Hollywood's top star of the time, Carole Lombard, but, as things turned out, the role went to Joan Fontaine, who, like Lombard, neither sang nor danced. The screenplay was to be based on a novel which an old colleague, PG Wodehouse, had co-written in 1919 with the English light author Ian Hay. This time there would be no problem about the title. Both picture and novel are called *A Damsel In Distress*.

A few days after his and Ira's options were taken up, George was shaken when his long-time friend and colleague, Bill Daly, died unexpectedly of a heart attack. He was forty-nine.

Still shaken by Bill's death, he embarked on another concert tour, conducting the 'Suite From *Porgy And Bess*' and playing, as usual, 'Rhapsody In Blue' and the 'Concerto In F'. This tour would cover a lot of ground, the first concert, on 17 December, being in Seattle. After it, he returned to California for the Christmas holidays, when his mother, his sister Frankie and her husband, Leopold Godowsky Jr, came on a visit.

During their visit, George did a bit of painting, producing portraits in oils of Arnold Schoenberg and Jerome Kern. Several visitors noticed that quite often while in Hollywood he would retreat from the social hubbub in the house, and paint in the peace and quiet upstairs.

Also during the family visit, preoccupied with his confusion of future plans, he told his sister Frankie (several times), "I don't think I've scratched the surface. I'm out here to make enough money with movies that I don't have to think of money anymore. Because I just want to work on American music: symphonies, chamber music, opera. This is what I really want to do."

As well as his uncertainty about where to head next in his music, Frankie also observed another change in George during her visit. As she said later, "George had always been so absorbed in his work... I felt when I saw him then that he was coming into his own as a rounded person... He asked about our daughter Sondra – about what we were doing. I felt that for the first time he had something going out and was not just taking in."

Certainly what was bothering George at this time was not just Hollywood and uncertainty about where to go musically. He was also lonely. In spite of his profusion of friends, he had never really let himself get close to anyone, and now he was beginning to feel isolated. Fearing to be alone, he encouraged people to visit the house, but social gatherings offered no real companionship and, as when he went upstairs to paint, he more and more felt the need to get away alone.

One way out of this mental trap he found himself in seemed to be to find a wife. Early in 1937 he told his cousin, Henry Botkin, "This year I've *got* to get married." He felt that Kay Swift was not the woman for him, but he made compulsive efforts to find someone who was. As well as having brief affairs with Hollywood stars like Simone Simon and Elizabeth Allen, he had more serious ones with several starlets, often asking them to marry him. None accepted. He even wrote letters to several old girlfriends in New York, asking them to come out and visit him in California. None came, and his sense of isolation deepened, making him even more despondent. As he said one day to Alexander Steinert, "I am thirty-eight, famous and rich, but profoundly unhappy. Why?"

The person in whom he confided most at this time was his old friend from the Paleys and from Paris, Mabel Schirmer, who was now back in New York. To her he wrote incessantly. Back in October he had written: "I miss New York and the things it had to offer quite a good deal, and will probably miss it more as time goes on." He did. The fewer distractions in Hollywood threw him more and more in on himself. Early in 1937 he was writing: "Perhaps dear Mabel this is our year. A year that will see both of us finding that elusive something that seems to bring happiness."

Also early in 1937, on 8 January, George and Ira went to Carmel, near Monterey, about two-hundred-and-fifty miles north of Los Angeles on the California coast. They were to stay for a few days with two old friends from the social world of New York, Mr and Mrs Sidney Fish. But this was not a simple social visit. There too were

Pandro Berman, director George Stevens, and a large staff of secretaries and studio minions, for Mr and Mrs Fish were hosting the first major conference on the production of *A Damsel In Distress*.

PG Wodehouse himself, who was not present at the conference, was at work on the screenplay, collaborating with SK Lauren and Ernest Pagano. He had not always been involved. As he told the story in his autobiographical book *Performing Flea*, the studio originally "gave [the book] to one of the RKO writers to adapt, and he turned out a script all about crooks – no resemblance to the novel. Then it struck them that it might be a good thing to stick to the story, so they chucked away the other script and called me in. But what uncongenial work picture-writing is. Somebody's got to do it, I suppose, but this is the last time they'll get me."

It had also been decided that, as leading lady Joan Fontaine was not a dancer, other actors must be cast who could dance a bit. It was suggested that supporting roles were given to the famous comedy team of George Burns and Gracie Allen.

Gracie had done quite a bit of hoofing in vaudeville and was a good dancer, but George Burns could only dance well enough to get along. As he said himself, "[I] was a sort of right-legged dancer. I could tap with my right foot, but my left foot wanted me to get into some other business."

It had been agreed that Fred Astaire had to approve the team's dancing and, not wanting to lose the job, Burns remembered a vaudeville act he once knew called Evans and Evans. They had a routine where they each danced with a whisk-broom, and Burns decided he could manage that, if only he could track down Evans and Evans to teach it to himself and Gracie. It turned out that one Evans had died, but the other came to California and taught them the dance. They did it for Fred Astaire, who not only liked their dancing enough to approve their casting, he liked the dance so much that he insisted the three of them dance it together in the film.

The story of *A Damsel In Distress*, as told in the film, is set in London. Jerry Halliday, played by Fred, is a matinee idol who is publicised by his press agent as a lady killer, but is actually shy and retiring. Somehow he gets the idea that a member of the English nobility, Lady Alyce (played by Joan Fontaine) is in love with him.

This idea is at first as repugnant to him as it is to her, and the film tells their story as this repugnance fades away and they fall in love.

Returning to Hollywood after the conference, George resumed his concert tour, playing in San Francisco (where the orchestra was conducted by Pierre Monteux), then across the bay at the University of California, in Berkeley. That was on 17 January, and three days later he was performing in Detroit, where the concert was so successful that the director of the Detroit Concert Society asked him to come back and repeat the programme in her 1937-38 winter season.

Before George got down to serious work on *A Damsel In Distress*, several other things happened. On 6 February he learned that Italy had given him the highest award it could give to a foreign composer, by electing him to the Royal Academy of Santa Cecilia, in Rome. On the ninth he was invited to premiere his next original composition at the Venice Biennale Festival the following September. And on the tenth and eleventh he gave his two concerts with the Los Angeles Philharmonic.

There had been some trouble finding a conductor. George had wanted Fritz Reiner to conduct, but Reiner was in Oslo. The formidable Otto Klemperer had been approached and, at first, had agreed to conduct, but then withdrew when he learned that the budget would permit only two rehearsals. So Alexander Smallens took over the podium.

As it happened, Klemperer need not have worried. George was so anxious for his music to be a success in the film capital that he paid for extra rehearsals out of his own pocket. He paid for so many that his own fee dropped from two thousand dollars to six-hundred-and-seventy.

Just before the concerts he wrote to Mabel Schirmer, saying: "They tell me that they've seen nothing like the excitement for a concert in years. My friend, Arthur Lyons [who was also his agent], is taking a room at the Trocadero and has invited two-hundred-and-fifty people to come in after the concert. He's going to great trouble to decorate the room and there will be two orchestras – one American and one Russian. I wish I could send a magic carpet for you, Emily and Lou..."

At the second of the two concerts, however, a disturbing thing happened, although possibly Oscar Levant was among a very few that noticed it. George had just launched into the 'Concerto In F' when Levant "noticed that he stumbled on a very easy passage in the first movement. Then in the andante, in playing the four simple octaves that conclude the movement above the sustained orchestral chords, he stumbled again."

Oscar was staggered. George was normally an impeccable pianist. What was wrong? Going backstage after the concert to see George, he wondered whether he should mention the missed notes but, as he entered the dressing room, George immediately greeted him by saying, "When I made those mistakes, I was thinking of you, you bastard."

He later told Oscar that something else had also happened during the concert. While conducting he had suddenly felt dizzy for a moment, and at the same time had felt a disagreeable sensation of smelling something like burning rubber.

And there had been a third thing. During rehearsal, while conducting the orchestra through the excerpts from *Porgy And Bess*, he had suddenly swayed on the podium and seemed about to fall off it. Paul Mueller, sitting in the front row, had leapt up and steadied him. "I'm all right, Paul," George had said. "I think I just lost my balance for a moment."

These three small mishaps worried George sufficiently for him to undergo a complete physical check-up a week or so later. He passed it without difficulty and was pronounced to be in excellent physical condition. More and more, however, the constant procession of visitors to the house on North Roxbury Drive began to bother him, and he took to working during the mornings at his friend Aileen Pringle's house in Santa Monica, where he could have peace and quiet.

He and Ira got down to work on *A Damsel In Distress* and, again, turned out some of their best songs, among them 'A Foggy Day' and 'Nice Work If You Can Get It'. In the film there was also a reference back to their early days of working with the Astaires, when Fred and Gracie danced the eccentric 'nut dance' that he and Adele had danced both in vaudeville and in *Lady Be Good*. This time it was called the 'Oom-Pah Trot'.

In mid-March, when the songs were almost finished, Merle Armitage came back to George. The two Los Angeles concerts had been such a success that he now wanted to present *Porgy And Bess* there. Negotiations to set this up began, and George was especially pleased because of various failures he had had in interesting the studios in his opera. All of them had shied away, fearing that a picture with an all-black cast would not be a commercial proposition.

Another cheering event in March was that he was invited by Edward G Robinson and his wife to a party given mainly in honour of Igor Stravinsky, whose autobiography had just been published. As well as Stravinsky, there were many Hollywood celebrities at the party, including Charlie Chaplin, Douglas Fairbanks Sr, Marlene Dietrich and Frank Capra (one can quite see why George missed feeling like a celebrity in Hollywood – as Mark Twain once said, "In heaven an angel is nobody in particular").

George was pleased to meet (and hear) Stravinsky, who played for the guests, but he was bowled over by Paulette Goddard, whom he sat next to at dinner, and who had been married to Chaplin since 1933. As he wrote to Mabel Schirmer: "Mmmmmm she's nice. Me likee." Which was putting it mildly, because he was so attracted to her that he came home convinced that she was the girl he would marry.

Paulette was, as it happened, not all that happy being married to Chaplin (they would divorce in 1942) and during the next few weeks she and George carried on a turbulent affair. She became a regular member of the group around the Gershwin pool on Sundays, and he would visit her in Palm Springs. He constantly asked her to marry him, but she was not then ready to leave Chaplin, and repeatedly turned him down. He began talking about buying a house of his own in Beverly Hills, where they could live together and about sending to New York for his furniture. Several of his friends, including Harold Arlen and Paul Mueller, tried to caution him about leaping into marriage, but all their warnings did was make him angry.

More and more his friends found him getting restless and irritable. And when it became obvious to him that he and Paulette Goddard were not going to get together, he completely reversed his thoughts about moving to Beverly Hills. In April he came to an arrangement with Ira that, when their work in Hollywood was finished, he would move back to New York, while Ira and Lee would buy a home in Beverly Hills and, alongside it, build a cottage-cum-studio for him to use on trips west.

As well as basing himself in New York, George also proposed to spend a lot of time in Europe, where he would play concerts, write his long-planned symphony and buy paintings. But before leaving Hollywood he wanted to write his string quartet (this idea had been inspired by his many conversations with Schoenberg). He decided that what he would do was rent a cottage somewhere up in one of the canyons, and write it there in peace and seclusion.

On 14 April, taking with him a new girlfriend, British actress Benita Hume, he attended a concert presenting pieces by Schoenberg's students (and an early piece, 'Pelleas And Melisande' by Schoenberg himself). America was now in the fourth year of Franklin D Roosevelt's presidency and, under his 'New Deal', was beginning to haul itself out of the Depression. As part of his plan to revitalise the country, Roosevelt had set up the WPA – the Works Progress Administration – whose brief was to fund people skilled in any field, from bridge-building to ballet, to do the jobs they were skilled to do. The Schoenberg student concert was funded by the WPA.

George, not being a student of Schoenberg's, did not have a piece in it, but Oscar Levant did. It was his 'Nocturne', the harmonically complex piece that George had found 'confusing'. Oscar, who was to conduct the piece, was as usual petrified with stage-fright. He stepped up onto the podium, gave the customary tap on the music stand with his baton to signify readiness – and the stand collapsed. This completely abolished his stage-fright and the performance proceeded flawlessly.

After the concert, Oscar and his own new girlfriend – the dancer and actress June Gale, who would become his second wife – went off to the fashionable Brown Derby restaurant, where George and Benita Hume were waiting for them. June Gale later recalled their meal, saying, "I remember how George looked and how he laughed at everything Oscar said, because Oscar was a little bit embarrassed about his piece and he was defending it in a way. And was squirming a little bit... And George was laughing... Everything went so well."

Three days later George again suffered a dizzy spell and, again, he smelt the smell of burning rubber. He became increasingly irritable, until Lee Gershwin told people they were not to indulge George's 'temper tantrums'.

It helped his irritability a little when during the same month (April), he was told that for *Porgy And Bess* he was to be awarded the David Bispham Memorial Medal by the American Opera Society in Chicago. In spite of its short run, and its failure to run at all in Europe, *Porgy* was beginning to look like an established piece, what with Merle Armitage's planned production in Los Angeles and now this medal.

At the end of April, *Shall We Dance?* was shown to an invited audience at the Pantages Theatre. George, who had been looking forward to seeing it, was disappointed. In a letter he wrote to biographer Isaac Goldberg he said: "The picture does not take advantage of the songs as well as it should. They literally throw one or two of the songs away without any kind of plug. This is mainly due to the structure of the story which does not include any other singers than Fred and Ginger and the amount of singing one can stand of these two is quite limited." Nor was he happy with the way the score was arranged and performed, feeling that much of its essential colour had been lost.

Later in the same letter to Goldberg, he wrote: "On account of the *Goldwyn Follies* Ira and I have had to postpone the Kaufman-Hart opus until next year." The 'Kaufman-Hart' opus was the proposed musical-about-a-musical, and the *Goldwyn Follies* was the revue film they had agreed to work on for Sam Goldwyn.

On 12 May, George again wrote to Isaac Goldberg: "We started this week on the *Goldwyn Follies*, a super, super, stupendous, colossal moving picture extravaganza which the 'Great Goldwyn' is producing. Ira and I should be taking a vacation by this time, having just finished eight songs for the second Astaire picture, *Damsel In Distress*, but unfortunately Goldwyn cannot put off half-a-million dollars' worth of principal salaries while the Gershwins bask in the sunshine of Arrowhead Springs."

Goldwyn Follies was to run for two hours, which was long for a film in those days, and it had a star-studded cast including Adolph Menjou, Kenny Baker (the singer, not the British trumpeter), Ella Logan, the Ritz Brothers, Edgar Bergen with Charlie McCarthy and comedian Bobby Clark.

Bobby Clark, who had been such a success with his friend and partner Paul McCullough in the second version of *Strike Up The Band*, was now working as a single. After *Strike Up The Band*, as well as their stage work, he and McCullough had made over twenty short films for RKO, stopping in 1935 to tour in a production of *George White's Scandals*. After the tour, McCullough, suffering from nervous exhaustion, entered a rest home in Medford, Massachusetts, while Clark went home to New York.

McCullough felt well enough to leave the rest home in March 1936, and a friend drove to Medford to collect him. As they were driving back to New York, they passed a barber's shop. McCullough said he needed a shave, so they stopped.He entered the barber's, chatted amiably to him for a moment, then grabbed a razor and slashed his throat and wrists. Rushed to hospital, he died a few days later. The only explanation anyone could ever give for his action was that he had become increasingly distressed by his friend's greater success with the public.

Also to be featured in the *Goldwyn Follies* was to be the American Ballet of the Metropolitan Opera, choreographed by the Russian-born George Balanchine. George had been keen to compose a film ballet for some time and, at last here was his chance. It was to be called *The Swing Symphony*.

Early in June, New York producer Eddie Warburg, hearing of *The Swing Symphony* and of George's enthusiasm for writing for ballet, contacted George to see if he and Ira would create a ballet for his company. But by now George's condition was beginning to deteriorate sharply, disturbing his friends even more. For instance, he developed a strange compulsion. As he sat in the back of his Cord, chauffeured by Paul Mueller, he would call out the name of every street as they passed it. If he missed one, he would insist Paul go back so he could try again.

He had begun to suffer from dizziness and crippling headaches. His friends could only assume they were caused by the stresses of working in Hollywood. And his vitality, once so legendary, seemed now to come in fits and starts. More and more often he would wake in the morning listless and confused and, once or twice, he was found crouched down between the beds in his bedroom, holding his head, with the shades drawn against the painful brightness of the day, too lethargic to move and with no clear idea of how long he had been sitting there.

Nonetheless, he drove himself to continue working. As well as composing for Sam Goldwyn, he was making plans to hold a one-man show of his own paintings in New York.

He didn't much enjoy working for Goldwyn, who was given to issuing a royal summons for George to present himself at the studio and demonstrate to Sam and his entourage whatever song he and Ira had just finished. Sam didn't like the first one or two he heard – possibly 'Just Another Rhumba' or 'I Love To Rhyme' – and kept demanding they write "hit songs you can whistle". But he perked up when he first heard 'I Was Doing All Right'. "Maybe that eight-bar bridge should be repeated," he suggested.

Ira was amused by this, but George was furious, saying later to SN Behrman, "I had to live for this, that Sam Goldwyn should say to me, 'Why don't you write hits like Irving Berlin?'"

His headaches and his loss of vitality grew worse, as did his jumpiness and irritability. One evening during dinner he became so upset by a conversation about Nazi Germany that he jumped up, shouted angrily and fled to his bedroom, where he remained, in bed, for two days, unable to summon the energy to rise.

Alarmed by his apparently worsening condition, George, like his friends, was due to put it down to stress and overwork. But just in case it was mental in origin, towards the end of the first week in June he consulted an analyst, Dr Ernest Simmel. After talking to George for some time, Dr Simmel came to the conclusion that, although he would continue seeing George on a regular basis, his problem was most probably physical. He suggested George consult a physician.

The physician George went to, on 9 June, was Dr Gabriel Segal. He gave him a thorough examination, but could find nothing physically wrong. However, in view of George's headaches and spells of dizziness, he brought in a neurologist, Dr Eugene Ziskind, to examine him as well. Between them, the only thing they could find wrong was a slight blockage of one nasal passage, caused in his boyhood by a kick from a horse. Still anxious to discover the root of George's problem, Dr Ziskind arranged that he should come to the Cedars of Lebanon Hospital in two weeks' time for further tests.

George went back to work. For the *Goldwyn Follies* he and Ira began work on two of their best-ever songs – first 'Love Walked In' and then 'Love Is Here To Stay'. This would be the last song they ever wrote together.

Some days George felt almost his old self. On Saturday 12 June, he went for a brief holiday to Coronado, down near San Diego, with his agent, Arthur Lyons and, during the holiday, he appeared to be almost as lively as ever.

On the next Saturday 19 June, Vincente Minnelli invited George to join him at dinner with a couple of "girls about town". George joyfully accepted and arrived at Minnelli's house full of high spirits. Minnelli introduced him, telling the girls, "This is George Gershwin", and even the fact that neither girl seemed to have ever heard of George Gershwin seemed to depress him. He played the piano and sang and seemed not to have a care in the world.

The next day Minnelli went to the usual Sunday gathering at North Roxbury Drive. George didn't appear and Minnelli was told he was unwell. That evening, however, he had recovered enough to go out to dinner at Irving Berlin's, although afterwards he complained to Lee of another blinding headache.

Two days later he had a luncheon date with Paulette Goddard, Constance Collier and his old friend George Pallay, the cousin of Lou Paley and the man who had been his first example of stylish living and his companion around the night spots of New York. George was so listless at the luncheon, so apathetic about everything, that his three friends were convinced there was something seriously wrong with him.

Next day was his medical appointment at the Cedars of Lebanon Hospital. Over three days the doctors there carried out every medical test they could think of. They X-rayed his skull, took blood samples and tested his reflexes. The one test that George vehemently refused to undergo was a painful and time-consuming lumbar puncture, to obtain a sample of his spinal fluid.

Once again, when he returned home, things seemed to have improved. But again it was only temporary. He went with Ira to a party at Samuel Goldwyn's but, on their way home, late at night, just before they reached their own house, George sat down on the kerb, holding his head. The headaches and the smell of burning rubber were more than he could bear.

Not long afterwards, he was eating dinner and the knife fell from his hand. He began to lose his motor co-ordination more and more – he dropped things, he spilled his food, he stumbled on the stairs and fumbled when playing the piano. Lee's reactions to all this veered alarmingly from concern to annoyance to embarrassment to revulsion. One day, when Oscar Levant and June Gale came to visit, she drew them aside and said, "It's disgusting. He's drooling out of the side of his mouth."

By now, Ira had asked Goldwyn to release them from work on his film. News that there was something wrong reached journalist Walter Winchell and, on 27 June, he announced on his radio programme that George was seriously ill. At once both the house in North Roxburgh Drive and his mother's house at 25 Central Park West, in New York, were swamped with letters and telegrams and phone calls asking for news and wishing him well.

Early in July, Harold Arlen and Yip Harburg, who were off to work on a show in New York, called by the house to say goodbye. They were appalled at the way George had deteriorated in the two weeks since they'd last seen him. He was weak and listless. "Do you have to go?" he said. "All my friends are leaving me."

It seemed to Yip that it might help George if he was moved somewhere more peaceful, away from all the activity at North Roxburgh Drive, and he offered George the use of his house, a few blocks away, to stay in. Dr Simmel, the analyst, agreed that this might be a good idea and George accepted. He and Paul Mueller moved in there, along with a male nurse, Paul Levy, whose job was to look after George whenever the other Paul was occupied elsewhere (it was up to Paul Mueller to shuttle between the two houses).

The move seemed at first to help. George seemed more relaxed, and even played the piano a bit, although his playing was uncertain and fumbling. But he was becoming unpredictable. One day Paul Mueller was driving George in the Cord to Dr Simmel for one of his continuing consultations, which George was convinced were proving useless. As they were speeding along, George reached across Paul, managed to open the driver's door and began trying to push him out.

Somehow, after swerving wildly, Paul managed to regain control of the car and get the door closed. He pulled in to the side of the highway and stopped, shaking. "What are you trying to do, kill us?" he said. "What have I ever done to you? Why did you do that?" George, perspiring, held his head in his hands and said, "I don't know."

Another disturbing incident happened at Yip Harburg's. Somebody George didn't much like sent him a large box of chocolates. He opened the box, gathered up all the chocolates in both hands, kneaded them into one gooey lump and then smeared the lump all over his body. Paul Mueller had to give him a bath.

Only a very few of George's friends were admitted to see him in his strange, secluded, almost silent existence in Yip Harburg's house. Oscar Levant was among them. One day he arrived with June Gale. Only George and the nurse, Paul Levy, were there. Oscar and June sat in the living room and George came downstairs to meet them, wearing a robe and pyjamas.

After some conversation, Oscar went to the piano and began to play and sing songs from *Porgy And Bess*. He always enjoyed singing the songs of Crown, using his deep chesty baritone and, while he was singing one of these, George was sitting by June, with his arm around her. As she later recalled, "He was looking at my face and hugging me and patting me. It made me very uneasy... Oscar would have been furious... I don't even know if he noticed, he was so busy singing away."

But Oscar had noticed and later he too recalled the incident: "George kept moving towards her. It was very strange. I don't know if it was part of the syndrome of sickness or not. Anyway, to use an old phrase, he was horny, as sick as he was. That didn't bother me. I loved George."

A few days later, Oscar accompanied Sam Behrman on what was to be Sam's last visit to George. George came downstairs with Paul Levy, and Berhman recorded in his diary: "I stared at him. It was not the George we all knew. The light had gone from his eye. He seemed old. He came to a sofa near where I was sitting and lay down on it. He tried to adjust his head against the pillows. The nurse hovered over him. I asked him if he felt pain. 'Behind my eyes,' he said, and repeated it: 'Behind my eyes.' I knelt beside him on the sofa and put my hand under his head. I asked him if he felt like playing the piano. He shook his head. It was the first refusal I'd ever heard from him."

The next day, on 6 July, a cable arrived from Paris asking what George's conditions would be for giving ten or fifteen European concerts later in the year.

On the morning of the ninth, he actually did spend a little time fumbling at the piano. Then he went back to bed. Ira and George Pallay dropped in to see him, but finding him asleep, went away again. At five in the afternoon, George awoke again. He was so weak that he had to call Paul Levy to help him to the bathroom. There he slumped and collapsed in a coma.

He was rushed to the Cedars of Lebanon Hospital, where he was examined by Dr Carl Rand, a neurosurgeon. His reflexes were gone, and all evidence pointed towards the cause being a brain tumour of unknown size and situation.

Prompt surgery was called for and the call was sent out for one of America's top neurosurgeons, Dr Walter Dandy of Johns Hopkins. He could not be traced at the hospital, at his office, or at home. It turned out he was vacationing on a yacht in Chesapeake Bay, south of Baltimore (the site of Johns Hopkins). George Pallay, frantic, phoned the White House and, on the afternoon after George's collapse, on Saturday, 10 July, two Navy destroyers were dispatched to find the yacht.

It was found and, soon, Dr Dandy with a motorcycle escort, was rushed to Cumberland, Maryland. From there he phoned the doctors at the Cedars of Lebanon and was asked to come and operate. Agreeing, he boarded a plane for Newark, where another plane, organised by Emil Mosbacher, would be waiting to fly him west.

Meanwhile, in the west, the hunt had gone on for another neurosurgeon. This was Dr Howard Naffziger, of the University of California Medical School. He too was on vacation, also out of telephone reach, at Lake Tahoe, not far from Reno, Nevada, on the eastern border of California. But he too was found and Paul Mueller was flown north to accompany him on the flight back to Los Angeles.

As they flew back, Paul asked Dr Naffziger what might bring on a brain tumour. The doctor suggested several possibilities, among them that a childhood head injury could lead to the formation of a clot around which tissue might grow.

It was nine-thirty in the evening when they arrived at the hospital.

Dr Dandy was still at Newark, waiting to take off, but Dr Naffziger examined George and found his pulse so low that he decided immediate surgery was imperative. There was no time to waste. Swiftly it was decided that he should perform the operation, while Dr Dandy remained at Newark, on the end of an open phone line connected to the theatre.

A ninety-minute preliminary operation was performed, then two-and-a-half hours of X-ray investigation. At three am Dr Naffziger began a major operation that was to last almost five hours. During all that time, George's agent, Arthur Lyons, was in the operating theatre, while George Pallay waited outside. Among those waiting downstairs were Ira and Lee, Henry Botkin, Moss Hart, Oscar Levant, Arthur Kober, Vincente Minnelli and Lou and Emily Paley, who had arrived in California two days earlier.

It turned out that George had suffered the cystic degeneration of a tumour in the right temporal lobe of the brain, in an area where it could not be touched. George Pallay was told by one of the doctors that there was not much hope of his recovery and, even if he did recover, it was likely that he would be blind or severely disabled.

Pallay told all this to Lee as they drove back to North Roxburgh Drive. Ira was driven back there by Paul Mueller and, when he arrived, Lee could not screw up her courage to pass the news on to him. Max Dreyfus phoned almost as soon as they had arrived back and Ira, in a state of exhaustion and shock, told him, "George will be all right, Max. The operation was a success. There is nothing to worry about."

But there was. At ten-thirty-five am, without regaining consciousness, George died. It was Sunday, 11 July 1937.

CHAPTER FOURTEEN

Epilogue

George's death stunned everyone who had ever known him or heard his music. Millions of people, in America and the rest of the world, found it unbelievable that, less than two years after writing his most ambitious work, *Porgy And Bess*, and when he was still at the height of his powers, he had died at the age of only thirty-eight.

Some of the projects he had been working on continued. On 18 December 1937, five months after he died, thirty-seven of his paintings were exhibited, as he had wanted, in a one-man show at the Harriman Gallery in New York. The art critic Henry McBride, reviewing the show, wrote: "He was not yet actually great as a painter, but that was merely because he had not yet had the time – but he was distinctly on the way to that goal."

Merle Armitage's planned production of *Porgy And Bess* did take place. It proved too expensive to mount only in Los Angeles and San Francisco, so it was also booked into several other western cities. Demand for it mounted, and eventually theatre managers asked for it to play not only in the far west, but in cities as far afield as Kansas City, Detroit and Cincinnati.

All the main members of the original cast agreed to appear in it, with one exception. The fee that John Bubbles asked was too high, so his role of Sportin' Life was taken over by Avon Long, who George himself had spotted performing at the Ubangi Club in Harlem, and who had been his second choice for the role. Reuben Mamoulian again directed (this time for no fee) and Alexander Steinert conducted.

The opera opened in Pasadena, playing for a single night before a celebrity audience, then moved to Los Angeles for eleven performances at the Los Angeles Philharmonic Auditorium, opening there on 4 February 1938. It was a great success. Members of the audience who had seen the original New York production found this one livelier and better.

Three more weeks were to follow, at the Curran Theatre in San Francisco, but during the first of those weeks California was struck by torrential rain, causing some of the worst floods in its history. Trains came to a standstill, and people from outlying communities, who might have been expected to attend the show, stayed at home. At the end of that first week, after playing to half-empty houses, Merle Armitage found himself unable to meet the payroll. The show folded, the cast were broke, and the tour to other cities never materialised. It was a sad end to Armitage's brave attempt to get *Porgy And Bess* the nationwide reputation he felt it deserved.

RKO's film *A Damsel In Distress* was released on 19 November, 1937, and the *Goldwyn Follies* was released by Goldwyn-United Artists on 23 February 1938. The last two songs that George and Ira had written for it, 'Love Walked In' and 'Love Is Here To Stay', had never been properly finished off while George was alive. Ira was helped to complete them by Oscar Levant and by Vernon Duke (who had been called in to take over the score for the film), using ideas and phrases they had heard George play. It is hardly surprising that in the stress of the time Ira accidentally left the word 'Our' off the registered title of what should have been 'Our Love Is Here To Stay'. George had never got round to writing the ballet, 'The Swing Symphony', and so the American Ballet of the Metropolitan Opera never appeared in the film.

Of all the hundreds of people who were desolated by George's death, Oscar Levant felt it more than most. He would devote much of the rest of his performing career playing George's concert works, beginning at a vast memorial concert, given on 8 September 1937, before an audience of twenty-two thousand at the Hollywood Bowl.

It was an enormous undertaking, involving "seven conductors, half a dozen singers, two piano soloists and a full symphony orchestra". Oscar was one of the two piano soloists. He played the 'Concerto In F', just as he had done for George at the Lewisohn Stadium, and the whole concert was broadcast around the world by CBS, whose founder, William Paley, had once tried to get Toscanini interested in conducting George's 'Second Rhapsody'.

Ira, who would live on until 1983, suffered worst. He had come to idolise his younger brother and, when George died, something in him seemed to die too. Three years went by before he came back to life sufficiently to attempt writing lyrics with anyone else. He and Lee bought the house next door to the one they had lived in with George, on North Roxburgh Drive, and they would live there for the rest of their lives, turning it into a George Gershwin shrine and devoting almost all their energies to keeping George's name alive.

From time to time Ira would pore through George's bulging files of unused or part-written tunes (there eventually turned out to be about sixty that were usable) and, often with the help of composer Kay Swift, would polish them up and write or rewrite lyrics to them. In this way he got together enough songs to provide the score for a 1947 film called *The Shocking Miss Pilgrim*, starring Betty Grable and Dick Haymes. And years later he wrote words to three tunes that had never had words, for use in Billy Wilder's 1964 film, *Kiss Me, Stupid*, which starred Dean Martin and Kim Novak.

Among the many other projects Ira involved himself in to perpetuate his brother's music, one was a stage production of *Porgy And Bess* that toured the world for several years in the fifties, and another was Vincente Minnelli's 1951 film, *An American In Paris*. To assemble the score for this picture, Ira and Vincente, with producer Arthur Freed and screenwriter Alan Jay Lerner, got together at Ira's house and ran through "somewhere between one-hundred-and-twenty-five and one-hundred-and-fifty songs" to choose the best to use.

The finished film pleased Ira greatly. It starred Gene Kelly and Leslie Caron, and Oscar Levant also had a role (as a struggling composer). In one of the best sequences in the film he plays a cutdown version of the 'Concerto In F', with both audience and orchestra composed entirely of Levants.

Oscar also appeared in another noteworthy Gershwin film, this time playing himself. This was *Rhapsody In Blue*, made by Warner Brothers in 1945, and purporting to be George's biography. It wasn't anything of the sort, of course. Every detail of his life was smoothed out and sanitised. Even his younger brother and sister, Arthur and Frankie, disappeared, and the 'Concerto In F' was moved, for dramatic reasons, to the end of his life. But much of his music, especially his concert music, was there, played well and at length. And because the film was made so soon after his death, several of his friends and colleagues were involved in the production. As well as Oscar, Al Jolson, George White and Paul Whiteman all appeared as themselves.

George had many friends and, in his short life, he wrote a lot of good music. The songs from his shows, and his concert pieces, and his opera, are today showing no sign at all of losing their popularity. At any given moment, something he wrote is undoubtedly playing somewhere in the world, even sixty years after his death. But as the writer John O'Hara said when he heard about it: "George Gershwin died on 11 July, but I don't have to believe it if I don't want to."

Bibliography

PRIMARY SOURCES

Hollis Alpert – *The Life And Times Of Porgy And Bess*
[Nick Hern Books 1991]

Merle Armitage (Ed) – *George Gershwin*
[Da Capo Press (US) 1995]

Guy Bolton & PG Wodehouse – *Bring On The Girls*
[Herbert Jenkins 1954]

David Ewen – *A Journey To Greatness: The Life And Music Of George Gershwin*
[WH Allen 1956]

Edward Jablonsky & Lawrence D Stewart – *The Gershwin Years*
[Robson Books 1974]

Sam Kashner & Nancy Schoenberger – *A Talent For Genius: The Life And Times Of Oscar Levant*
[Villard Books (US) 1994]

Deena Rosenberg – *Fascinating Rhythm: The Collaboration Of George And Ira Gershwin*
[Lime Tree 1992]

ADDITIONAL SOURCES

Joe Adamson – *Groucho, Harpo, Chico And Sometimes Zeppo*
[WH Allen 1973]

James Agate – *Immoment Toys*
[Jonathan Cape 1945]

Fred Astaire – *Steps In Time*
[Harper (US) 1959]

Djuna Barnes – *I Could Never Be Lonely Without A Husband*
[Virago Press 1987]

Nathaniel Benchley – *Robert Benchley*
[Cassell 1956]

SN Behrman – *People In A Diary; A Memoir*
[Little, Brown (US) 1972]

George Burns – *The Third Time Around*
[WH Allen 1980]

William & Rhoda Cahn – *The Great American Comedy Scene*
[Monarch (US) 1978]

Bennett Cerf – *Try And Stop Me*
[Dennis Dobson Ltd 1947]

James Lincoln Collier – *Duke Ellington*
[Pan Books 1989]

Alistair Cooke – *Letters From America 1946-51*
[Penguin Books 1981]

David Ewen – *Great Men Of American Popular Music*
[Prentice Hall (US) 1972]

James R Gaines – *Wit's End: Days And Nights At The Algonquin Round Table*
[Harcourt Brace Jovanovich 1977]

Douglas Gilbert – *American Vaudeville*
[Dover (US) 1963]

Douglas Gilbert – *Lost Chords: The Diverting Story Of American Popular Songs*
[Cooper Square Publishers (USA) 1970]

Abel Green & Joe Laurie, Jr – *Show Biz From Vaude To Video*
[Permabooks (USA) 1953]

Moss Hart – *Act One*
[Secker & Warburg 1960]

Leonard Maltin – *Movie Comedy Teams*
[Signet (US) 1970]

Scott Meredith – *George S Kaufman And The Algonquin Round Table*
[George Allen & Unwin 1977]

Ethel Merman – *Don't Call Me Madam!*
[WH Allen 1955]

Vincente Minnelli – *I Remember It Well*
[Angus & Robertson (UK) Ltd 1974]

Robert Redding – *Starring Robert Benchley*
[The University of New Mexico Press (US) 1973]

Brian Rust – *My Kind Of Jazz*
[Elm Tree Books 1990]

David Thompson – *A Biographical Dictionary Of Film*
[André Deutsch 1995]

ES Turner – *Roads To Ruin*
[Penguin Books 1966]

Mark White – *You Must Remember This*
[Frederick Warne 1983]

PG Wodehouse – *Performing Flea*
[Herbert Jenkins 1953]

Ean Wood – *Born To Swing: The Story Of The Big Bands*
[Sanctuary 1996]

Maurice Zolotow – *It Takes All Kinds*
[WH Allen 1953]

Indexes

SHOWS INVOLVING GEORGE AND/OR IRA

INDEX OF PERSONS